VISION AND VALUES

ETHICAL VIEWPOINTS IN
THE CATHOLIC TRADITION

VISION AND VALUES
ETHICAL VIEWPOINTS IN THE CATHOLIC TRADITION

Edited by

Judith A. Dwyer

GEORGETOWN UNIVERSITY PRESS/WASHINGTON, D.C.

Georgetown University Press, Washington, D.C. 20007
©1999 by Georgetown University Press. All rights reserved.
Printed in the United States of America
10 9 8 7 6 5 4 3 2 1 1999
THIS VOLUME IS PRINTED ON ACID-FREE OFFSET BOOKPAPER.

Library of Congress Cataloging-in-Publication Data

Vision and values: ethical viewpoints in the Catholic tradition /
edited by Judith A. Dwyer.
p. cm.
Includes index.
ISBN 0-87840-742-1 (pbk.)
1. Christian ethics—Catholic authors. I. Dwyer, Judith A.
BJ1249.V54 1999
241'.042—dc21   99-19947
CIP

CONTENTS

INTRODUCTION

Vision and Values: Ethical Viewpoints in the Catholic Tradition brings to-gether various essays that demonstrate both the richness and the vitality of the Catholic theological tradition. The text, which emerged as a response to the renewed emphasis on ethics in the undergraduate curriculum at Villanova University, deliberately attempts to present not only founda-tional issues but also the practical implications of analyzing contemporary issues from the vision and values embraced by the Catholic community.

Professor Paul Danove's essay on the scriptural sources investigates two major approaches to this important Christian heritage: the fundamentalist approach and the historical critical method. He then demonstrates the limitations and deficiencies within both methods. While the fundamental-ist approach yields a series of clear statements on various ethical issues, it provides no mechanism for generating a truly comprehensive statement of ethics in the scriptures. On the other hand, while the historical critical method does provide such a mechanism, it requires training for its proper use, since it yields more nuanced results.

Professor Michael Scanlon's chapter on Christian anthropology exam-ines the evolving understanding of human existence by inspecting Old Testament and New Testament contributions, as well as those of such fig-ures as Augustine, Aquinas, Luther, Schleiermacher, Rahner, and Lonergan, all situated within the complex historical and philosophical context from which these figures and their various understandings of human existence emerged. He concludes with an analysis of the postmodern situation in which today's students find themselves.

Chapter 3, titled "Turn to the Heavens and the Earth: Retrieval of the Cosmos in Theology," authored by Professor Elizabeth A. Johnson of Fordham University, attempts to address an important theme largely absent from contemporary North American theology, namely, the significance of the cosmos in theology. Tracing this theme through the historical "remembering and forgetting" of the cosmos, she demonstrates how cosmology contributes to both the intellectual and moral integrity of theology as she persuasively fortifies her argument that cosmology be a framework within which all theological topics be rethought.

The chapter on "Reverence for Human Life" constitutes Professor James McCartney's contribution to this volume. After a brief analysis of fundamental questions, such as the concept of health and healing itself, McCartney investigates certain specific contemporary questions. These include abortion, assisted suicide and euthanasia, brain death, the criteria for legitimate refusal of medical treatment, and the artificial delivery of nutrition and hydration.

Professor Marie Giblin's essay presents a feminist critique of current approaches to bioethics. After developing six characteristics of a feminist approach, including a focus on the oppression of women and its concrete forms in the health care system, she then notes two important tasks for the future: analysis of the current metamorphosis of contemporary systems of health care and a more explicit use of stories to ground ethical reflection on the struggle of women today.

Chapter 6, contributed by Professor William Werpehowski and titled "Sexuality and Intimacy," situates the topic within the context of the methodological debate currently unfolding in Catholic moral theology today. How do "traditional" and "revisionist" understandings of marital love, sexuality, and reproduction differ? What virtues and practices need to permeate a mutual relationship of love? How is fidelity understood today? To these questions and others, Werpehowski provides insights both from traditional and contemporary ethical analysis.

Professor Sarah-Vaughn Brakman's essay identifies family life as the first experience of community and relationships, as well as the place in which individuals learn how to treat others. With special emphasis on the obligation that adult children have to parents, the author inspects such virtues as love, compassion, charity, self-sacrifice, and gratitude. She concludes her study by citing practical implications and the countercultural dimensions of the teaching.

My own essay traces the evolution of Roman Catholic hierarchical thought on the concept of peace in the modern world. The chapter examines the fact that, while both the traditional just-war theory and pacifism share a presumption against the use of force, they differ dramatically concerning the legitimacy of overriding this presumption against war. After an inspection of such issues as deterrence, disarmament, and development, the study concludes by articulating components of an emerging theology of peace.

Professor Sally Scholz's contribution on economic ethics focuses on legal and moral rights and the corresponding responsibilities entailed with those rights. She then takes up the question of the dignity of work and its impact on the worker, the family, and the broader community.

Professor David Hollenbach of Boston College examines a key challenge for Catholic higher education today: how to retain and strengthen its distinctive religious identity while educating students for life in an increasingly pluralistic world. He then offers key concepts such as justice, the common good, and the virtue of solidarity as critical foundations upon which Catholic higher education can build.

I want to thank John Samples, Director of Georgetown University Press, and his competent staff for their invaluable assistance with this volume. Frances Hart, S.S.J., also assisted in the preparation of the text, as did Katarina Schuth, O.S.F., and Catherine Slight. For their help, I am especially grateful. Finally, James McCartney and Jane Mary Zwerner gave assistance with the text's development and I am grateful for their help as well.

—Judith A. Dwyer
University of St. Thomas
St. Paul, MN

CONTRIBUTORS

SARAH-VAUGHAN BRAKMAN, PH.D., is Assistant Professor of Philosophy at Villanova University, where she teaches ethics, medical ethics, and philosophy of medicine. Dr. Brakman also serves as an ethics consultant for hospitals and long-term care facilities and she is the chairperson of the Devereux Foundation's National Ethics Committee. She writes on familial obligations and long-term care, ethical issues in reproductive technologies, and philosophy and psychiatry.

PAUL DANOVE is an Associate Professor of New Testament Studies in the Department of Theology and Religious Studies at Villanova University. He received his M.Div. and S.T.L. from the Jesuit School of Theology in Berkeley and Ph.D. from the Graduate Theological Union (Berkeley, CA). Dr. Danove is the author of *The End of Mark's Story: A Methodological Study* (Leiden: E. J. Brill, 1993), "The Narrative Rhetoric of Mark's Ambiguous Characterization of the Disciples," *Journal for the Study of the New Testament* 70 (1998) 21–38, and "The Characterization and Narrative Function of the Women at the Tomb (Mark 15, 40–41, 47; 16, 1–8)," *Biblica* 77:3 (1996) 375–397. He is an active lecturer, both on and off campus, and the Director of the M.A. Program in Theology at Villanova University.

JUDITH A. DWYER, PH.D., is Executive Vice President of the University of St. Thomas, St. Paul, MN, and Professor of Moral Theology there. Her previous works with Georgetown University Press are *Questions of Special*

Urgency: The Church in the Modern World Two Decades after Vatican Two (1986) and *The Catholic Bishops and Nuclear War: A Critique and Analysis of the Pastoral "The Challenge of Peace"* (1984). She also initiated and edited the award-winning *New Dictionary of Catholic Social Thought* (Liturgical Press, 1994). Dr. Dwyer has served on the Committee on International Policy of the United States Catholic Conference and as Editor of the *Proceedings* of the Catholic Theological Society of America.

MARIE J. GIBLIN teaches Christian social ethics and health care ethics at Xavier University in Cincinnati, Ohio. She received her Ph.D. in Christian Ethics from Union Theological Seminary in New York City. Professor Giblin lived and worked in Tanzania, and taught at Maryknoll School of Theology in Maryknoll, New York, before moving to Xavier. Her articles have appeared in *Horizons, Quarterly Review, The Way, Listening*, and other journals. She serves as an ethics consultant to Mercy Health Partners in Greater Cincinnati.

DAVID HOLLENBACH, S.J., is the Margaret O'Brien Flatley Professor of Catholic Theology at Boston College, where he teaches theological ethics and Christian social ethics. His research interests are in the foundations of Christian social ethics, particularly in the areas of human rights, theory of justice, the common good, and the role of religion in social and political life. His publications include *Catholicism and Liberalism: Contributions to American Public Philosophy* (1994), *Justice, Peace, and Human Rights: American Catholic Social Ethics in a Pluralistic World* (1988), *Nuclear Ethics: A Christian Moral Argument* (1983), and *Claims in Conflict: Retrieving and Renewing the Catholic Human Rights Tradition* (1979). In 1998 he received the John Courtney Murray Award for distinguished achievement in theology from the Catholic Theological Society of America.

ELIZABETH A. JOHNSON, CSJ, is Distinguished Professor of Theology at Fordham University in New York City. In addition to numerous essays in scholarly journals, encyclopedias, edited books, and popular journals, she has authored these books: *Consider Jesus: Waves of Renewal in Christology* (NY: Crossroads, 1990); *She Who Is: The Mystery of God in Feminist Theological Discourse* (Crossroads, 1992); *Women, Earth, and Creator Spirit* (NY: Paulist Press, (1993); *Friends of God and Prophets: A Feminist Theological Reading of the Communion of Saints* (NY: Continuum, 1998). Her work has been translated into German, Portuguese, Spanish, Italian, Dutch, French, and Korean. A former President of the Catholic Theological Society of

America and on the Steering Committee of several American Academy of Religious Groups, she serves on the editorial boards of *Theological Studies* and *Horizons: Journal of the College Theology Society.* Dr. Johnson has lectured widely at colleges and universities as well as to church, women's, and clergy groups throughout the United States and abroad, including South Africa, Mexico, Canada, Lithuania, England, and Australia. Deeply involved in the life of the Church, she has served as a theologian on the national Lutheran-Catholic Dialogue; as a consultant to the U.S. Catholic Bishops' Committee on Women in Church and Society; and now on the core committee of the Common Ground Initiative started by Cardinal Bernardin.

JAMES J. MCCARTNEY is an Augustinian priest who serves as Chair of the Department of Philosophy at Villanova University and teaches courses in health care ethics, bioethics and the law, philosophy of biology, and philosophy of law. He is also a faculty associate at The University of Pennsylvania Center for Bioethics and an Adjunct Professor at the Villanova School of Law. Professor McCartney is Ethicist Consultant for the Holy Redeemer Health System and Ethics Consultant for Catholic Health East Health System, and serves on the editorial boards of *Catholic Studies in Bioethics* and *HEC Forum.* He has authored numerous articles, a book (*Unborn Persons: Pope John Paul II and the Abortion Debate*), and has co-edited an anthology dealing with the philosophy of medicine (*Concepts of Health and Disease: Interdisciplinary Perspective*).

MICHAEL J. SCANLON, O.S.A., is a Past President of the Catholic Theological Society of America and currently holds the Josephine C. Connelly Chair of Christian Theology at Villanova University. He received the S.T.D. degree from the Catholic University of America. Professor Scanlon is the Chair of the Graduate Committee of the Department of Theology and Religious Studies. He has taught and published in the areas of fundamental theology, systematic theology, and Augustinian studies.

SALLY J. SCHOLZ is Assistant Professor of Philosophy at Villanova University. She has published articles on systemic oppression, domestic violence, ethics, and feminist theory in *The Thomist, Teaching Philosophy, The Journal of Social Philosophy*, and numerous other venues. Her current research focuses on language in the thought of Simone de Beauvoir and questions the role of language in social solidarity. She and Judith Presler are currently editing *Peacemaking: Lessons from the Past/Visions for the Future.*

WILLIAM WERPEHOWSKI teaches Christian ethics at Villanova University, and is currently the Director of Villanova's Center for Peace and Justice Education. He is the co-editor (with Edmund N. Santurri) of *The Love Commandments* (Georgetown, 1992) and (with Stephen D. Crocco) *The Essential Paul Ramsey* (Yale, 1994). Dr. Werpehowski is an Associate Editor of the *Journal of Religious Ethics*, and a member of the Board of Directors of the Society of Christian Ethics.

1

SCRIPTURAL
SOURCES

PAUL DANOVE

Villanova University

As the title "Scriptural Sources" indicates, Christians hold that the biblical writings constitute valued sources for ethical reflection and guidance. The title also implies a foundational distinction between Christian ethics, the study of the ethics of Christian communities, and biblical ethics, the study of the ethics in the scriptures.[1] Christian ethics is distinct from biblical ethics because it must grapple with many issues never envisioned in the Christian scriptures. The Mosaic Law offers no directly applicable regulations about genetic engineering; the Hebrew prophets who frequently rail against the abuse of the poor by the rich never envisioned the economic impact of the operation of multinational corporations; Jesus' teachings and actions do not give direct guidance concerning when or if it is appropriate to turn off the respirators of terminal patients; and Paul's many instructions on Christian living never envisioned a social situation in which men and women enjoy true equality and slavery is deemed immoral.

While such examples confirm the distinction between biblical ethics and Christian ethics, they also raise the question of what is the appropriate way for the Christian scriptures to be used as sources in ethical discussion. Traditionally this question has occasioned much discussion and debate among Protestant Christians, for whom the scriptures hold the position of primacy in ethical inquiry and reflection. In contrast, Roman Catholic ethical writing, especially during the last two centuries, gave primacy to the guidance provided by natural law, which sometimes was identified with the law that God writes in human hearts (Rom 2:14–16).[2] A precedent for the use of natural law was seen in the use of the ethical codes of contemporary non-Christian Stoic philosophers by the apostle Paul and other New Testament writers (1 Cor 14:33b–35; cf. Eph 5:21; Col 3:18–4:1; 1 Tm 2:11–12; 3:4–5; 1 Pt 2:13–3:17). Roman Catholic reliance on natural law continued to grow until the Second Vatican Council, which stated that moral theology's "scientific exposition should be more thoroughly nourished by scriptural teaching."[3] Thus today, both Protestant and Catholic Christians are faced with answering the question about how the scriptures may be used as sources to inform ethical reflection.

The distinction between biblical ethics and Christian ethics indicates that the use of the scriptures as sources for Christian ethics will entail a two-stage process of investigation. Since the Christian scriptures are to serve "as sources" for Christian ethics, the first stage of investigation will require a rigorous and open study of the ethical statements and assertions in the scriptures and a careful compilation and systemization of the results of this study. This investigation, if it is to be rigorous and open to collaborative effort and critique, will need to employ generally accepted methods of biblical analysis and principles for systematizing the results of the analysis. Such methods of analysis, honed and developed over time, will provide rigorous procedures for studying the precise content of the scriptures. Similarly, the principles of systemization will ensure that the differing emphases and concerns of the various biblical authors are identified and clarified and that both specific and broad themes within the biblical writings may be understood and developed. That is, the application of biblical methods of analysis and principles of systemization of the Christian scriptures will permit the formulation of a comprehensive and systematic statement of biblical ethics that reflects the themes and emphases provided by the scriptures themselves.[4]

Once the preliminary study and systemization of the statement of the ethics in the scriptures is completed, the second stage of the investigation may begin. Since the Christian scriptures are to serve as sources "for Christian ethics," the second stage, like the first, will need to employ rigorous and open methods of analysis and principles of systemization. At this second stage of the investigation, however, the object of analysis is no longer the scriptures themselves, but the comprehensive and systematic statement of the ethics in the scriptures derived in the first stage. Likewise, the systemization of the results of this second stage will not be based primarily on scriptural themes, but on issues and topics of vital concern to contemporary Christians. That is, the application of ethical methods to the statement of biblical ethics will permit a formulation of Christian ethics that reflects the issues and concerns of contemporary Christians, whose ethical questions and problems may be very different from those envisioned by the original biblical writers.

Although the use of the scriptures as sources for Christian ethics requires a two-stage process of investigation, the present discussion focuses specifically on the first stage of the process, the one concerned with developing a comprehensive and systematic statement of the ethics in the scriptures. Statements applicable to the second stage will be suggestive only of potential possibilities and difficulties. The actual application of the implications of the present discussion will be used to varying degrees and in differing ways by subsequent contributors to this volume.

Many possible approaches have been proposed concerning the appropriate use of the scriptures as sources for Christian ethics. The use of one or another approach generally does not depend on an objective determination of the inherent superiority of one method over another, but on a series of presuppositions concerning the nature of the Christian scriptures themselves. These presuppositions frequently exclude certain methods of inquiry, relegate some to secondary status, and elevate others to preferred status. The following discussion distinguishes two broadly conceived approaches for using the scriptures as sources for Christian ethics—the fundamentalist approach and the historical critical approach. These are the two most commonly employed approaches in contemporary attempts to formulate a comprehensive statement of the ethics in the scriptures. The discussion of these approaches focuses on the presuppositions for their use, their preferred methods for analyzing biblical texts, and their principles for systematizing the results of analysis. This investigation permits the formulation of a preliminary statement of biblical ethics with respect to specific scriptural terms or themes. The discussion concludes with a review of the possible limitations of both approaches for constructing a comprehensive exposition of the ethics in the scriptures.

In order to facilitate a comparison and contrast of these methods, the discussion of each approach centers on the examination of the same four sets of biblical texts: the Genesis creation accounts (Gn 1:1–2; 4a; 2:4b–25); statements concerning sexual relations between two men from Leviticus (Lv 18:22; 20:13) and the New Testament Letters (Rom 1:27; 1 Cor 6:9; 1 Tm 1:10); stories of miraculous feeding in the Gospels (Mk 6:34–44; 8:1–9; Mt 14:13–21; 15:32–39; Lk 9:10–19); and statements concerning the proper role of women in the Christian assembly and family (1 Cor 14:34–35; 1 Tm 2:9; 1 Pt 3:1, 3). The choice of these texts reflects a desire to study passages for which fundamentalist and historical critical analyses yield divergent interpretations while at the same time addressing issues of interest in contemporary Christian ethical writing and debate.

The Fundamentalist Approach to Scripture

Fundamentalist Presuppositions

In its historical origins, the foundational presupposition of the fundamentalist approach to scripture is that the biblical writings are inerrant, that is, the scriptures are without error in matters of theological, ethical, historical, and scientific fact.[5] The presupposition of strict inerrancy is based on a view of inspiration (guidance of the Holy Spirit). Using this view, the role of the biblical author is minimized, thereby precluding the encroachment of possible human error, and the role of God is maximized, thereby ensuring absoluteness and timelessness of the pronouncements of scripture. Within this review of scripture, the biblical writer is seen to approximate a stenographer whose task is to record the explicit verbal communications of God to human beings.

The presupposition of inerrancy implies a rejection of the possibility of both the historical development and the literary conditioning of the original written documents of the scriptures. The rejection of the historical development of biblical writings denies that the scriptures are a product of oral and written transmission and modification over time and that they reflect particular historical or cultural predispositions and biases.[6] The rejection of literary conditioning of the scriptures frequently minimizes the significance of the differing literary genres within the scriptures: thus, what would be considered a law code, a poem, or a story with a moral at the end in other literature is deemed to be a source of theological, ethical, historical, and/or scientific facts in strict fundamentalist interpretation. The presupposition of inerrancy holds only for the original written documents of the scriptures that have long since been lost. Thus the fundamentalist approach recognizes the possibility that errors or mistakes may have entered the biblical texts during the centuries in which they were hand-copied and passed on.

Fundamentalist Methods of Biblical Analysis and Their Application

The fundamentalist presupposition that the Christian scriptures are inerrant, without historical development and without literary conditioning, supports methods of biblical analyses that stress the investigation of individual, brief biblical texts in isolation from other texts. There are several reasons for this. First, since the biblical writings constitute absolute verbal communication of God, not only the scriptures as a whole, but each and every sentence and verse of the scriptures, constitute an inerrant communication from God to human beings. Second, inerrancy and the rejection of the historical development of texts combine to grant each statement of scripture an everlasting validity that is not influenced by the particular historical context or circumstances in which it arose. Third, inerrancy and the rejection of historical development join with a rejection of literary conditioning to minimize the need or value of analyzing particular statements within their larger narrative contexts.

Although fundamentalist presuppositions deny the usefulness of most methods of historical criticism and literary analysis in the study of the scriptures, they are compatible with the goals of linguistic analysis. Since each sentence of scripture provides direct access to God's will and intentions, the meaning of the Hebrew, Aramaic, or Greek words of the original texts takes on great significance. Fundamentalist linguistic analysis frequently seeks to determine a single, precise, and universally applicable connotation for each word and phrase of the scriptures. In so doing, fundamentalist linguistic analysis diverges from traditional forms of linguistic analysis, which recognize that the meanings of words and phrases generally evolve or change over time and that the meaning of words can differ from author to author. Thus, the explicit fundamentalist rejection of the historical development within the original written texts of the scriptures frequently extends to an implicit rejection of the notion of the historical development of biblical languages, at least in the way they are used in the scriptures, and to an implicit rejection of differing meanings for the same words in the various books of the Bible.

Application of the fundamentalist method of biblical analysis produces a series of autonomous historical (/scientific) and theological (/ethical) statements related to specific brief texts. Fundamentalist analysis of Genesis 1:1–2:25, for example, generates statements indicating that the world was created in seven days (Gn 2:3), that the man was created before the woman (Gn 2:23), that woman was created to be a "partner" or "helper" for men (Gn 2:20), and that man and woman were created to be joined to each other in marriage (Gn 2:24). The investigation of the Levitical statements concerning sexual relations between two males indicates that such activity is always morally wrong (Lv 18:22) and should be punished (Lv 20:13). Study of the feeding stories in Mark (6:34–44; 8:1–9) indicates that Jesus twice fed crowds miraculously during his ministry and that the disciples of Jesus are called upon to share in this activity (6:41; 8:6). The fundamentalist inquiry into the statements concerning the role of women in the Christian assembly and family indicates that women in the Christian assembly should remain silent (1 Cor 14:34–35; 1 Tm 2:9) and that women should be subordinate to their husbands (1 Pt 3:1). These statements are held to communicate assured historical (/scientific) facts or unchanging theological (/ethical) regulations from God.

Fundamentalist Principles of Systemization and Their Application

Within the fundamentalist approach to the scriptures, the individually derived statements of historical and theological fact remain largely autonomous; that is, the fundamentalist method of analysis includes no objective, universally applicable set of principles for organizing and systematizing the results of biblical analysis. A frequently used principle of systemization is based on the repetition of a given word or words. For example, bringing together the various scriptural genealogies in which the word "year" appears permits a determination that the universe was created between six and seven thousand years ago. This principle of organization is limited, however, by the linguistic composition of the scriptural texts that were written in three different languages and in which there are few, if any, cases of the repetition of identical words throughout the scriptures. Even the word "year," which would seem to be a straightforward example of a clearly defined parallel unit from language to language, reveals some variation in meaning. For example, contemporary Christian, Jewish, Islamic, and Chinese calendars reveal differences in the number of days per year and/or the method of dividing years into smaller segments. Outside of such apparently clearly defined words as "year," the problems of carryover from one language to another become significant.

Another frequently used principle of systemization combines the repetition of words or ideas with the presence of commands (imperative forms of verbs) to establish regulations concerning human behavior. For example, bringing together the various biblical statements in which commands are joined with the word "woman" permits the systemization of a series of regulations governing the conduct of women in the Christian assembly and family.[7] This principle of organization is also limited by the noted problems involved in linguistic repetition, the frequent difficulty of distinguishing statements from commands in the original languages, and the absence of a specific word for "women" in certain texts.

The primary fundamentalist principle for systematizing the results of biblical inquiry is guidance of the Holy Spirit. The assertion here is that—since the Holy Spirit, who guided the composition of the scriptures, is present in each Christian—each Christian, under the guidance of the same Holy Spirit, may systematize the results of biblical inquiry for him or herself.[8] This principle is deemed subjective because the source of guidance is the individual's experience of the Holy Spirit, and neither this experience nor the manner of the Spirit's guidance is visible or made explicit for public discussion and critique.

Toward a Preliminary Fundamentalist-Based Formulation of Biblical Ethics

Fundamentalist discussion of the creation accounts offers significant insight into the nature of the fundamentalist systemization of biblical ethics. Since the principle of inerrancy requires that the scriptures, as originally written, not contain factual contradictions, fundamentalist discussion tends to harmonize apparent divergences between the two accounts of creation. The chronology of the second account, in which the male human being is created before the animals (Gn 2:7) and the female human being is created after the animals (Gn 2:21–22), is harmonized to conform to the seven-day chronology of the first account, in which both human beings are created after the animals (Gn 1:26–27). This harmonization is accomplished by translating certain Hebrew verbs in particular ways.[9] Similarly, the inherent equality of males and females implied by their simultaneous creation in the first account (Gn 1:27) is harmonized to conform to the second account in which the creation of the male precedes that of the female (Gn 2:7, 21–22) and the female is designated as a "helper" of the male. This implied precedence of the male over the female is then seen to be explicit and mandated by God in the story of Adam and Eve's sin in the garden (Gn 3:12–13, 17).

The fundamentalist systemization of the legislation concerning sexual relations between two men recognizes the Levitical laws (Lv 18:22; 20:13) as everlasting valid injunctions against such activity and sees the New Testament statements on the same subject (Rom 1:26–27; 1 Cor 6:9; 1 Tm 1:10) as an ongoing validation of these same injunctions.

The fundamentalist study of the two feeding stories in Mark (Mk 6:33–44; 8:1–9) and Matthew (Mt 14:15–21; 15:32–38) may harmonize all of the accounts to the Matthean statement that those who were fed were followers of Jesus (Mt 14:13), that is, Jesus' disciples. In some fundamentalist writings, this is taken to indicate that the biblical imperative to feed the hungry applies specifically or primarily to fellow believers. This conclusion then may be joined to other stories in which Jesus heals those who have faith to establish the basis of an exclusive or preferential "ethic" that requires that Christians give exclusive or primary assistance to those who share the same faith.

The fundamentalist systemization of the noted New Testament passages concerning women (1 Cor 14:34–35; 1 Tm 2:9; 1 Pt 3:1, 3)—as supported by the fundamentalist interpretation of the creation accounts and other passages—recognizes that women are to be subservient to men in the Christian assembly and family, that women may not occupy positions of authority over men in the Christian community, and that women may not be teachers of men in matters of the faith. Apparent statements of the equality of men and women—such as Paul's statement that " . . . there is not male or female, for you are all one in Christ" (Gal 3:28) and the exhortation to the Ephesians, "Being subordinate to one another out of reverence to Christ, wives . . . husbands . . . " (Eph 5:21–27)—are interpreted to refer to a spiritual equality, not a practical equality.

In each of these examples, the systemization of the results of funda-mentalist methods of biblical analysis is seen to be primarily an additive process. That is, systemization consists of grouping together all the perti-nent statements and legislation on a particular topic or concerning particu-lar individuals, groups, or all human beings in general. The resulting groupings of statements may be organized under the headings of history, science, theology, or ethics, and the same statements may appear under one or more headings. In general, however, there is no concerted attempt to integrate the resulting groupings or larger headings into a more compre-hensive synthesis.

The Historical Critical Approach to Scripture

Historical Critical Presuppositions

The foundational presupposition of most contemporary Christian writers who employ the historical critical approach to the scriptures is that the biblical writings are infallible. Here "infallibility" asserts that the scriptures are without error in matters of faith but not in matters of historical or scientific knowledge or facts. In distinction to the notion of inerrancy, infallibility grants a greater role to the writer of scripture, who is recognized as influenced by historical and cultural considerations. The presupposition of infallibility recognizes that the scriptures can reflect their writers' scien-tific understanding and cultural attitudes and biases, that much of the present biblical text has undergone a long process of oral transmission and modification prior to being written down, and that biblical writers used differing narrative forms to communicate different types of knowledge and teaching. Because of this, infallibility asserts that the Bible is a book about faith, not about history or science, and that the inspired writers of the scriptures were limited in writing the scriptures by the horizons of their historical and cultural circumstances.

Historical Critical Methods of Biblical Analysis
and Their Application

The presupposition of infallibility and the acceptance of the historical de-velopment and literary conditioning of the biblical writings supports the use of the historical critical methods of analysis that are geared to exegesis, that is, the interpretation of texts in their original contexts. The exegesis of scriptural texts clarifies precisely which issues are being addressed in a particular text and the biblical assertions concerning those issues. Historical critical methods are "historical" in that they provide access to the historical processes that gave rise to the biblical texts. In doing so, they address questions such as "Which stages of development did these texts go through?" and "What were the cultural and religious presuppositions of the hearers of these texts during the differing times and stages of their development?" These methods are "critical" in that each step of their application is governed by objective or scientific criteria that help to reduce the subjectivity of the inquiry. That is, these methods follow procedures that are open to public critique at each stage of their application.

Of the many historical critical methods of analysis, the following discussion treats only four methods at length: textual, source, form, and redaction criticism. Additional information from other historical critical methods and from complementary methods of analysis is also included when helpful. Textual, source, form, and redaction critical methods tend to be applied sequentially to a given scripture passage, for each contributes specific information that is necessary for proper investigation by subsequent historical critical method(s).

Of the noted historical critical methods, textual criticism attempts to determine the original wording of biblical texts as they were first set down by their writers. Textual criticism is deemed necessary because there are no original copies of any of the biblical books and even the oldest handwritten copies of parts of the Bible reveal significant differences in wording from one ancient document to another. By comparing all of the available ancient manuscripts, textual critical method permits a reconstruction of the most probable original wording for each set of divergent readings in the biblical manuscripts. For example, textual critical analysis establishes the exact location (after verse 33) and wording of the statement that appears in most contemporary English translations as 1 Corinthians 14:34–35. In some ancient manuscript, this sentence appears after verse 40 and has a slightly different wording.[10] In addition, significant textual critical evidence suggests that someone (not the writer of the letter) added these verses to 1 Corinthians long after its original composition.[11] Here both the exact order and wording of this text and a determination of the authenticity of its statements are essential for understanding the apostle Paul's proposed norms of governing women's behavior in the Christian assembly and family. Though textual criticism, in this example and in general, does not lead directly to the exegesis of biblical texts, it does establish the exact ordering and wording of texts, which is a prerequisite for applying the other historical critical methods of analysis.

Source criticism provides procedures for identifying the presence of pre-existing materials or sources that have been incorporated into present scriptural texts and for establishing at which point these sources begin and end. Source criticism is deemed valuable because it permits the recognition of the composite nature of biblical texts and provides the basis for further study through form and redaction criticism. For example, source critical analysis suggests that Mark has used two different sources for the feeding stories in Mark 6:34–44 and 8:1–9 and that Mark's versions of these stories served as sources in the composition of the Gospels of Matthew and Luke. Likewise, source criticism establishes that many of the New Testament statements governing the relationships among different groups (1 Cor 14:33b–35; cf. Eph 5:21; Col 3:18–4:1; 1 Tm 2:11–12; 3:4–5; 1 Pt 2:13–3:17) are borrowed from pre-existent Greco-Roman ethical lists. Such results establish a foundation for form critical and redaction critical analyses of these texts.

Form criticism studies the literary genres or forms and the historical backgrounds of the sources determined by source criticism. Form criticism is deemed valuable because differing literary genres convey information and assertions of truth in different ways. For example, both a legal command and a story with a moral at the end may communicate that one should not steal, but they do so in very different ways. Form critical analysis also grants a window into the past to understand the cultural and religious presuppositions of the original writers of texts, the nature of the situations that these writers wished to address, how particular compositions addressed these situations, and the stages through which texts developed into their present written forms.

Form criticism offers considerable insight into both the form and the historical and cultural backgrounds of each of the noted scripture passages. Form critical analysis of the first creation account (Gn 1:1–2:4a) indicates that it is an example of the genre or form of "saga," that is, a highly embellished story built around a real or necessary historical event, in this

case the "creation." The second account (Gn 2:4b–25) is characterized by a
closely related form, "the origins story," that deals with many of the same
issues. Form critical analysis reveals that the first creation account is of
much more recent composition (probably after the Babylonian Exile in the
sixth century B.C.E.) than the composition of the second creation story
(probably during the early monarchy in the tenth century B.C.E.). The
post-Exilic concern for cultic matters appears in the seven-day duration of
the creative act that culminates in the creation of human beings and in the
greater transcendence ascribed to God. In distinction, the early monarchi-
cal writings tend to emphasize a more triumphal and potentially more
androcentric (male-centered) view of human beings and a more anthropo-
morphic view of God. This view gives insight into the order of creation in
which the male human being is created before the female and into the
imagery of portraying God as a potter fashioning God's creatures (Gn 2:7).
The form of both stories would preclude their use as sources of historical
and/or scientific knowledge of the creative act itself, for these forms deal
with primordial realities and are not employed to communicate particular
historical facts. Rather, both creation accounts are seen to make complementary theological assertions that God is the author of creation at each
and every stage of creation, that God is the creator of all, and that God is
actively involved with God's creation.

Form critical analysis of the setting of the legislation concerning sexual
relations between two males (Lv 18:22; 20:13) reveals that these statements
are part of larger literary units (Lv 18:1–30 and 20:1–27) called "legal codes."
In particular, these regulations are parts of religious legal codes that reflect
the religious and ethical understanding of a given community at a particular
point in time. Form critical investigation, as augmented by archaeological
research and sociohistorical criticism, reveals that the historical setting in
which these codes arose was the period of the settlement of Palestine. At
that time, the two primary factors operative in the development of Israel's
sexual ethics were a concern for cultic purity and for procreation. Both of
these concerns are apparent in the two laws from Leviticus. The concern for
cultic purity manifested itself in a concerted attempt by the Israelites to
define their cultic practices in contrast to those of the original inhabitants
of the land and in contrast to certain pagan elements of their own former
practices. One such cultic practice was the fertility rite, in which males
engaged in sexual relations with cultic male prostitutes as a means of

ensuring fertility for the land. From an Israelite point of view, participation in such rites constituted an "abomination" (Lv 18:22), that is, an action that is deemed loathsome for religious or cultic reasons. Recourse to male prostitutes within the context of pagan fertility cults was deemed an abomination because it involved the Israelites in the performance of actions directed to win the blessing of fertility from a pagan god, a form of idolatry. Such idolatrous actions are specifically condemned by the first commandment of the Decalogue (Ex 20:2–6; cf. Dt 5:7–10). Second, the concern for procreation reflected both practical necessity—the need to secure a sufficiently large population to displace their pagan neighbors—and religious faith—the belief that God fulfilled the promise of many descendents to Abraham by granting large families to the Israelites.[12] The study of the vocabulary used in the New Testament condemnations of sexual relations between two males reveals that, like the Levitical laws, these statements are directed specifically to the practice of cultic prostitution, this time in Greco-Roman temples. The situation being condemned in the New Testament, however, is made even more onerous by the fact that, unlike their ancient equivalents, who were mostly adult members of a priestly caste, Greco-Roman temple prostitutes were predominantly young, adolescent male slaves (1 Cor 6:9 and 1 Tm 1:10). Thus the Levitical laws and the New Testament statements condemn sexual relations between two males in the specific context of idolatrous actions. The New Testament also indirectly condemns pederasty. However, neither the Levitical laws nor the New Testament statements offers a general consideration or condemnation of sexual relations between two males.

Form critical analysis indicates that the two feeding stories in Mark are examples of the form "miracle story" and represent two different versions of the same original story. The first Marcan feeding story (Mk 6:45–44), with its references to the exodus (6:40) and its use of the significant Jewish number "twelve" (6:43), finds its life setting in the early period of Jewish Christian proclamation; whereas the second (Mk 8:1–9), with its exodus and Jewish allusions removed and its use of the significant Greek number "seven" (8:8), constitutes a later version of the same story for use in Greek Christian proclamation.[13] Analysis of the form of these feeding stories highlights the stories' central theological concerns of Jesus' (and his disciples') attitudes toward and actions on behalf of the hungry and the overarching eucharistic interpretation of the event (Mk 6:41; 8:6; cf. 14:22); however, it also indicates the secondary nature of the changeable parts of the story (Jewish or Greek imagery and numbers).

Form critical analysis of the various statements concerning the conduct of women indicates that each of these statements is part of a larger formal unit called a "household code." These codes present a series of guidelines for the smooth functioning and interaction of the recognizable groups within a society or state. Household codes appearing in the New Testament offer regulations governing interaction between and mutual obligations of state/family, husbands/wives, men/women, parents/children, and masters/slaves. The New Testament household codes were either borrowed without modification from or patterned on contemporary Greco-Roman household codes.[14] Thus they reflect Greco-Roman society's patriarchal and androcentric world view and widespread reliance on slave labor.

Redaction criticism studies the process of editing particular sources with their given forms into the finished works that appear in the Bible. Redaction criticism is deemed valuable because it grants access to the manner in which the biblical writers modify their sources to address the particular theological needs of the communities for which the sources were written. When joined with composition criticism, which studies the overall contribution of writers to pre-existent sources and not just their editorial revisions, redaction criticism gives us a snapshot of the biblical writers' particular theological and ethical concerns. This permits a better understanding not only of overarching theology of a biblical book, but also of the particular theological emphases present in the various parts of that book.

Redaction critical analysis of the two creation accounts reveals that the final editor(s) of the Book of Genesis saw no apparent difficulty with including two back-to-back stories with very different perspectives and chronologies. This decision indicates that the theological assertions of both accounts were deemed compatible with the editor's general theological position.

Redaction critical analysis of the legislation governing sexual relations between two males establishes that the two Levitical passages are related in that the first law gives the statement of the transgression (Lv 18:22) and the second (Lv 20:13) gives its punishment. This relationship confirms the cultic setting of both regulations through the presence of the cultic word "abomination" (Lv 18:22). Redaction critical study of the context of Romans 1:27 reveals that, although it does not specifically include the word designating young male prostitutes, the overall concern that undergirds the entire narrative context of the passage is idolatry. This interpretation indicates that Romans 1:27, like 1 Corinthians 6:9 and 1 Timothy 1:10, involves a specific condemnation of the use of male Greco-Roman cult prostitutes by Christian males. Romans 1:26, the only scriptural statement concerning sexual relations between two females, occurs in the same context and involves a parallel condemnation of the use of female Greco-Roman cult prostitutes by Christian females.

Redaction critical analysis of the editing of Mark's stories by Luke and Matthew highlights the particular theological emphases of each Gospel. Luke combined Mark's two stories into a single story (Lk 9:10–19) that reduces the exodus reference but maintains the Jewish number "twelve" (9:19). Luke also changes the emphasis of the story by removing statements indicating Jesus' lack of knowledge (Mk 6:38; 8:5) and by adding a statement highlighting the disciples' activity in the feeding (9:14). The latter statement makes explicit the more implicit Marcan emphasis of the need for action by the disciples. In contrast, Matthew employs Mark's two stories separately, removes the exodus reference from the first story, and emphasizes Jesus' authority by having Jesus seat the crowds without the assistance of the disciples (Mt 14:9; 15:35). Each of these noted modifications (as well as many others not noted) has an impact on the overall theological assertion and ethical implications of these stories. Redaction critical analysis together with composition analysis would identify the statement that those who were fed were followers of Jesus (Mt 14:13) as being a Matthean composition that needs to be interpreted within the overall Gospel emphasis on the need for the disciples of Jesus to care for all human beings, whether or not they are fellow believers (Mt 25:31–46).

Redactional analysis of the use of Stoic household codes that have been incorporated into the New Testament Letters (1 Cor 14:34–35; 1 Tm 2:9; 1 Pt 3:1, 3) reveals that, in all but one case, the New Testament writers have included theological statements concerning the inherent equality of men and women in the immediate context of the citations of the original Greco-Roman household codes. The inclusion of these theological statements of equality, usually at the beginning or end of the household code, serves to relativize the more extreme statements of inequality and to justify the disparity between the sexes as an accommodation to the need to spread the gospel within a given social context. Thus, the original Greco-Roman assertions of male dominance over women in the society and the home (1 Cor 1:33–34; 1 Tm 2:11–12; 1 Pt 3:1) are qualified by the recognition of the mutual interdependence of men and women (1 Cor 11:11–12) and the need for husbands to understand and honor their wives "who are joint heirs of the gift of life in Jesus" (1 Pt 3:7). Again, the statement of the need for wives to be subservient to their husbands in 1 Peter 3:1 is addressed specifically to the Christian wives of non-Christian husbands who are to remain subservient according to Greco-Roman custom so that their husbands "may be won over without a word by their wives' conduct" (1 Pt 3:1b).

Historical Critical Principles of Systemization and Their Application

The historical critical approach offers a diverse set of principles for systemizing the data for analysis. Textual critical method, with its concern to establish the exact wording and ordering of the statements of the original texts of the scriptures, raises the possibility of employing linguistic repetition as a basis of study. Here the problems centered on the biblical languages, already discussed under the principles of fundamentalist systemization, are complicated by the historical critical recognition that languages evolve over time and words may have differing meanings at different times and in different writings. However, the use of the formal unit—that is, any continuous and coherent extension of text characterized by a single literary genre or form—as the basic unit of study within source, form, and redaction criticism opens new avenues for systemization by determining the exact meaning of particular words within an extended literary context. This usage permits systemization centered on meaning and not simply on particular words.

Since the formal unit can vary in length from a few verses (as in the Gospel feeding stories) to a complete chapter (the Levitical legal codes) or even longer (the first creation account), it provides a very fruitful foundation for the systemization of the results of analysis according to particular biblical themes and/or forms. For example, the form critical determination that both the Levitical laws and New Testament statements concerning sexual relations between two males (or two females) are directed against participation in idolatrous pagan cultic rites permits systemization under the scriptural theme of idolatry in general and of idolatry as expressed in sexual activity in particular. Again, the two creation accounts in Genesis reveal that the first has the formal characteristics of a saga and that the second has the formal characteristics of an origins story. These related forms are concerned primarily with explaining the primordial origins of created reality as it presently exists. This recognition permits systemization either according to the theme, "creation," or according to form itself.

The possibilities for systemizing the results of historical critical analysis are significantly augmented by the inclusion of complementary methods of analysis and systemization that presuppose a complete biblical book or even the entire Bible as the basic unit of investigation. Several such "synchronic" methods received explicit attention in the foregoing discussion (e.g., composition and sociohistorical criticism), while others were employed without special mention (e.g., structural, semiotic, and canonical criticism). These methods, like historical critical methods, employ procedures that are open to public discussion and critique. They differ in that they provide objective criteria and procedures for investigating disparate texts and principles for systemizing the results of such analysis. The use of such methods is essential for any study of the ethics in the Bible conducted under a presupposition of the infallibility of the scriptures. The objectivity and scientific character of the historical critical and synchronic approaches help to constrain the subjectivity of those who study the scriptures and so ensures that the scriptures will be able to assert their own truths and make their own demands.

Toward a Preliminary Historical Critical-Based Formulation of Biblical Ethics

As noted above, the study of the two creation accounts in Genesis reveals that the first has the formal characteristics of a saga and that the second has the formal characteristics of an origins story. These two stories deal with the question of origins by attributing the existence of all created reality directly to the God of the Hebrews, who remains intimately involved with creation. The stories also clarify the nature of the relationship between God and humans as well as between one human being and another. The formal similarity of these stories permits systemization based on both theme and form. There are two other partial examples of the saga in the Hebrew Bible: the creation stories that present God as either the slayer of the sea serpent, the principle of chaos

(Jb 26:7–13; cf. Is 27:1; Ps 89:11), or the architect of creation (Jb 38:4–11). These stories, too, present God as the sole source of all created reality and emphasize God's ongoing involvement with God's creatures. Thus both the form of these stories and their central theological assertions become the basis for further systemization of the scriptural witness.

The use of the formal unit offers significant insight into the meaning of the Levitical legislation and New Testament statements concerning sexual activity between two males (or two females) by clarifying that what is being condemned is idolatry, specifically as manifest in the arena of sexual activity between two persons of the same sex. This clarification of the exact nature of the condemned activity permits a systemization with respect to other scriptural statements and legislation (specially within the same Levitical law code) dealing with idolatry as manifest in sexual activity between a male and a female. This clarification also serves as a check on an overly facile extension of laws pertaining to specific cultic acts to more general norms of governing sexual relations between two people of the same sex or of the opposite sex.

The historical background of the two Marcan feeding stories reveals that the early Christian community deemed culturally specific elements of their proclamation as changeable and adaptable to new cultural contexts. The interrelation of Jesus' (and the disciples') concern for the hungry, the need for action on behalf of those who are hungry, and the underlying eucharistic interpretation of these actions establish the basis for a theological systemization that grounds action on behalf of the hungry, both believers and nonbelievers, in the Eucharist. Although the precise nature of this systemization must await the application of other methods of analysis, the contours of such systemization are already implicit in these stories.

The form critical analysis of the various teachings on the role of women in the Christian assembly and family reveal the influence of culture on recommended behavior. Form and redaction criticism establish that, in all but one case, the same New Testament passages that propose a subservient role for women also presuppose that men and women share a basic equality. In these passages, the sole justification for tolerating specific instances of subservience is to spread the gospel more easily. This interpretation establishes the foundation for systemizing a scriptural understanding of the relationship between men and women that stresses their underlying equality (from Gn 1 to the New Testament Letters), that attributes concrete manifestations of inequality to human sinfulness (Gn 3), and that tolerates a temporary subservience of women to men, specifically their husbands, only as a freely chosen means of spreading the gospel more effectively (1 Pt 3).

Proposed Limitations and Deficiencies of the Fundamentalist Approach

The foregoing discussion indicated that both the fundamentalist approach and the historical critical approach to the scriptures provide presuppositions for study, methods of biblical analysis, and principles for systemizing the results of analysis. Both approaches, however, reveal limitations or deficiencies in their application. Some of these limitations and deficiencies are intrinsic to the approaches themselves, that is, they arise from the nature of the presuppositions, methods of analysis, and principles of systemization within the approach. Others are extrinsic to the approaches and find their origin in those who use the approaches. The following discussion reviews several of the more significant intrinsic limitations and deficiencies apparent in the application of the fundamentalist and historical critical approaches. Each review then concludes by examining one significant extrinsic limitation for the noted approach.

Proposed Limitations and Deficiencies of the Fundamentalist Approach

The fundamentalist approach to the scriptures, in conjunction with a literalist principle of interpretation, permits the construction and articulation of a systematic statement of ethics in the scriptures. The fundamentalist approach to scripture is employed in many contemporary Christian communities in the United States, some of which identify themselves as conservative evangelicals.[15] Proposed limitations and deficiencies of the fundamentalist approach focus on the presupposition of inerrancy, the character of the methods of analysis, and reliance on guidance of the Holy Spirit in the systemization of the results of analysis.

The most commonly proposed deficiency concerning the fundamentalist presupposition of inerrancy is the presence of apparently unresolved and potentially unresolvable contradictory statements within the scriptures. As noted previously, the fundamentalist approach employs a principle, of harmonization to deal with apparent contradictions. The application of this principle, however, is frequently very complicated, and the rationale for a particular harmonization is rarely self-evident. Examples of this appeared in the discussion of the two creation accounts. Here the chronology of the second account was harmonized to agree with the first, whereas the particular sequence of events involved in the creation of the man and the woman in the first account was harmonized to agree with the second. Also problematic is the fundamentalist tendency to discount or even ignore many such apparent contradictions.

A second challenge to the presupposition of inerrancy is the apparent presence of examples of historical development and modification within the scriptures themselves. Although the fundamentalist approach accepts the possibility that a subsequent statement or law may overturn a prior statement or law in the scriptures, the previous discussion of the fundamentalist approach to the two creation accounts noted that in this case the assertions of a more recently composed story (Gn 1:1–2:4a) are harmonized to those of the earlier one (Gn 2:4b–25). Here the rejection of historical critical methods results in "subsequent" being interpreted as "appearing later in the present text of the Bible" rather than as "of more recent composition."

The proposed limitations to the fundamentalist methods of analysis generally are joined with the fundamentalist use of a literalist interpretation of the scriptures. The potential limitation in using the repetition of vocabulary is the difficulty of deriving a single meaning for particular words over time and in different books. The potential limitations engendered by a literalist reading of the scriptures becomes apparent in the historical critical study of the Levitical legislation concerning sexual relations between two men and of the New Testament statements on the role of women. In the former case, the presence of specifically cultic vocabulary in the condemnation of sexual relations between two males does not receive mention in the literalist reading that takes these condemnations to apply to all sexual relations between two males. In the latter case, the isolation of specific commands concerning the role of women in the Christian assembly and family seems to neglect equally assertive statements of the inherent equality of men and women that appear elsewhere in the scriptures.

The most serious challenge to the fundamentalist principles of systemization concerns the reliance on the guidance of the Holy Spirit as the preeminent basis for relating the disparate scriptural statements on a given topic. This principle grants a radical autonomy to each interpreter, whose experience of the guidance of the Holy Spirit in interpreting the scriptures is not open to direct critique by other interpreters. This approach results in two major potential limitations. First, lacking explicit procedures for distinguishing between the guidance of the Holy Spirit and the guidance of human subjectivity, the fundamentalist approach produces widely variant interpretations and systemizations of theology and ethics in the scriptures. Second, since it provides no mechanisms for ensuring that all pertinent passages on a particular topic receive investigation, fundamentalist systemizations often neglect large portions of the biblical text and instead concentrate on a limited selection of particular texts. The fundamentalist principles of systemization also contain an implicit claim that rarely receives explicit attention: each interpreter must assume a level of inspiration equal to that of the original writers of the scriptures in order to interpret them as they were originally intended to be interpreted. Acceptance of this claim would remove the unique and privileged status granted to the scriptures by most Christians. This implicit claim, joined with the noted deficiencies in the presupposition of inerrancy, constitutes the most challenging potential limitation for the application of the fundamentalist approach.

The primary extrinsic deficiency of the fundamentalist approach is a direct consequence of its reliance on the guidance of the Holy Spirit as its basic principle of systemization. Since there are no objective principles for systemizing the results of a fundamentalist study of the scriptures, consensus of interpretations generally is built around the interpretations offered by a particular biblical scholar, theologian, or evangelist. Since the fundamentalist approach provides no objective mechanisms for dialogue between consensus groups, these people and their interpreted tend to remain largely autonomous. This approach has the practical result of removing the possibility of a fundamentalist theological or ethical synthesis at least until one set of interpretations wins general acceptance.

Proposed Limitations and Deficiencies of the Historical Critical Approach

The historical critical approach establishes presuppositions, methods of analysis, and principles of systemization that permit the formulation of a comprehensive statement of the ethics in the scriptures. This approach to the scriptures is employed in a majority of contemporary Christian communities in the United States: recent documents of the Presbyterian Church in this country employ both historical and literary methods in their new statement of faith;[16] only one of the traditional Lutheran Synods maintains a position of inerrancy;[17] and the most recent Roman Catholic document on the study of the scriptures explicitly rejects the fundamentalist presupposition on inerrancy, methods of biblical inquiry, and principles of systemization.[18]

The proposed limitations of the historical critical approach differ markedly from those proposed for the fundamentalist approach. The general competency of the historical critical methods for analyzing literature receives widespread recognition even in many fundamentalist circles. This competency is especially true of textual criticism that receives significant use in fundamentalist analysis. Proposed limitations and deficiencies focus on the presupposition of infallibility, the propriety of using historical critical methods for analyzing scripture texts, and the use of principles of systematization that do not presuppose commitment of faith.

The most commonly proposed deficiency concerning the historical critical presupposition of infallibility is that it undermines the unique claims of authority and respect that Christians grant to their scriptures. Accepting the possibility that the scriptures may contain historical and scientific errors seems to limit or call into question the validity of the theological assertions tied to these erroneous historical and scientific statements. For example, historical critical investigation of the creation stories produces a series of theological assertions about the role of God in creation and the implied relationship of God and human beings without requiring the historical or scientific accuracy of the particular statements of the creation stories.

The potential limitations posed by the use of the historical critical methods, excluding textual criticism, stem from the complexity of the methods themselves and from the centrality they grant to the historical, cultural, and literary concerns in interpreting the scripture texts. First, the complexity of these methods limits their usefulness to a small group of trained scholars. The resulting exclusivity seems to undermine a widely held Christian conviction that the scriptures and their truths should be available to everyone. Second, investigations into the historical development and the cultural and literary conditioning of the assertions of the scriptures remove the apparent clarity of scripture statements by revealing differing emphases and positions on particular issues and topics in different writings. This interpretation limits the possibility of using the scriptures for clear and unambiguous guidance in many areas of Christian life. For example, the historical critical analysis of the legislation and statements concerning sexual relations between two males (or two females) limits the applicability of these scriptural assertions to the specific context of idolatrous or pederastic activity. In so doing, any basis for universally applicable scriptural guidance on the topic of same-sex sexual relations is removed. Again, analysis of the Genesis stories and New Testament Letters would indicate occasions of ambivalence about the role of women. The recognition of a more basic and general assertion of the equality of men and women must acknowledge the presence of contravening statements and assumptions, which will make the formulation of a universally applicable statement on the relationship of men and women and the inherent status of women very difficult.

The primary proposed limitation or deficiency in using historical critical methods does not concern their inherent inadequacy for analyzing literature in general, but instead, the propriety of their use in the study of Christian scriptures in particular. These methods were developed for the study of literature in general, and there is no claim that literature in general is written under the special guidance of the Holy Spirit. Since these approaches do not address the topic of inspiration itself, their use in the study of scriptures appears to discount the significance of inspiration in their composition. This understanding would have the practical effect of undermining the unique status that Christians grant their scriptures. The difficulty with this challenge is that it usually is posed as an intrinsic problem when, in fact, it is an extrinsic problem. In granting no explicit attention to the question of inspiration, historical critical methods are in no way different from fundamentalist methods; both sets of methods deal only with analyzing written texts. The question of how to respect the inspired status of the scriptures resides in the area presuppositions and principles of systemization. The actual concern that underlies this challenge to the historical critical approach is the recognition that, since historical critical methods are scientific, they have the potential to be employed not only by believers, but also by nonbelievers. In this case the potential extrinsic limitation concerns the possibility of unsympathetic and even hostile use of historical critical methods for studying the scriptures. However, the public nature of these methods ensures that any potentially hostile use of them would be open to public discussions and critique by believers employing these same methods.

Concluding Remarks on Formulating a Comprehensive Statement of the Ethics in the Bible

The foregoing discussion investigated the two major approaches for studying the Christian scriptures in this country today. The investigation revealed that Christians tend to choose one or the other approach based on their presuppositions concerning the nature of the scriptures themselves. Christians who hold a presupposition of inerrancy generally adopt fundamentalist methods of analysis; and those who hold a presupposition of infallibility generally adopt historical critical and complementary methods of analysis. The adoption of one or the other of these approaches produces significant differences in the nature of the resulting formulation of the ethics in the scriptures. While the fundamentalist approach produces a series of clear statements on various ethical topics and issues, the results of its analysis diverge widely from interpreter to interpreter, providing no mechanism for generating a truly comprehensive statement of the ethics in the scriptures. While the historical critical approach provides mechanisms for addressing divergent interpretations and for constructing a truly comprehensive statement of the ethics in the scriptures, it requires training for its proper use. The application of historical critical and complementary methods also yields results that are much more specific and nuanced than those yielded by fundamentalist methods of analysis. The complexity of many contemporary Christian ethical questions and issues reveals the pressing need for a comprehensive and nuanced statement of Christian ethics. Such a statement of Christian ethics will require an equally comprehensive and nuanced statement of ethics in the scriptures if the scriptures are to serve as adequate sources for Christian ethics. Of the approaches discussed, only the historical approach establishes the required basis for formulating a comprehensive statement of ethics in the scriptures.

Endnotes

1. J. M. Gustafson, "The Place of Scripture in Christian Ethics: A Methodological Study," in C. E. Curran and R. A. McCormick, eds., *Readings in Moral Theology No. 4: The Use of Scripture in Moral Theology* (New York: Paulist, 1984) 151.

2. J. Fuchs, *Natural Law: A Theological Investigation* (New York: Sheed and Ward, 1965) 3–13.

3. W. M. Abbott, ed., "The Decree on Priestly Formation (Optatam Totius)," in *The Documents of Vatican II* (New York: Guild Press, 1966) 452.

4. R. F. Collins, *Christian Morality: Biblical Foundations* (Notre Dame, IN: University of Notre Dame, 1986) vii.

5. D. W. Bebbington, "Evangelicalism in Its Settings: The British and American Movements since 1940," in M. A. Noll, D. W. Bebbington, and G.A. Rawlyk, eds., *Evangelism: Comparative Studies of Popular Protestantism in North America, the British Isles, and Beyond, 1700–1990* (New York: Oxford University, 1994) 371–373.

6. D. M. Rosman, *Evangelicals and Culture* (London: Croom Helm, 1984) 226.

7. R. Balmer, *Mine Eyes Have Seen the Glory: A Journey into the Evangelical Subculture in America* (New York: Oxford University, 1989) 40–41.

8. J. Wolffe, "Anti-Catholicism and Evangelical Identity in Britain and the United States, 1830–1860," in M.A. Noll, D. W. Bebbington, and G. A. Rawlyk, eds., *Evangelism: Comparative Studies of Popular Protestantism in North America, the British Isles, and Beyond, 1700–1990* (New York: Oxford University, 1994) 183.

9. J. Rogerson, *Genesis 1–11: Old Testament Guides,* 1 (Sheffield: Academic Press, 1991) 63.

10. B. M. Metzger, *Textual Commentary on the Greek New Testament* (Stuttgart: Biblia-Druck GmbH, 1975) 565.

11. G. D. Fee, *The First Epistle to the Corinthians* (Grand Rapids, MI: Eerdmans, 1987) 696–710.

12. Collins, 172–176.

13. P. Perkins, *Reading the New Testament* (New York: Paulist, 1988) 54.

14. Perkins, 129–130.

15. Balmer, 6, 97.

16. W. C. Placher and D. Willis-Watkins, *Belonging to God: A Commentary on A Brief Statement of Faith* (Louisville: Westminster, 1992) 148, 156.

17. E. C. Nelson, *Lutheranism in North America* (Minneapolis: Augsburg, 1972) 165–166.

18. The Pontifical Biblical Commission, "The Interpretation of the Bible in the Church," *Origins* (January 1994) 509–510.

2

CHRISTIAN ANTHROPOLOGY AND ETHICS

MICHAEL J. SCANLON

Villanova University

Christian anthropology is an understanding of human existence from the perspective of the Christian faith. It attempts to interpret humanity in relation to God's self-disclosure in Jesus Christ. Fundamental to this interpretation is the perception of Christianity itself, not primarily as a system of doctrines, but as a *way of life* based on following Jesus in the power of the Holy Spirit. In the gospel of John, Jesus himself is the Way (Jn 14:4ff), and the Acts of the Apostles refers to Christian discipleship as the "new way" (Acts 9:2).

Christian faith, then, is not to be identified with beliefs. Rather, faith is a radical trust in the God of Jesus, a trust that manifests itself in what St. Paul names as the "obedience" of faith. Here obedience is to be taken in the etymological sense of "hearing," as the faithful person assumes an attitude of attentiveness and of listening for the call of God in deciding on courses of action in life. Christian faith implies an *ethos,* a certain style of living, guided by the living memory of Jesus.

Christians ethics (or "moral theology") is a tradition that goes back to the early Church as Christians reflected on the *practical* implications of following Christ in the ever-changing concrete circumstances of life in history. This tradition developed in a continuous conversation with philosophy as

Western civilization unfolded under the influences of "Athens" (philosophy) and "Jerusalem" (theology). Obviously, it is the latter influence that distinguishes Christian ethics from moral philosophy. Christian ethics had a prehistory in the Old Testament. It is rooted in the ethical traditions of Israel and Judaism. Before considering the Christian tradition itself, it is important to appreciate its Old Testament roots.

The Old Testament

Central to the Hebrew scriptures is the Covenant between God and the people, Israel, which took place at Sinai after the Exodus from Egypt. It can be summed up in the formula "You shall be my people, and I will be your God." This divine election of Israel was based on Yahweh's initiative, not on the merits of the people. The very name of Israel's God, *Yahweh,* means "I will be for you who I will be for you." God is a God of promise, but the fulfillment of the promise is not without conditions. These conditions are elaborated in the Decalogue (the "Ten Commandments"). God's fidelity to the people cannot be manipulated—divine fidelity is embraced by divine freedom. The moral core of the Covenant demands obedience to God's Law on the part of the elected people. As the biblical story continues, God's fidelity is more and more in tension with the infidelity of the people. Especially through the evil deeds of the rich, the wise, and the powerful (often in collusion), the people betray the Covenant. This betrayal, this pervasive "social sin," reaches a pitch that is disclosed and indicted by the great prophets of Israel.

Sociologists of religion often portray the religion of a people as "a sacred canopy," a divine legitimation of the status quo, which functions to conserve the social order in place. But religion does not always function in such a conservative manner. Religion can be a massive critique of the status quo, and this function is poignantly illustrated in the prophets of Israel. A prophet, literally, is one who speaks for is a spokesperson for God. The prophet is so attain to the divine will or the divine *pathos* that God's feelings for God's people become the feelings of the prophet.[1] The use of the word *feelings* here is important, prophets are overwhelmed by their experience of God's call—they cannot avoid speaking in the name of Yahweh. As the prophet Jeremiah graphically put it: "O Lord, thou has seduced me, and I am seduced. Thou has raped me, and I am overcome" (Jer 20:7). Try as he might to avoid speaking in God's name because of the suffering entailed, Jeremiah exclaimed that "within me there is something like a burning fire shut up in my bones. I am weary with holding it in and I cannot" (Jer 20:9).

The fundamental message of the prophets is that there cannot be any authentic worship of God without love, care, and concern for one's neighbor, especially the oppressed and the marginalized—"the widow, the orphan, and the stranger" (Dt 27:19). Any use of religious language or practice is idolatry if it is divorced from the active search for justice, love, and mercy in the land. It is precisely this prophetic teaching that we find radicalized in Jesus of Nazareth. The "logic" behind this prophetic tradition is plain. The God of the Bible is God *for us, our* God, and *this* God cannot be reached except in and through each other.

The prophetic critique of injustice in Israelite society is a lucid example of passionate religious faith working to overcome what today we call "social sin." Social sin is a pervasive atmospheric conditioning of social, political, and economic structures. These unjust structures endure because people do not discern the injustice and the violence built into them. The Bible calls this "blindness," and it is a blindness that demands a symbolic "cover-up" so that people continue to accept this illegitimate situation. Cultural and religious symbols can supply this pseudo-legitimation of social evil—through the power of these symbols, people come to think that what is wrong is right. They accept the status quo as "the way things should be." But in the midst of this social blindness, some people (a few) begin to suspect that all is not right in the land. Thus emerges the prophet, the one profoundly shaped by the authentic religious traditions of the people, with a call for repentance, conversion, and change. This call often falls on deaf ears (this blindness makes people deaf as well) and/or on hostile ears on the part of those who are profiting from the unjust structures of society—the rich, the wise, and the powerful. That is why the prophetic indictment on these people is most severe. All are sinners, but these sinners are the most powerful, so that their sins have dire consequences for the majority (the poor, the uneducated, the politically impotent). These sinners recognize the danger for them in the prophetic accusation; thus, the prophets are silenced by murder, imprisonment, and exile. It is always so, everywhere, down to our own day. But without the prophet, there is no hope.

What has been said above about the sins of the powerful illustrates the fact that there is a dialectical relationship between social sin and personal sin. Regarding the latter, an extremely significant development takes place among the prophets of Israel—the emergence of that structure of human existence that we call *personhood*. Personhood, as a way of being human, is the discovery of the *responsible self*. The Personal God (or the God of freedom) calls the Israelites into personhood as they become aware of themselves as summoned by the prophets into ethical responsibility for themselves and for others. The prophet Jeremiah is perhaps the clearest example of the birth of personhood beyond the "collective personality" of the undifferentiated "we" (the previous pre-personal stage of human consciousness when unreflective, uncritical obedience to laws and customs ruled the day). Without this prophetic breakthrough to personal existence, the message of Jesus of Nazareth would have been inaudible.

Frustrated over and over again by the apathetic responses of their people, the prophets came to realize our powerlessness to obey the moral demands of God. Their "ethical monotheism" (love of God and love of neighbor are one) created a terrible tension between the clarity of the divine command and the human incapacity to fulfill it. Jeremiah longed for a "new covenant," written by God *on the heart,* a new divine empowerment from *within* the human spirit (Jer 31:33). Similarly, the prophet Ezekiel hoped for a new heart of flesh to replace the heart of stone, when God would put the divine Spirit *within* the people (Ez 11:19). For Christians this yearning is fulfilled through the redemptive mediation of the divine Spirit through Jesus Christ.

The New Testament

The New Testament is for Christians the normative articulation of the new way of life inaugurated by the words, the deeds, and the destiny of Jesus of Nazareth. From its beginning, the life of Jesus is one of conflict and rejection. He comes to his own, but his own receive him not. He is the light shining in darkness. He begins a movement of ethical egalitarianism in which the accepted standards and the religion-cultural mores of his people are overturned. His followers are the poor, women, and outcasts—the despised of this world. His central symbol is the "Kingdom of God," a way of talking about God *for us.* He fleshed out his new vision of God in his parables ("The Kingdom of God is like . . . "), those metaphoric stories so "ordinary" at first glance, but marked by an extraordinary or extravagant twist in each case. The God of Jesus is a God in love with human be-ings—our concerns are God's concerns, our interests are God's interests. As St. Irenaeus (second century) put it so beautifully: "The glory of God is humanity fully alive."

Jesus strongly condemned all forms of hypocritical, legalistic, and de-humanizing religion. While, as a Jew, he had reverence for the Torah (the Law of Moses), he exercised a sovereign freedom in interpreting it. Not only did he perform cures on the Sabbath, but he claimed that the Sabbath (the "Lord's day") was made for human beings and not human beings for the Sabbath. His moral demands went beyond the Law in his astonishing way of "comparing". "You have heard it said to you (i.e., by the Law), . . . but I say to you . . . " Whatever it may be, Christian morality can never be merely a matter of obedience to law.

For what he said and what he did, Jesus was condemned to death in the name of the Law by the leaders of the people of the Law with Roman collaboration. He was crucified, suffering the worst of Roman penalties. He seemed to die a failure, but God raised him from the dead, thus validating and confirming Jesus and his message. His follower Paul would reflect on the cross and resurrection of Jesus, and from this destiny he would con-struct a "soteriological anthropology."

St. Paul and Christian Morality

The Christian anthropology of the Western Church is rooted in the teach-ings of Paul, the converted persecutor of the early Christians. Pauline theology is both dynamic and dramatic—he loves to describe the Christian life in terms of "before" and "after." For example, he distinguishes between life according to the "flesh" and life according to the "spirit." It is very important for us to understand that by "flesh" Paul does *not* mean the human body and that by "spirit" he does *not* mean the human soul. Body/soul anthropology is of Greek philosophical derivation; it is an ana-lytic anthropology that distinguishes the "parts" of the human being. Paul's anthropology ("Hebrew of the Hebrews," as he claimed to be in Phil 3:5) was Semitic and, therefore, synthetic. Flesh and spirit do not name the "parts" of the human being—they name the whole person from different perspectives. Flesh is the whole human being without the Spirit (or grace) of Christ (i.e., the sinner); spirit names the whole person who is now a "new creation," vivified by the spirit of Christ. Christians are those who have "died" (the cross) to the "flesh" (their sinful past) and have been born anew (resurrection) to a new way of life, the "spiritual life" (or life in the power of the Risen Christ).

Paul's understanding of the work of the Holy Spirit in us is *the distinctive characteristic* of Christian anthropology and, hence, of Christian ethics. The Spirit of God is the divine, life-giving power in the world. Paul tells us that this Spirit of God has become the Spirit of Christ because Jesus Christ is the concrete revelation of what God's spirit effects in human beings. Filled with the Holy Spirit, Jesus lived and died as *the* Image of God, as God intends all of us to live and die. In his resurrection from the dead, Jesus is the definitive disclosure of the Spirit at work as "the Lord and Giver of life." As the Risen Lord, Jesus mediates to us that same Spirit as *empowerment* to reproduce Christ's life in our different ways down through the centuries. Jeremiah's hope for a "new covenant" written within us and Ezekiel's yearning for a new "heart" have been fulfilled with the gift of the Holy Spirit.

In one sentence, Paul combines the "Christian indicative" and the "Christian imperative"— "Where the Spirit of God is, there is freedom" (2 Cor 3:17). The Spirit is given (the "good news," or the "indicative"); now we are empowered to act (freedom, or the "imperative"). Paul tells us that we are freed *from* sin, death, and the Law. By the "Law," he means the moral law of Judaism (the Ten Commandments). This declaration sounds quite radical, and it is! For Christians, the Law can have only a pedagogical function; the Law alerts us to our responsibilities. But we must choose to do the good not because it is commanded, but because it is good. When Paul goes on to tell us what we have been freed *for,* he cannot find words: "We have been freed for freedom!" (Gal 5:1). If the divine power, the Spirit, is the source of our freedom, no one can delimit the potential range of this freedom. "I live now, but Christ (or the Spirit) lives in me" (Gal 2:20). Co-constituted by the Spirit and one's self, the Christian finds nothing impossible. Hyperbole, yes, but mysteriously true. If, according to the Old Testament nothing is impossible for God, then, according to the New Testament, nothing is impossible for *humanity.*

Freedom is not to be confused with "free will." Free will is the ability to choose or not, to choose this or that, to choose good or evil. Free will has to do with specific acts. Freedom, however, is the Spirit-empowered ability to be oneself, to determine oneself, to enact oneself over a lifetime. Each of us at any moment the product of his or her freedom. When our time is up, we die to discover that we have created our eternity out of our time. This act is possible only because we have cocreated ourselves in the eternal power, the Holy Spirit.

With all Christians, Paul gives the same answer to the question, how do I enact my freedom authentically? The answer is love; love is the "how" of freedom. If time is the raw material of freedom, then love can be defined easily—it is giving away our time. Whenever we respond to the needs of others, we "lose" our time—which is to say, we "lose" ourselves, for we *are* our lifetime. But, according to Jesus, if we "lose" ourselves in this way, we "find" our true selves—ultimately, at the Last Judgment, the only criteria for this is active love of neighbor: "I was hungry, and you gave me to eat; I was thirsty . . . " (Mt 25:35–36).

A final Pauline theme, crucial for Christian ethics, is his notion of Christian *phronēsis*. This notion requires further elaboration in dialogue with the practical philosophy of Aristotle.

Aristotle and Praxis

Pervasive in practically all of contemporary ethical studies in the retrieval of Aristotle's practical philosophy. Aristotle distinguished various kinds of knowledge. Theoretical knowing strives for *epistēmē*, or "scientific" knowledge of the unchanging structures of reality. This speculative knowledge of the metaphysician is the highest kind of knowledge. But because this kind of knowing pertains to immutable structures, it is unable to provide practical know-how regarding those concrete circumstances of human life that occupy the majority of people. For the different forms of human "making," which constitute the world of work or labor (poiēsis), Aristotle specified *technē* as the requisite "technical" know-how. But this type of practical knowledge is secondary to the kind of knowing necessary for human "doing," or human action, which he called *praxis* (ethical and political action). The kind of knowledge necessary to guide *praxis* he called *phronēsis* (ethical know-how). Contemporary authors ordinarily do not translate *praxis* and *phronēsis* into English—"practice" is too general, and "prudence" has devolved into meanings like "calculated self-interest."

Phronēsis is the moral wisdom that regulates life according to the virtues. It is first among the "cardinal" (from the Latin *cardo,* meaning "hinge") virtues. It can be defined as the habitual, quasi-instinctual ability of the *phronimos* (the morally sagacious person) to discern the right thing to do in the ever-changing circumstances of daily life with others in the *polis* (the city, Athens). The source of this practical wisdom is the "common sense" of the community, or what we would call "culture" (a system of shared meanings and values). Thus, morality finds its genesis in a process of "socialization" or education wherein the values of one's community become one's own. Thus, ideally, one becomes an "apprentice" of a publicly recognized ethical "master," thereby appropriating the master's moral wisdom as one's own.

Since the New Testament was written in Greek, it is interesting to see if the word *phronēsis* is used and, if so, how it is used. The noun itself occurs only twice in the New Testament: in Luke 1:17, in which the task of John the Baptist is described as "bringing back the disobedient to the wisdom *(phronēsis)* of the righteous," and in Ephesians 1:8, in which it is claimed that "through the grace of Christ God richly endows us with wisdom and insight *(phronēsis)*." In verbal form, the word appears at the beginning of the famous hymn in Paul's Epistle to the Philippians: "Let the same mind *(touto phroneite)* be in you as was in Christ Jesus . . . " (Phil 2:5). Paul tells us that we are true disciples ("learners") of Jesus when *phronēsis* of Jesus becomes our own. For Aristotle, *phronēsis* is a matter of appropriating the cultural values of Athens (the virtues). For Paul, Christian *phronēsis* is, similarly, a matter of appropriating the mind of Christ in the "school" of Christ's Church. But, despite the similarity between Aristotle and Paul on the "genealogy" of morals, there are major differences. For Aristotle, *phronēsis* is an intellectual virtue, albeit a virtue of the practical intellect. His ethics is elitist; it is a possibility limited to the well-off, educated, male citizen of Athens. The rest of humanity is dismissed as "barbarians." Pauline *phronēsis* is primarily a matter not of the intellect but of the *kardia,* the heart. In the Bible, psychic activity is usually associated with various organs of the body; the chief of these and the one most frequently mentioned is the heart. The heart is the bodily focus of *emotional* activity—the heart feels joy and sorrow, worry and anguish, fear and anger, love and courage. The heart is also the seat of mental and volitional activity: thoughts, desires, deeds, wisdom, discernment, and knowledge. For Paul, *phronēsis* might be called "the reasoning heart." St. Augustine will develop this *kardia* ethics.

The Ethics of St. Augustine

No thinker has had more influence on the development of the Christian understanding of human existence than Augustine of Hippo (now Bone in Algeria). He was born in North Africa, then a Roman province, in 354 during the early decades of the "Christian Empire." Although born of a Christian mother, he was not baptized in childhood. He taught rhetoric in Rome and Milan, where he was received into the Church by St. Ambrose, Bishop of Milan, in 387. His conversion experience is the central theme of his great classic "autobiography," *The Confessions.*[2] Returning to North Africa, he was ordained a priest and later Bishop of the diocese of Hippo, where he lived the remainder of his relatively long life. He died in 430 as the first stage of the "Christian Empire" was falling apart.

Augustine's moral teaching is scattered throughout his enormous literary output: more than 100 books (some short, some quite long), over 200 articles, and more than 500 letters, thus creating an immense arsenal for theologians of all subsequent centuries. Augustine's theology has been considered a perfect blend of Athens and Jerusalem, but when we focus on his anthropology, the influence of Jerusalem is predominant. First of all, Augustine mediated to the West the biblical understanding of personhood. He did this through what is called his characteristic "voluntarism," which holds that the will, not the intellect, is the central power of the human being—and it is the will that is the core of personhood. "What are we but wills?" Augustine asks rhetorically. He was the first philosopher of the will.

For Augustine, human beings are infinitely erotic—desire is the key to understanding humanity. Throughout life, our hearts are restless in search of happiness and fulfillment. This happiness has a name: God. God is the infinite satisfaction of the yearning, the hunger, the desire that we are. Augustine has given us the best preliminary description of the meaning of the word God, using human desire as the chief clue. Augustine never forgets the passion that we are. Throughout his intellectual career, he never thinks of the human mind as a detached spectator—all authentic human knowing must be a passionate engagement with the reality we seek to know. This anthropological insight continues in the great thinkers of the Christian tradition through the ages. Even the atheist philosopher of the twentieth century, Sartre, agrees with Augustine—for Sartre we *are* passion, but we are "useless passions," condemned to ultimate absurdity because there is no God to fill our hearts.

Augustine wrote in defense of "free will" against the Manichaeans, a dualistic sect he had once joined. The Manichaeans identified human beings with their spiritual nature and condemned their material or bodily nature as evil. But later Augustine was faced with the problem of Pelagianism. Pelagius was a moral rigorist for whom free will was everything; it was the basis for the possibility of a sinless existence. For Pelagius, Christ was the great "facilitator" of our salvation, but not its "enabler." Christ was the great example to be followed by human free will. This position Augustine could not accept. Following the Pauline teaching that Christ is our redeemer, Augustine maintained that we are all in need of this redemption. Free will alone is de facto the heart turned in on itself. This understanding is the theological foundation for Augustine's elaboration of the doctrine of "original sin." To express our universal need for the liberating grace of Christ (the gift of the Holy Spirit), Augustine used a biological metaphor—we are *born* sinners. The Christian community recognized the truth of Augustine's teaching that without Christ we are *unable* to move toward God, our ultimate happiness, and this teaching became Church doctrine. Augustine was right. He named the basis for the moral impotency that Jeremiah and Ezekiel discovered, but we are not committed to Augustine's biological metaphor in expressing a doctrine of original sin. Today we have different ways to formulate this doctrine through modern psychology, sociology, and the evolutionary advance from the state of "nature" to the complexities of "culture." But Augustine affirmed the basic position of the Christian tradition that, without empowerment by the Spirit, there is no real freedom to do the good.

For the West, Augustine is the great "Doctor of Grace." He understood the grace of the Holy Spirit as God's saving work on human interiority, or on the "soul." But, by "soul," Augustine did not mean Aristotle's "substance." Soul for Augustine meant what today is referred to as the "subject"—the human person characterized by consciousness and freedom. This understanding makes Augustine the first "modern man." He initiated a new language for the exploration of human beings as persons, not things. Grace is primarily "operating grace"— what God does in us *without* us. But he also recognized the need to respect human action. Here he speaks of "cooperating grace"—what God does in us *with* us. This latter understanding is the point of departure for Christian ethics.

St. Thomas Aquinas

Up until the thirteenth century, Augustine's theology was equivalent to "orthodoxy" in the West. The "textbook" for all medieval theologians was Peter Lombard's *Sentences,* a collection of Patristic opinions, most of them Augustine's. But most distinctive of medieval theology was the rediscovery of the works of Aristotle, translated into Latin by Arabic philosophers. Aristotle provided medieval thinkers with a new ideal of "science" just as they were constructing the great European universities. Theology itself became a science as theologians worked to formulate the "essence" of the articles of faith by way of Aristotle's "four causes." This new type of philosophical theology came to be known as Scholasticism. Scholastic theologians brought Christian doctrine into the "world of theory." Previously, theologians approached Christian beliefs functionally—they asked, for instance, "What is grace *for;* why is it necessary?" The Scholastic approach moved beyond functional questions to ask speculative or theoretical questions. They asked, for example, "What *is* grace; what categories can be used to articulate its essential structure?"

The greatest of Scholastic theologians was Thomas Aquinas (1225–74). His greatest work was the *Summa Theologiae,* which encompassed all Christian doctrine by way of the architectonic scheme of emanation and return—all things have their source and their goal in God. The *Summa* is divided into three parts: Part I, God and the emergence of all things from God; Part II (itself divided into two parts), the return of all things to God through humanity; and Part III, Christology, Christ as the Way, the Truth, and the Life. Thomas's "moral theology" is found in Part II of the *Summa.*

Thomas's anthropology is concerned with "humanity"—all human beings as members of the human species, what he calls "human nature" *(natura humana).* As an anthropological term, "nature" is the essential structure of the human being *as oriented to action.* Thus, human nature is the source of human action, and human action is oriented to a goal. As it exists, human nature is a composite of body and soul. The soul is "the form" of the body—for example, the soul gives vital "shape" to the body. The clearest way to state Thomas's anthropology is to say that the human being is a "living body." Thomas moves away from any "Platonic" temptation, to define the human being as "soul." Indeed, the "soul" is presented as "adjectival" to the body. Though formulated in Aristotelian philosophical language, this Thomistic anthropology is very close to the synthetic anthropology of the Bible.

This philosophical anthropology becomes explicitly theological when Thomas notes that human nature has no connatural human goal. According to Christian faith, the only goal that humanity has is God, a goal obviously beyond the capacities of human nature to reach. In Thomas's language, this goal is "supernatural." It is here that the humanism of Thomas comes to the fore: the creator cannot be honored at the expense of the creature. If God graciously makes God our goal, then God must graciously *make us capable* of reaching God by our own actions. Here is a new, thoroughly humanistic, understanding of grace—grace is the elevation of human nature to parity with its goal! Grace makes us God's friends, and friends are "equal"! Graced nature (nature "supernaturalized") is now a new source of human action, an action that "merits" its goal, God. Merit here is not a psychological category (reward/punishment motivation). It describes human action itself as "divinized" by its "elevated" or divinized" source. Thomas tells us, "You *are* your grace!"

Thomas develops his Christian ethics by combining Aristotle's notion of *phronēsis* (in Latin, *prudentia*) with the Stoic notion of "natural law," both theologically grounded in charity. Natural law is our participation in God's eternal law through reason. Its basic principle is "good must be done; evil must be avoided." What is good is good because it perfects human nature; what is evil is evil because it destroys human nature. "Good is good not because it is commanded; it is commanded because it is good. Evil is evil not because it is forbidden because it is evil." Thomas' ethical humanism rejects all forms of legalism. Nature (the way we *are*) determines what we *ought* to do.

Natural law ethics, however, is very general. It is not of immediate help in facing the changing complexities of everyday life. Thomas employs the notion of natural law to construct an explicitly theological ethics—natural law is our rational participation in God's eternal law, which orders all of creation. The first principles of natural law are for Thomas the first principles of practical reason. For the concrete, particular decisions of everyday life, Thomas retrieves Aristotle's notion of *phronēsis*, which was sufficient for Aristotle's "naturalistic" ethics in search of the good life in the *polis*. Prudence for Thomas is the *recta ratio agibilium* (right reasoning regarding action), whose source, like Aristotle's, is *community*, but a community that is Christ's Church, not a pagan *polis*. We must be careful here. Thomas did not have our "modern" understanding of Church as a special institution alongside the other institutions of sociopolitical life. Thomas lived in a "Church civilization," wherein the Church encompassed all other institutions of human sociality in a fragmentary but real anticipation of the Kingdom of God. Thus, Christian *phronēsis* was mediated by the whole atmosphere of Christian medieval culture. Never was Paul Tillich's dictum more true: "religion is the *substance* of culture; culture is the *form* of religion."[3] Natural law grounds ethics in the creative ordering of the world by God. *Phronēsis* guides Christian *praxis* in the concrete. And *phronēsis* is enlivened by charity (the *kardia* of the New Testament). Like the *kardia* ethics of Augustine, Thomas's ethics is in harmony with the Pauline ethics of the New Testament. Thomas has also appropriated Paul's insistence that we are freed from the Law by the grace of Christ. Asking whether the "New Law" (the "Law" of Christ) is a written law, Thomas answers in the negative. The New Law is interior transformation by grace, and this New Law will last until the end of time. And, again, "Anyone who does the good because it is commanded is not free; anyone who avoids evil because it is forbidden is not free."

The ethical teaching of Thomas Aquinas has begotten a long history of interpretation. In recent years, moral theologians have attempted to retrieve his natural law ethics with attention to contemporary historical consciousness. Thomas's virtue ethics is attactively retrieved in the work of the moral philosopher, Alasdair MacIntyre,[4] and Thomas's teaching on prudence is a major concern in contemporary attempts to construct a communal ethics.[5]

Modern Thought

The anthropocentric cast of Thomas Aquinas's practical theology of grace was a significant factor in the movement into distinctively modern thought. The thinking of the modern era is characterized by the "turn to the subject," the philosophical concern to explore human interiority or subjectivity: consciousness and freedom. This modern philosophy begins with Descartes, who focuses on the "thinking" subject. This thinking subject throughout the modern period is the individual male thinker—for Descartes, this individual thinker in his study was in search of certitude in knowledge through "clear and distinct ideas." A bias against tradition and authority is evident in this modern turn from its beginning. Descartes essayed a "methodical doubt" about everything he had learned from others so that he could reach truth on his own. This bias against tradition becomes most explicit during the Enlightenment, as evidenced in Kant's famous essay, "What is Enlightenment?" The motto of Enlightenment according to Kant is *sapere aude*—dare to use your own head! While this modern "turn to the subject" is obviously influenced by previous moments in the history of thought (Augustinian interiority, for example), its identification of tradition with backwardness and ignorance rendered it basically inimical to religion and, specifically, to Christianity, which is so obviously a tradition.

The rationalistic self-sufficiency of the modern cast of mind did not invite Christian theologians to develop a "modern theology." Coinciding with the beginnings of the modern period was the tragic fragmentation of Western Christianity into the Roman Catholic and the many Protestant churches. Theology became polemical, and, as if that were not bad enough, the polemical attitude led to real *polemos* (war!) in the disgraceful "wars of religion" that convulsed Europe in the seventeenth century.

"Early modern" (at least in terms of dating) was the theology and anthropology of Martin Luther (1483–1546). The center of Luther's theology was the Pauline theme of the "justification of the sinner" by God through Christ. Luther accented the radical depravity of humanity in sin in order to celebrate the total graciousness of God's mercy. The only path to justification was the way of faith or trust in God's saving work as disclosed in the cross of Christ. Reacting to what he discerned to be a rebirth of Pelagianism in parts of Europe in his day, Luther condemned the placing of any confidence in human "works." God alone, through Christ alone, by grace alone, attested by Scripture alone, accepted by faith alone, does the saving work. Through his study of the scriptures, Luther recovered the biblical understanding of God for *us;* at the same time, he revived the biblical understanding of the human being as *person* with a new found *freedom* in Christ. While these Lutheran emphases are indeed positive, they are rather individualistic. They envision the Christian as standing alone before God without the mediation of the Church. This touch of individualism is, of course, consonant with the modern spirit. For Luther, faith had ethical consequences: works do not make us just, but the justified do good works.

But Luther's central emphasis on what *God* does for us lessens his concern to develop a Christian ethics.

It was Friedrich Schleiermacher, the Father of Liberal Protestantism, who produced a modern Christian ethics on the basis of his Christomorphic ("Christ shaped") anthropology. Departing from classical theology, which begins with God and the Trinity, Schleiermacher's great work, *The Christian Faith*,[6] begins with human nature. His emphasis is on the likeness of redeemed humanity to Christ. Employing the Johannine metaphor of friendship, he always speaks of Christ and Christ's disciple ("friend") together. Conformed to Christ in the Christian community, the disciple is called to be a responsible moral agent in the historical world. This Christomorphic understanding of morality is similar to the Christian anthropologies of recent Catholic theologians.

The Transcendental Thomists

In the twentieth century, Christian anthropology becomes a central concern with those Catholic theologians known as the "Transcendental Thomists." The word *transcendental* is used here in the Kantian sense. Kant called his philosophy transcendental because, instead of focusing immediately on objects to be known, he turned to the human knower as the "transcendent" agent in the production of knowledge. The famous question of Kant's critical philosophy is "What are the *a priori* conditions in the knowing subject that make actual knowing possible?" Kant wanted to delineate the range of human knowing, and he did so by exploring the possibilities and the limits of the human knower. In Kant, the "turn to the subject" takes a critical twist.

The Jesuit theologian, Karl Rahner (1904–84), set out to "modernize" Catholic theology. To do so, he read Thomas Aquinas with a Kantian lens.[7] Convinced of the Thomistic realism (the mind can know reality), Rahner retrieved the thought of Thomas by employing the Kantian transcendental question. Far from limiting the human mind to the phenomenal world, as Kant had done, Rahner held that the *a priori* condition for the possibility of human knowledge of reality ("categorical" knowledge) was a preconceptual, athematic "knowledge" of Being itself. Pursuing his theological interests, Rahner quickly moved from the language of Athens to the language of Jerusalem. The *a priori* pre-grasp of Being becomes the *a priori* pre-grasp of

God. As the sun is to the physical eye, God, the eternal light, is to the "inner eye" of the mind. This understanding is Rahner's transcendental retrieval of Catholic tradition on the "natural" know ability of God—God is "known" by all human beings, not as an object of knowledge, but as the presupposition of knowing anything at all.

Rahner went on to develop a "transcendental theology." Instead of the philosophical concern with constructing a foundation of human *knowing,* he focused on the theological concern about the possibility of the act of *faith.* He used Kantian language to raise the question of "What are the *a priori* conditions in the human person that make the act of faith possible?" His answer to this question had enormous consequences for Catholic belief and practice—making Rahner the "Church Father" for the twentieth century. He delineated two basic conditions for the act of faith. The first is the "natural" constitution of the human knower as "infinite in outreach" toward an Infinite Horizon (his philosophical anthropology). The second is "supernatural"—the gracious presence to the human subject of that Reality (God) who is the unreachable goal of our natural striving left to itself. The transcendent God is immanent to the human spirit always and everywhere because God "desires everyone to be saved and to come to the knowledge of the truth" (1 Tm 2:4). Focused on the universal salvific will of God, Rahner's theology celebrates a world of grace.

As we have seen, Thomas Aquinas employed a body/soul anthropology that did not subordinate the body to the soul. Following Thomas, Rahner modernizes his anthropology by substituting *history* for body and *transcendence* for soul. Just as Thomas insisted on the intrinsic relationship of body and soul (the soul is the form of the body), Rahner presents a mutual conditioning between transcendence and history. This is the anthropological key to Rahner's thought: transcendence is the condition that makes history possible; history is the concrete mediation of transcendence. Just as the Holy Spirit (the divine immanence in the world) is the condition that makes Christ (the historical savior) possible, so Christ is the mediator of the Holy Spirit. That same Spirit dwells in the human spirit as the condition that makes human history potentially Christomorphic ("Christ shaped"). The anthropology here is quite concrete and quite simple to formulate—every human being is his or her lifetime, or every human being *is* a person to *become* one.

This anthropology has obvious ethical consequences. One way to elaborate these consequences is through the notion of the "fundamental option."

The "fundamental option" is an ethical term for "person." Instead of a moral evaluation of human actions taken discretely (this act, that act), the notion of the "fundamental option" evaluates human actions as they form a pattern, a particular and personal self-enactment in a lifetime. The "fundamental option" is not *an* option—it is the cumulative result of all actions to date; it is the moral character of the person. Every significant human deed *expresses* the moral character of the person and, in and through that expression, creates the person. Here is a contemporary way to emphasize the ethical role of the human *body* through which all human self-expression comes to be and through which bodily self-expression the human person comes to be. Here, body is the appropriate *symbol* of the person as historical self-enactment in word and deed. The meaning of the biblical metaphor of hope, the resurrection of the body, can be clarified by this kind of "body theology."

Among the Transcendental Thomists is another Jesuit, Canadian Bernard Lonergan (1904–84). Although a theologian, Lonergan spent much time on the philosophical prolegommena for theology. He refers to the anthropological component of his theology as "transcendental method."[8] This transcendental method is the way, or the path (literal meaning of "method"), toward authentic existence. It is based on the human being's "conscious intentionality" (self-awareness, reaching out to reality). Lonergan constructs a fourfold dynamic movement of the human spirit toward reality, and reality is differentiated in accord with the human movement toward it. The first movement is experience, which intends reality as perceptible. The second movement is understanding, which intends reality as intelligible. The third movement is judgment, which intends reality as true. The fourth movement is decision, which intends reality as good and valuable. The first three movements describe consciousness; the fourth movement describes conscience. Cognition begets conation (action striving for the good). While this transcendental method has relevance for all particular methods of inquiry, it itself is the method to follow in order to become an authentic, ethical person. For Lonergan, this transcendental method brings to language the path authentic persons have always followed, albeit without their spelling it out. Lonergan invites his readers to find themselves within his method so that they may become reflexively aware of what they have been doing at their best. If this happens, his readers are invited to embrace his "transcendental precepts," which merely restate the fourfold movement of conscious intentionality in the imperative mood: "Be attentive; be intelligent; be rational or critical; be responsible." In other words, be true to yourself, for these imperatives are not imposed from without—they are the very "law" of being human.

Lonergan's transcendental method is a modern form of Thomas's understanding of the natural law as the "law" built into our human constitution. As a Christian, Lonergan has been instructed by Augustine as well. He knows the moral impotency that describes us as sinners. The only way we can be true to ourselves is through that empowerment by the Spirit of Christ that is grace, the freedom to love. Here we can recall Paul's teaching that love is the fulfillment of the law and the famous words of Augustine: "Love and do what you want." Lonergan's transcendental precepts can be sublated into one: "Be loving."

The "turn to the subject" in recent Catholic theology was soon followed by the "sociopolitical turn." When the "subject" is the "person," the social context of human personhood is implied. People become persons only with other persons in communities that are structured to promote personal flourishing. From what we have seen so far in Rahner and Lonergan, our attention has been focused on personal *praxis*. With the "sociopolitical turn," we move to the broader context wherein persons are formed by the social, political, economic, and religious institutions of public life. To the extent that these institutions are just, communities thrive. To the extent that they are unjust, communities decline. In our imperfect world, the public structuring of life displays differing degrees of justice and injustice. While Aristotle's teaching on *praxis* and *phronēsis* was quite helpful when our attention was focused on personal ethics, we turn to different mentors for insight on social ethics: the nineteenth century promoters of "historical consciousness," Hegel and Marx.

Hegel alerts us to the fact that human beings create their own history. Everything that appears in culture (as distinct from nature) is a human creation. Freedom is our ability to determine all the social, political, economic, and religious structures of public life. Human consciousness is creative of the human world. Marx, in turn, informs us that the opposite is also true. The concrete circumstances that human beings have created are themselves determining factors for the ongoing shaping of human consciousness. Historical consciousness is the recognition of this dialectic—we are the producers of history; we are the products of history. And, of course, we are "products" before we are "producers."

Historical consciousness is clearly illustrated by a famous "thesis" of Marx: "Up till now, philosophers have merely *interpreted* the world in their various ways, but the point is to *change* it." Marx's challenge is the end point of a tradition of German philosophy, from the practical philosophy of Kent through the philosophy of history of Hegel to the humanistic atheism of Feuerbach that has been called "the modern history of freedom." With the sociopolitical turn in theology, Christian thinkers are brought into dialogue with this tradition.

Historical consciousness has significant consequences for Christian faith and action. Christianity has been at times excessively otherworldly. But historical consciousness means the end of any literal otherworldliness. Heaven is not "above" but "ahead." Eternity is not timelessness, but the fullness of time. Eternity is the fruit, the issue of history. With historical consciousness, theologians begin to resonate with Marx's challenge to change the world. European theologians after Rahner concentrated on the construction of a "political theology" to bring the gospel effectively into the arena of public life. The wars of religion between Catholics and Protestants had made European Christianity into a private matter, focused on interior "spirituality."

Inspired by compelling theologies of freedom such as Rahner's, Latin American theologians translated their historical consciousness into liberation theology, which would transform the dire economic situation of the poor of that continent. In North America, liberation theologies focused on other social evils, such as sexism and racism. The world in which these evils exist must be changed. It is interesting in this regard to note that the Catholic theology of grace has characteristically used the word *change* to express the efficacy of grace. For Augustine, grace changed the human will; for Aquinas, grace meant a change in human nature; for Rahner, grace was a "change" in human consciousness; for contemporary political and liberation theologians, there is need of a social grace to change the life-world. But changing the world demands a communal *praxis* and communal *phronēsis*. The next major "turn" in Christian theology would begin to address these issues.

The "linguistic turn" has had an enormous effect on contemporary theology. While modern thought was centered on human knowing (epistemology), contemporary, postmodern thought has centered on language as *the* anthropological key. Once again, Aristotle is helpful. His famous anthropology, the "rational animal," was translated into English from the Latin translation of the Greek, *animal rationale.* But in the original Greek, Aristotle defines the human as, literally, "the animal having speech." Language is *the* distinctive human trait. Thought is derivative from language—thinking "logically" is literally "thinking with words." Language constructs the mind. To learn a language is to annex the whole culture. To learn a religious language is to absorb the religious meanings and values of a culture. To study the religious language of the Christian religion is to encounter the Christian imagination with its world of narrative, metaphor, symbol, and analogy.

Contemporary Christian anthropology has rediscovered the centrality of the human imagination for human *praxis.* In dialogue or, better, polemic, with Enlightenment rationalism, Catholic theology became narrowly conceptual. Orthodoxy was identified with acceptance of doctrine in its propositional forms. John Henry Cardinal Newman tried to give to theologians an appreciation of the primacy of the imagination for the understanding of revelation and faith in the last century, but to little avail. It was the contemporary turn to the study of language that led theologians to perceive the prominent role of the imagination in religious living. Primary religious language, the language of worship and confession, is metaphorical and symbolic and is found in the biblical narratives that give identity to the Christian community. These narratives are addressed to the imagination, the fundamental human power to negotiate life. Imagination renders accessible what is physically or logically inaccessible. Imagination gives us the past in the mode of memory. It gives us the future in the mode of anticipation. Imagination gives us the ineffable God through images. It is the seat of revelation and the springboard for the life of faith. The "faculty" of the imagination is an ability, a skill, a way of acting that allows one to *do* something. The English Romantic writer Coleridge saw "God's eternal act of creation" as the primary meaning of imagination. Human, or secondary, imagination is an "echo" of God's imagination. Human beings are created in the image and likeness of God (Gn 1:26). Sin has distorted our theomorphic ("God shaped") potential. But, according to Paul, Jesus Christ is *the* Image of God, and through him we can become "images in the Image" (Rom 8:29)—we can become "Christomorphic" and, thereby, "theomorphic."

Catholicism has traditionally had a "high" ecclesiology. It holds that the Church (the people of God) is the continuation of the Incarnation or the continuing Sacrament (effective manifestation) of Christ. As Jesus was the Sacrament (the "Epiphany") of God for us, so the disciples of Jesus are called to an "analogical imagination," whereby they see the presence of God in all things and seek new ways to disclose the divine presence for others. Ethical life *is* this imaging of Christ, this witnessing to the power of the Spirit in the most powerful way. Catholicism agrees with all Christians that the message of the gospel must be proclaimed, but it insists that it must also be *embodied* in the concrete way of life in the Christian community. This communal *praxis* must have a *centrifugal* orientation—the Church does not exist for itself, but for the world, just as Jesus was not for himself, but "for us and for our salvation" according to the Creed. The source of the communal *phronēsis* necessary to guide communal Christian *praxis* is primarily the story of Jesus, "the pioneer of our faith" (Heb 12:2).

Recent years have seen a veritable explosion of books and articles on "the historical Jesus." This "historical Jesus" is a contemporary construct that attempts to know as much as possible about what Jesus actually said and did, his style of life, and so forth. Indeed, there are many contemporary reconstructions of the "historical Jesus," as many as the reconstructing authors themselves. Despite significant disagreement among these authors, there are some areas of consensus. Here we are concerned with the *ethical consequences* of knowledge about Jesus. We concur with the whole tradition that we are saved by *faith* in Jesus, but this faith can be enlightened by what we can know about Jesus. After all, faith does demand a practical "know-how" if we are to "cooperate" (Augustine) with God's work in the world—if we are not merely passive recipients of the divine favors. This practical knowledge, this *phronēsis,* this skill, is mediated to us in the School of Jerusalem (the Church) as we hear the story of Jesus at least every week and as we encounter "other Christs" (saints) in the Christian community. This "schooling" is effective as our imaginations are transformed and we see things in a new way and notice things that we did not notice before. Aristotle was a very intelligent ethicist, but he did not notice the plight of the poor of Athens as an ethical issue. His imagination had not been formed by association with the God of the prophets. Here are a few illustrations of the ethical consequences of knowing Jesus.

Perhaps the most important lesson to learn is that knowing Jesus is knowing the God of Jesus. As the prophets of Israel had felt the *pathos,* the "passion" of God, Jesus discloses a God of *compassion,*— a loving, caring

God who delights in our joys and who suffers in our sorrows. Jesus teaches and exemplifies the central moral quality of compassion in a life centered in God. He commands us, "Be compassionate as God is compassionate" (Lk 6:36). A church without compassion is not the church of the God of Jesus.

In everything he said and did, Jesus exemplified unbounded love and compassion. He surrounded himself with all the wrong people according to the standards of his day—women, the poor, prostitutes, publicans, outcasts of all kinds"as Paul put it, "nobodies," or in the Greek, "non- beings" (1 Cor 1). These followers of Jesus formed an egalitarian community in total disregard of the accepted standards of honor, worth, class, and so forth of the larger community. Especially significant for us is the fact that women were not only equal to men in the Jesus movement, but they held leadership roles as well. Mary Magdalene is a striking example—she was the first to experience Easter, becoming the apostle to the apostles.

Jesus is the "concrete universal" of Christian ethics.[9] By the appropriation of his story through the imagination, Jesus becomes paradigmatic for our ethical sensibility, our motivation, and our very identity. Like Jesus, we receive our identity from personal prayer and communal worship. We come to experience ourselves as living from God through Christ and in the Spirit. Christian morality must have this mystical foundation. We must come to experience what we say when we claim to be empowered by the Spirit. Otherwise, our morality is indistinguishable from the dedicated social worker. To use Rahnerian language, our mystical attunement to God's presence is the condition for the possibility for effective prophetic action in imitation of Jesus.

Our Postmodern Situation

Reflective people today concur that we are in a new era. The modern era with its spatial metaphors of "higher" and "lower" (male over female, spirit over body, mind over heart, the white race over other races, etc.) is "over" in principle. Postmodern thinking is focused on "alterity" on "otherness"—"the other person, 'man's' other, other species, the other of the West," etc.[10] This new emphasis on alterity resonates with the emphasis of Christian anthropology, which has much to gain from many postmodern thinkers. Postmodern thought is too historically conscious to pretend that we can dismiss tradition. In its deepest theological meaning, tradition is the lived sense of faith of the people of God—it is the presence of the Spirit in the Church, the living memory of Jesus. But tradition in its ordinary sense of the transmitted meanings and values of a human culture is always ambiguous—as are the people who shape and are shaped by their culture. We cannot escape tradition, but we must receive it with a "hermeneutics of suspicion" before we venture a "hermeneutics of retrieval."

The postmodern "other" *par excellence* is women, the more than half of the human race who have suffered varying degrees of subordination to men for centuries in our patriarchal, androcentric culture. The feminist movement of today at its best is a prophetic movement, inspired by the Spirit. It has uncovered the terrible social sin called sexism. The moral imperative for the Christian community is obvious. Its self-indictment must come from its own tradition, especially from the suppressed and forgotten voices of the tradition. We must begin from our ethical paradigm, Jesus, and learn from his association with women that women are equal disciples with men. The famous words of Paul, describing the Christian community, must call us to repentance and transformation: "There is no longer Jew or Greek, there is no longer slave or free, there is no longer male and female; for all of you are one in Christ Jesus" (Gal 3:28). The subordination of women to men in the Church was the result of excessive adaptation to the patriarchal culture of the Greco-Roman world. Knowing that, we must change. Reform in the Church results from growing awareness that Church structures contradict the gospel we preach: women as images of God, Jesus, the liberator of women, male and female no longer.

Contemporary ethics recognizes a need for a global ethics, but it also recognizes the tremendous obstacles in the way of elaborating such a "universal" ethics. As a result of the linguistic and hermeneutical turns, there is a general suspicion of any rational "foundation" for such an ethics. In any case, we have learned that universalist, rational theories of morality are not effective in making people moral. Kant tried it. The great transcendental philospher gave us a deontological ethics that we see as purely formal, offering no concrete guidance for particular, concrete circumstances. Every ethical tradition is *a* tradition, offering a particular ethical perspective different from other perspectives. It seems that we are left with mere relativity—coexistence without cooperation. One proposal that seems attractive is "discourse ethics." This approach to ethics by way of conversation and argument, with hope for some consensus in the future, is illustrated by the "communicative *praxis*" ideal of Jurgen Habermas.[11] The conversation has begun, and the tradition of Christian ethics has much to bring to the discussion. Christian anthropology has material content to bring into dialogue with secular ethics: an appreciation of the great but not absolute value of human life, a respect for all God's creatures, a sense of responsibility for the ecosystem God has provided—in sum, an ethics of responsibility.

The core ethical themes of Christian anthropology have much to offer. Jesus is the paradigm of active love of neighbor. The *kardia* ethics of the New Testament begets a long tradition with essential continuity: Augustine's "reasoning heart," Thomas' prudence grounded in charity, Rahner's theology of freedom actualized in the unity of love of God and love of neighbor, Lonergan's transcendental precepts summarized in "be loving," and contemporary liberation movements of practical love for the poor, the oppressed, and the marginalized.

Moral theories and ethical rules have their place. But they do not make people moral. Morality finds its source and its nourishment in community. A community supplies an accumulated moral wisdom as its tradition expands to meet the ever-changing conditions of human life. People become moral through relationships, through cooperation in common projects, through the intersubjective power of language, through experience brought to reflection, and through the example of others. People become moral when they are transformed by a moral tradition with its "dangerous memories" of love overcoming hatred, of justice prevailing over injustice, of peace avoiding conflict, and of care triumphing over indifference. Fundamentally, people become moral by the grace of God. For a final Catholic touch—our moral lives are *wholly* God's gift and *wholly* our deed.

Endnotes

1. See Abraham J. Heschel, *The Prophets* (Philadelphia: Jewish Publication Society of America, 1962).

2. Saint Augustine, *Confessions,* Henry Chadwick, trans. (Oxford: Oxford University Press, 1991).

3. Paul Tillich, *Theology of Culture* (New York: Oxford University, 1959) 42.

4. See Alasdair MacIntyre, *After Virtue: A Study in Moral Theory* (Notre Dame: University of Notre Dame, 1981) and *Whose Justice? Which Rationality?* (Notre Dame: University of Notre Dame, 1980).

5. See Daniel Mark Nelson, *The Priority of Prudence* (University Park, PA: Pennsylvania State University, 1992).

6. Friedrich Schleiermacher, *The Christian Faith*, H. R. Mackintosh and J. S. Steward, trans. (Edinburgh: T & T Clark, 1928).

7. See Karl Rahner, *Foundations of Christian Faith* (New York: Seabury, 1978).

8. Bernard Lonergan, *Method in Theology* (New York: Herder & Herder, 1992) 3–25.

9. William C. Spohn, "Jesus and Ethics," in *Proceedings of the Catholic Theological Society of America* 49, 40–57.

10. John D. Caputo, "The Good News About Alterity: Derrida and Theology" in *Faith and Philosophy* 10/4 (October 1993) 453–70.

11. Jurgen Habermas, "What is Universal Pragmatics" in his *Communication and the Evolution of Society* (Boston: Beacon, 1979) and *The Theory of Communicative Action* Vol 1. (Boston: Beacon, 1987) chapter 3.

3

TURN TO THE HEAVENS AND THE EARTH: RETRIEVAL OF THE COSMOS IN THEOLOGY*

ELIZABETH A. JOHNSON

Fordham University

As the twenty-first century rapidly approaches, there is a vital theme largely absent from the thinking of most North American theologians, namely, the whole world as God's good creation. There are a few notable exceptions among our members, but surveying our work as a whole would quickly make this absence clear. This neglect of "the cosmos" by recent decades of mainstream Catholic theology has two deleterious results. It enfeebles theology in its basic task of interpreting the *whole* of reality in the light of faith, thereby compromising the intellectual integrity of theology. And it blocks what should be theology's powerful contribution to the religious praxis of justice and mercy for the threatened earth, so necessary at this moment of our planet's unprecedented ecological crisis, thereby endangering the moral integrity of theology. In this address I am going to try to persuade you of the following thesis: as theologians of the twenty-first century, we need to complete our recent anthropological turns by turning to the entire interconnected community of life and the network of life-systems in which the human race is embedded, all of which has its own intrinsic value before God. In a word, we need to convert our intelligence to the heavens and the earth.

Remembering and Forgetting the Cosmos

It is instructive to remember the long-standing Catholic heritage that held high the importance of the cosmos in theology, and to examine how and why it got lost.

Theology is potentially the most comprehensive of fields. If there is only one God, and if this God is the Creator of all that exists, then everything is encompassed in the scope of theology's interest. Traditionally this is expressed in the idea that theology deals with three major areas: God, humanity, and world, a metaphysical trinity, so to speak. Nor can these elements be separated, for, as the history of theology makes evident, every understanding of God corresponds to a particular understanding of the natural world and the human.

Early Christian and medieval theologians took this view of things for granted, interpreting the natural world as God's good creation, a revealing pathway to the knowledge of God, and a partner in salvation. It was common for them to say that God has put two books at our disposal, the book of sacred scripture and the book of nature; if we learn how to read the book of nature aright, we will hear God's word and be led to knowledge about God's wisdom, power, and love.[1]

The conscious endeavor to integrate the cosmos into theology reached its zenith in the twelfth and thirteenth centuries. Inspired by the translation of ancient Greek scientific works along with works by Jewish and Muslim scholars, medieval theologians applied themselves to constructing an all-embracing Christian view of the world, writing innumerable treatises on the universe, on the world, on the picture of the world, on the philosophy of the world, on the nature of things. Their endeavor to interpret the whole world in the light of Christian faith gave vitality to their work and inspired impressive systems in which cosmology, anthropology, and theology of God formed a harmonious unity. Some examples:

- In her *summa* of Christian doctrine *(Scivias)* Hildegard of Bingen sees the whole universe imbued with the love of Christ, the sun of justice, who shines with "the brilliance of burning charity of such great glory that every creature is illumined by the brightness of this light."[2] In the midst of this marvelous vision stand human beings, "made in a wondrous way with great glory from the dust of the earth, and so intertwined with the strengths of the rest of creation that we can never be separated from them."[3]

• Bonaventure instructs the soul journeying toward God to see the universe as a wonderful work of art in which one recognizes traces of its Maker:

> Whoever is not enlightened by the splendor of created things is blind; whoever is not aroused by the sound of their voice is deaf; whoever does not praise God for all these creatures is mute; whoever after so much evidence does not recognize the First Principle is a fool [*stultus est* = an idiot].[4]

• Aquinas believes that theologians ought quite consciously to study nature and include a consideration of nature in their work. His own writing is pervaded with a cosmic sense as well as instructive analogies from the natural world, from fire to urine. Indeed, the whole cosmos itself is an astonishing image of God.

> God brought things into being in order that the divine goodness might be communicated to creatures and be represented by them. And because the divine goodness could not be adequately represented by one creature alone, God produced many and diverse creatures, that what was wanting in one in the representation of divine goodness might be supplied by another. For goodness, which in God is simple and uniform, in creatures is manifold and divided. Thus the whole universe together participates in divine goodness more perfectly, and represents it better, than any single creature whatever.[5]

Medieval theology brought God, humanity, and the world into an order harmony. The resulting synthesis not only shaped art, architecture, liturgy, and poetry, it also remained for centuries a guiding influence in Catholic theology even when its underlying world picture was discredited by scientific advance.

And scientific advance there was, as the names of Copernicus, Galileo, Newton, and later Darwin, Einstein, Heisenberg, and many others imply. Strange as it may seem in the light of a fifteen-hundred-year-old heritage, after the Reformation neither Catholic nor Protestant theology kept pace with new scientific worldviews. Instead, they focused on God and the self, leaving the world to the side.

Why this should have been the case has not been sufficiently studied. One factor frequently cited is the seventeenth-century ecclesiastical censure of Galileo whose investigations challenged the medieval picture of the universe as geocentric, static, and perfectly ordered. According to John Paul II, speaking on the occasion of Galileo's rehabilitation, at the heart of the conflict was the fact that to Church leaders "geocentrism seemed to be part of scriptural teaching itself."[6] Wedded as they were to a literal interpretation of scripture, they thought that since the Bible assumes the centrality of the earth, this was a doctrine of the faith. To have avoided the conflict, "it would have been necessary all at once to overcome habits of thought, and to devise a way of teaching capable of enlightening the people of God." But most of them did not know how to do so.

Under pressure of ecclesiastical censure, Catholic theologians largely ignored the questions arising from a heliocentric and evolutionary world. Theology became estranged from ongoing thought about the universe. Even so, even as the medieval world picture disintegrated and was no longer available as a cosmological framework for Christian doctrine, the spirit of that great synthesis lingered like a ghost in the neoscholastic manuals. Those of us in the Catholic Theological Society of America of a certain age, who first studied theology before the Second Vatican Council, imbibed a sense of the cosmos with our first lessons. The implicit world picture may have been untenable, but at least there was a natural world there worthy of some consideration before God.

Vatican II marked a turning point in the saga of Catholic theology, directing thought with new openness toward dialogue with the modern world and with ecumenical and interreligious partners. Far from putting Catholic thought in touch with Christian theology that had kept pace with scientific advance, however, our first contacts with Protestantism heightened our own absorption with anthropology. For under pressure of the Reformation's great *solas*—Christ alone, faith alone, grace alone, scripture alone—Protestant thought had taken an intensely anthropocentric turn. Revelation discloses a gracious God bent over our sinfulness and justifying us in Christ: theology's vision stays focused on humanity. Furthermore, the Protestant thought we met was grappling with the modern discovery of history. History, interpreted through the lens of the Bible as linear time, was the locus of God's mighty acts. By contrast, nature was the realm of cyclic time where pagan deities were invoked. Nature thus came to be treated as simply a stage on which salvation history was played out. With the outstanding exception of American process thought, cosmology, for all practical purposes, had disappeared as a partner and subject of theology.

In the decades since the council, Catholic theology has moved rapidly away from neoscholasticism, going through a series of turns: the turn to the subject in transcendental theology; the turn to the subject under threat or defeated, in political theology; the linguistic turn, reintegrating the subject to community; the turn to the nonperson through the praxis of justice in liberation theologies as well as in feminist, womanist, mujerista, and Third World women's theologies. In this richness of theology's flourishing, however, it seems to me that something has been lost, namely, even that ghost of outdated cosmology that used to hover in our vision. Today one could go through a whole course of study in college, seminary, or university and never encounter the subject. And yet nature is one of the three main pillars of theology, along with God and humanity. What is needed now, I am convinced, is yet one more turn, a fully inclusive turn to the heavens and the earth, a return to cosmology, in order to restore fullness of vision and get theology back on the track from which it fell off a few hundred years ago.

At least two reasons persuade us to make this turn: the intellectual integrity and the moral integrity of theology, one not strictly separable from the other.

Cosmology and the Intellectual Integrity of Theology

Since theology is the study of God and all things in the light of God, shrinking attention to humanity apart from the rest of creation simply does not do justice to theology's intrinsic mission. Even more, ignoring the cosmos has a deleterious effect insofar as it paves the way for theology to retreat to otherworldliness, disparage matter, body, and the earth, and offer interpretations of reality far removed from the way things actually work. We must engage the world.

When theology today opens its door to the natural world, it is met with a wondrous array of insights. Medieval cosmology, which saw the world as geocentric, static, and unchanging, hierarchically ordered and centered on humanity, is gone. But gone too is the Enlightenment prejudice that held a mechanistic and deterministic view of nature inimical in many ways to religious values. Instead, contemporary science is discovering a natural world that is surprisingly dynamic, organic, self-organizing, indeterminate, chancy, boundless, and open to the mystery of reality. There are still many gaps and uncertainties, but enormous discoveries are being made in our day.[7]

- The world is almost unimaginably *old:* about fifteen billion years ago a single numinous speck exploded in an outpouring of matter and energy, shaping a universe that is still expanding. Five billion years ago an aging, first-generation star exploded, spewing out elements that coalesced to form our sun and its planets, including Earth. (The human race is only recently arrived.)

- The world is almost incomprehensibly *large:* more than 100 billion galaxies, each comprised of 100 billion stars, and no one knows how many moons and planets, all of this visible and audible matter being only a fraction of the matter in the universe. (We humans inhabit a small planet orbiting a medium-sized star toward the edge of one spiral galaxy.)

- The world is almost mind-numbingly *dynamic:* out of the Big Bang, the stars; out of the stardust, the earth; out of the earth, single-celled living creatures; out of the evolutionary life and death of these creatures, human beings with a consciousness and freedom that concentrates the self-transcendence of matter itself. (Human beings are the universe become conscious of itself. We are the cantors of the universe.)

- The world is almost unfathomably *organic:* everything is connected with everything else; nothing conceivable is isolated. In the words of scientist and theologian Arthur Peacocke,

  > Every atom of iron in our blood would not have been there had it not been produced in some galactic explosion billions of years ago and eventually condensed to form the iron in the crust of the earth from which we have emerged. (We are made of stardust.)[8]

- We are also biologically interconnected: human genetic structure closely parallels the DNA of other creatures—bacteria, grasses, bluebirds, horses, the great gray whales. We have all evolved from common ancestors and are kin in the shared history of life.

These and other discoveries of contemporary science coalesce into a picture of the world calling for new interpretations, especially as classical dualisms can no longer be maintained. What, for example, is the proper relationship of spirit and matter if they are in effect the inside and outside of the same phenomena?[9] And—a burning question—what is humanity's place in the great scheme of things? The ancient concept of the hierarchy of being ranks things according to their participation in spirit, from nonorganic to grades of organic life, all under the sway of the Source of Being (from the pebble to the peach to the poodle to the person to the powers and principalities). In this hierarchy, human beings with their rational souls are superior to the natural world, a ranking that easily gives rise to arrogance, one root of the present ecological crisis. Consider for a moment, however, green plants. Predating the human race by millennia, green plants take in carbon dioxide and give off oxygen. Through this process of photosynthesis they create the atmosphere that makes the life of land animals possible. Human beings could not exist without these plants that neither think nor move. They, on the other hand, get along fine without us. Wherein, then, lies superiority?[10] In an interdependent system, no part is intrinsically higher or lower. Yes, more complex life represents critical evolutionary breakthrough, but not such as to remove humanity from essential dependence upon previously evolved creatures. The challenge is to redesign the hierarchy of being into a circle of the community of life. With a kind of species humility, we need to reimagine systematically the uniqueness of being human in the context of our profound kinship with the rest of nature.

In addition to prodding us to rethink basic categories, the new cosmology also offers a new framework within which to consider typical theological questions.[11] Each of our subspecialties is profoundly affected. In such an old, vast, dynamic, and organic world, how and for what reasons does one come to belief in God (foundational theology or apologetics)? What wisdom about the world can be found in biblical and historical authors and the writings of the world's other religious traditions? What does the book of nature in our day teach us about the mystery of God, the Creator of this magnificence, who continues to work creatively within its open and unpredictable systems? How to interpret the irreversible entrance of God into precisely *this* world through the incarnation of divine Wisdom and the transformation of *this* flesh in the resurrection of Jesus Christ? How to understand that the love revealed in Jesus' healings and feedings and poured out on the cross is the very same "Love that moves the sun and the other stars,"[12] so that Dante's vision is no pious lyricism but a theological truth? How to interpret the Spirit of the baptismal font as none other than the very Giver of Life to all the creatures of the rain forest (another undeveloped aspect of pneumatology to which this convention's theme has been drawing our attention)? Whence evil is such a self-organizing universe, and how does sin gain a foothold? Why suffering? How to preach salvation as healing and rescue for the whole world rather than an a-cosmic relation to God? How to let go of contempt for matter, the body and its sexuality, and revalue them as good and blessed? How to interpret human beings as primarily "earthlings" rather than tourists or aliens whose true home is elsewhere?[13] How to conceive of the church, its mission and structures in an evolving universe? How to recognize the sacraments as symbols of divine graciousness in a universe which is itself a sacrament? How to hope for the eschatological redemption of the whole material universe, even now groaning? What paths of spirituality does the new cosmology suggest?

Not least, how is moral decision-making affected? In the classic synthesis, there is a natural order in the world established by God and knowable by the human mind. To act morally or "in accord with natural law" is to transpose the order in the cosmos into human conduct, doing or avoiding acts according to their coherence with that order. How is this pattern of thought affected by the realization that the laws of nature are themselves not eternal principles but only approximations read off from regularities, and that their working is shot through with chance and indeterminacy?

Bringing cosmology into view, I am suggesting, shifts the axis of all theological questions, setting an agenda for years to come. Notice that one does not have to deal with the cosmos directly; rather, it provides both framework and substantive insights useful for *fides quaerens intellectum*. The intellectual integrity of theology, as public discourse of a North American community responsible to articulate faith in a global society, requires vigorous response to this intellectual challenge.

TURN TO THE HEAVENS AND THE EARTH

Cosmology and the Moral Integrity of Theology

Besides an intellectual reason for theology's turn to the heavens and the earth, there is a compelling moral reason as well. In our day the human race is inflicting devastation on the life-systems and other living species of our home planet, havoc that has reached crisis proportions and even in some places ecological collapse. Due to the unceasing demands of consumerist economies on the one hand and burgeoning population on the other, we are exploiting earth's resources without regard for long-term sustainability.

This assault on the earth results now in damage to the systems that sustain life: holes in the ozone layer, clear-cut forests, drained wetlands, denuded grasslands and soils, polluted air, rivers, and coastal waters, poisoned oceans, disputed habitats, and hovering over all the threat of nuclear conflagration and the reality of nuclear waste. The widescale destruction of ecosystems has as its flip side the extinction of species with a consequent loss of earth's biodiversity. By a conservative estimate, in the last quarter of the twentieth century (1975–2000), twenty percent of all living species will have become extinct. We are living in a time of a great dying off. Life forms that have taken millions of years to evolve, magnificent animals and intricate plants, are disappearing forever, due to human actions. Their perishing sends an early warning signal of the death of the planet itself as a dwelling place for life. In the blunt language of the World Council of Churches Canberra assembly, "The stark sign of our times is a planet in peril at out hands."[14]

This ongoing destruction of God's good earth, when perceived through the lens of theology, bears the mark of deep sinfulness.[15] Through greed, self-interest, and injustice, human beings are violently bringing disfigurement and death to this living, evolving planet which ultimately comes from the creative hands of God who looks upon it as "very good" (Gen 1:31). Ecocide, biocide, geocide—these new terms attempt to name the killing of ecosystems and species that are meant to reflect the glory of God but instead end up broken or extinct. One of the "books" that teaches about God is being ruined, and this is a matter for theological concern, having even the character of a moral imperative.

In light of the devastation, the turn to the heavens and the earth bears the marks of genuine conversion of mind and heart, with repentance for the lack of love and the violence visited on the living planet. As we turn, we will be looking for thought patterns that will transform our species-centered-ness and enable us to grant not just instrumental worth but intrinsic value to the natural world. This is a condition for the possibility of extending vigorous moral consideration to the whole earth, now under threat.[16] If nature with its own inherent value before God be the new poor, then our compassion is called into play. Solidarity with victims, option for the poor, and action on behalf of justice widen out from human beings to embrace life-systems and other species to ensure vibrant communion in life for all.

Moral reflection about the natural world under threat becomes more complex when we take into consideration the organic links that exist be-tween exploitation of the earth and injustice among human beings them-selves. The voices of the poor and of women bring to light the fact that structures of social domination are chief among the ways that abuse of the earth is accomplished. Attending to these voices prevents retrieval of the cosmos from being tagged as the interest of only a first-world, male, aca-demic elite.

The Poor. Economic poverty coincides with ecological poverty, for the poor suffer disproportionately from environmental destruction.[17] In so-called Third World countries, the onset of development through capitalism brings deforestation, soil erosion, and polluted waters, which in turn lead to the disruption of local cycles of nature and the sustenance economies on which most poor people depend. Sheer human misery results. Again, plan-tation farming of commodity crops for export not only destroys biodiver-sity but also creates wealth for a few from the backbreaking labor of a class of poor people. Correlatively, lack of land reform pushes dispossessed rural peoples to the edges of cultivated land where, in order to stay alive, they practice slash-and-burn agriculture, in the process destroying pristine habi-tat, killing rare animals, and displacing indigenous peoples. To give a North American example, United States companies export work to factories across the Mexican border *(maquiladores)* that cheaply employ thousands of young, rural women to make high-quality consumer goods for export while they live in unhealthy squalor in an environment spoiled by toxic waste.

In a global perspective, these conditions result from an economic sys-tem driven by profit whose inner logic makes it prey without ceasing on nature's resources and seek cheap labor to turn those resources into con-sumer products. The beneficiaries are the wealthy classes and nations, including ourselves, who consume without ceasing a disproportionate amount of the earth's resources not out of need to stay alive but out of need to be pleasured and entertained. Even in these wealthy countries, ecological injustice runs through the social fabric. The economically well-off, for example, can choose to live amid acres of green, while poor people are housed near factories, refineries, or waste processing plants that heavily pollute the environment; birth defects, general ill health, and disease result. The bitterness of this experience is exacerbated by racial prejudice as environmental racism pressures people of color to dwell in these neighborhoods.

In sum, social injustice has an ecological face: ravaging of people and of the land go hand in hand. To be truly effective, therefore, the turn to the cosmos in theology needs to include commitment to a more just social order within the wider struggle for life as a whole, for healthy ecosystems where all living creatures can flourish.

Women. Exploitation of the earth also coincides with the subordination of women with the system of patriarchy. Female symbolism for nature generally pervades human thought, arising from the fact that women are the lifegivers to every human child as the earth itself, Mother Earth, brings forth fruits. Feminist scholarship today points out how classical Christian theology has consistently used this symbolic affinity to interpret both women and the natural world in terms of hierarchical dualism, separating them from and subordinating them to the men they bring forth and sustain. While granted their own goodness before God, both women and nature are identified with matter, potency, and body more than with spirit, act, and mind. They are assigned mainly instrumental value in this world and excluded from direct contact with the sphere of the sacred, which is construed in analogy with transcendent male consciousness beyond the realm of coming to be and passing away. Women whose bodies mediate physical existence to humanity thus become the oldest symbol of the connection between social domination and the domination of nature.[18]

While the construals of Greek philosophy that undergird traditional subordinationist theologies may be superseded by other philosophies, the mentality that sees nature as something to be dominated continues to draw on the imagery and attitudes of men's domination of women. We speak of "the rape of the earth," revealing the extent to which exploitation of nature is identified with violent sexual conquest of women, and of "virgin forest," as yet untouched by man but awaiting his exploration and conquest. These and other linguistic metaphors point to the reality that ruling man's hierarchy over women extends also to nature, who is meant for his service while *he,* in his nobility, has a duty to control and a right to use her.

The contribution of women from cultural positions other than white feminists is instructive here. For example, womanist theologian Delores Williams makes a telling connection between the violation of nature and the practice of breeding black women under slavery, both defilements leading to exhaustion of the body and depletion of the spirit created by God.[19] Describing the Chipko movement to protect local trees in India and the Green Belt movement for reforestation in Kenya, both led largely by women, Asian theologian Aruna Gnanadason analyzes how the women are affirming the life of their own bodies in the process.[20] Indeed, in our day, women's bodily self-confidence, women's psychological and spiritual self-confidence, flows against the tide of ecological collapse, but meets mighty opposition in the process.

In sum, sexism too has an ecological face, and the devastating consequences of patriarchal dualism cannot be fully addressed until the system is faced as a whole. To be truly effective, therefore, the turn to the cosmos in theology needs to cut through the knot of misogynist prejudice in our systematic concepts, shifting from dualistic, hierarchical, and atomistic categories to holistic, communal, and relational ones.

The argument of this section has been that the moral integrity of theology demands that it extend its concern to embrace the great family of earth as a supreme value, now under threat. The vision motivating such theology is that of a flourishing humanity on a thriving earth, both together a sacrament of the glory of God.

Ellery and Participation

Having scanned the history of the cosmological theme in theology and having argued for its retrieval on the grounds of theology's intellectual and moral integrity, I would like to engage you in a simple thought experiment, one that may whet your appetite for the work that lies ahead. Let us juxtapose a goldfish with Aquinas's notion of participation, and ask what might result if theology interpreted the former in the light of the latter.

We begin with nature writer Annie Dillard's description of her goldfish Ellery.

This Ellery cost me twenty-five cents. He is a deep red-orange, darker than most goldfish. He steers short distances mainly with his slender red lateral fins; they seem to provide impetus for going backward, up or down. . . . He can extend his mouth, so it looks like a length of pipe; he can shift the angle of his eyes in his head [to] look before and behind himself, instead of simply out to his side. His belly, what there is of it, is white . . . and a patch of this white extends up his sides . . . as though all his [upper] brightness were sunburn.

For this creature, as I said, I paid twenty-five cents. I had never bought an animal before. It was very simple; I went to a store in Roanoke called "Wet Pets"; I handed the man a quarter, and he handed me a knotted plastic bag bouncing with water in which a green plant floated and the goldfish swam. This fish, two bits' worth, has a coiled gut, a spine radiating fine bones, and a brain. Just before I sprinkle his food flakes into his bowl, I rap three times on the bowl's edge; now he is conditioned, and swims to the surface when I rap. And, he has a heart.[21]

As Sallie McFague comments, "the juxtaposition in this passage of twenty-five cents with the elaborateness, cleverness, and sheer glory of this tiny bit of matter named Ellery is frankly unnerving. For the intricacy of this little creature calls forth wonder, and suddenly we see that it is priceless."[22] What would be an appropriate theological interpretation of Ellery? I suggest that Aquinas's notion of participation is a resource with great and largely untapped potential to help answer that question. According to Aquinas, all creatures exist by participation in divine being.[23] This is an awesome concept, suggesting an intrinsic, ongoing relationship with the very wellspring of being, with the sheer livingness of the living God who in overflowing graciousness quickens all things. Exemplifying the catholic imagination at work, Aquinas works with a fine analogy to explain this.[24] God's presence among creatures awakens them to life the way fire ignites what it brushes against. We know that fire is present wherever something catches on fire. Just so, everything that exists does so by participation in the fire of divine being. Everything that acts is energized by participation in divine act. Everything that brings something else into being does so by sharing in divine creative power. Every act of resistance to the history of radical suffering is fueled by the inexhaustible source of new being. Conversely, thanks to the relation of participation, we can affirm of God in surpassing and originating sense all the vitality, radical energy, spontaneity, and charm encountered in the world. In turn, we can see that creatures themselves in some way resemble God.

Does Ellery exist by participation in divine being? Is this glorious little fish in some way an image of God? Is he a word in the book of nature that reveals knowledge of God? Is God intimately present to this goldfish preserving him in existence at every moment? Does he have his own intrinsic value which we are called upon to respect? If so—and I hope you are answering "Yes" to these questions—then we can ill afford to neglect him. Including Ellery, and by extension the whole universe, in theological reflection is of critical importance.

Conclusion

This address has been seeking to persuade you that theology needs to complete the many recent worthy turns to the subject with a turn to the heavens and the earth. Whatever our subdisciplines, we need to develop theology with a tangible and comprehensive ecological dimension. I am not suggesting that we just think through a new theology of creation, but that cosmology be a framework within which all theological topics be rethought and a substantive partner in theological interpretation. There is hard work ahead. We need to appreciate all over again that the whole universe is a sacrament, vivified by the presence of the Creator Spirit. We need to realize that its destruction is tantamount to sacrilege. And we need to fathom that human beings are part of the mystery and magnificence of this universe, not lords of the manor but partners with God in helping creation to grow and prosper.

Recovering the cosmocentric power of the fuller Christian tradition puts us in line with our ancient and medieval forebears and fosters the intellectual and moral integrity of theology. Not doing so would be to make our theologizing increasingly irrelevant. It would also be to fail in responsibility to our profession, to the Church, and to generations yet unborn, human and nonhuman species alike. Doing so sets theology off on a great intellectual adventure, one where both wisdom and prophecy will intertwine on the way to a new theological synthesis and praxis. This, friends and colleagues, is a monumental challenge as the Catholic Theological Society of American begins its second half-century of Catholic talk.[25]

Endnotes

*This essay first appeared in *The Catholic Theological Society of America PROCEEDINGS* of the Fifty-first Annual Convention, San Diego, California, June 6–9, 1996, and is used with permission.

1. For this and what follows, see the study by Max Wilder, *The Theologian and His Universe: Theology and Cosmology from the Middle Ages to the Present*, trans. Paul Dunphy (New York: Seabury, 1982).

2. Hildegard of Bingen, *Scivias*, trans. Mother Columba Hart and Jane Bishop (New York: Paulist, 1980) 94.

3. Ibid., 98; adapted for inclusivity.

4. "Qui igitur tantis rerum creatarum splendoribus non illustratur caecus est; qui tar clamoribus non evigilat surdus est; qui ex omnibus his effectibus Derum non laudat mu est; qui ex tantis indiciis primum principium non advertit stultus est." *Itinerarium mer in Deum*, c. 1, no. 15; adapted from *The Mind's Journey to God*, trans. Lawrence Cunningham (Chicago: Franciscan Herald Press, 1979).

5. *Summa theologiae* I, q. 47, a. 1. The first chapters of the *Summa contra genti* book II are even entitled this way: "That the consideration of creatures is useful instruction of faith" (ch. 2); "That knowledge of the nature of creatures serves to destroy errors concerning God" (ch. 3), wherein it is written that "errors about creatures sometimes lead one astray from the truth of faith" (3.1).

6. Quotations from John Paul II: "Lessons of the Galileo Case," *Origins* 22/22 (12 November 1992): 369–73. For what follows, see also Cardinal Paul Poupard, "Galileo: Report on Papal Commission Findings," ibid., 374–75.

7. Several key works that deal directly with scientific concepts are Ian Barbour, *Religion in an Age of Science*, 2 vols. (San Francisco: Harper & Row, 1990–1991); Arthur Peacocke, *Theology for a Scientific Age: Being and Becoming—Natural, Divine, and Human* (Minneapolis: Fortress, 1993); Ted Peters, ed., *Cosmos as Creation: Theology and Science in Consonance* (Nashville: Abingdon, 1989); John Polkinghorne, *One World: The Interaction of Science and Theology* (Princeton: Princeton University Press, 1986); and the series edited by Robert Russell et al. and published by the Vatican Observatory (Vatican City) and the Center for Theology and the Natural Sciences (Berkeley): *Physics, Philosophy, and Theology: A Common Quest for Understanding* (1988), *Quantum Cosmology and the Laws of Nature: Scientific Perspectives on Divine Action* (1993), and *Chaos and Complexity: Scientific Perspectives on Divine Action* (1995).

8. Arthur Peacocke, "Theology and Science Today," in *Cosmos as Creation*, ed. Peters, 32.

9. See the insightful essay of Karl Rahner: "The Unity of Spirit and Matter

in the Christian Understanding of Faith," *Theological Investigations,* vol. 6, trans. Karl and Boniface Kruger (New York: Crossroad, 1982) 153–77. The works of Teilhard de Chardin are prophetic in this respect: cf. *The Divine Milieu* (New York: Harper & Row, 1960) and *Hymn of the Universe* (New York: Harper & Row, 1965).

10. This example is taken from Rosemary Radford Ruether, *To Change the World: Christology and Cultural Criticism* (New York: Crossroad, 1981) 67. This scholar has contributed early, insightfully, and voluminously to ecological theology: see her *New Woman, New Earth* (San Francisco: Harper & Row, 1975) ch. 8; *Sexism and God-Talk: Toward a Feminist Theology* (Boston: Beacon, 1983) chs. 3, 9, 10, and postscript; and *Gaia and God: An Ecofeminist Theology of Earth Healing* (San Francisco: HarperCollins, 1992).

11. It is good to report that the work has already begun. See, e.g., university symposiums: David Burrell, ed. *God and Creation: An Ecumenical Symposium* (Notre Dame IN: University of Notre Dame Press, 1990) and Kevin Irwin, ed., *Preserving the Creation: Environmental Theology and Ethics* (Washington, DC: Georgetown University Press, 1994); pivotal essays: David Tracy, "Cosmology and Christian Hope," in his *On Naming the Present* (Maryknoll, NY: Orbis, 1994) 73–81, and Michael Himes and Kenneth Himes, "Creation and an Environmental Ethic," in their *Fullness of Faith* (New York: Paulist, 1993) 104–24; and book-length treatments: John Haught, *The Promise of Nature: Ecology and Cosmic Purpose* (New York: Paulist, 1993); Tony Kelly, *An Expanding Theology: Faith in a World of Connections* (Newtown, Australia: E. J. Dwyer, 1993)—a little summa; and Denis Edwards, *Jesus the Wisdom of God: An Ecological Theology* (Maryknoll, NY: Orbis, 1995).

12. Dante, *The Divine Comedy,* trans. Dorothy Sayers and Barbara Reynolds (Harmondsworth, England: Penguin, 1962) canto 33, line 145.

13. This is the expression of Sallie McFague, "An Earthly Theological Agenda," in *Ecofeminism and the Sacred,* ed. Carol Adams (New York: Continuum, 1993) 84–98.

14. "Giver of Life—Sustain Your Creation," in *Signs of the Spirit,* official report of the WCC's seventh assembly in Canberra, ed. Michael Kinnamon (Geneva: WCC, 1991) 55.

15. See Sallie McFague's shrewd analysis of ecological sin in her *The Body of God: An Ecological Theology* (Minneapolis: Augsburg/Fortress, 1993) 112–29; her earlier work, *Models of God: Theology for an Ecological, Nuclear Age* (Philadelphia: Fortress, 1987) is filled with data about the ecological crisis and offers a rethinking of God in its light.

16. This intrinsic value is well attested in biblical theologies. God covenants with the earth as well as with humans; prophets invoke judgment over all that destroys life; Wisdom's playful delight in the natural world is not dependent on human participation. As oppressed people cry out to God, so too the earth can groan, lament, and shout out; conversely, rejoicing clothes the hills, the desert blossoms, the meadows and valleys sing with gladness. See Richard Clifford, "The Bible and the Environment," in *Preserving the Creation,* ed. Irwin, 1–26.

17. See David Hallman, ed., *Ecotheology: Voices from South and North* (Geneva: WCC; Maryknoll, NY: Orbis, 1994); Leonardo Boff and Virgil Elizondo, eds., *Ecology and Poverty, Concilium* 1995/5 (Maryknoll, NY: Orbis, 1995) esp. Eduardo Gudynas, "Ecology from the Viewpoint of the Poor," 106–14; Leonardo Boff, *Ecology and Liberation: A New Paradigm* (Maryknoll, NY: Orbis, 1995); Mary Heather MacKinnon and Moni McIntyre, eds., *Readings in Ecology and Feminist Theology* (Kansas City: Sheed and Ward, 1995) esp. H. Paul Santmire, "Ecology, Justice, and Theology: Beyond the Preliminary Skirmishes," 56–62, and Vandana Shiva, "Development, Ecology, and Women," 161–71; and Vitor Westhelle, "Creation Motifs in the Search for a Vital Space: A Latin American Perspective," in *Lift Every Voice: Constructing Christian Theologies from the Underside*, ed. Susan Thistlethwaite and Mary Potter Engel (San Francisco: Harper & Row, 1990) 128–40.

18. In addition to the writings of Ruether and McFague, see Anne Primavesi, *From Apocalypse to Genesis: Ecology, Feminism, and Christianity* (Minneapolis: Augsburg/Fortress, 1991); Elizabeth Johnson, *Women, Earth, and Creator Spirit* (New York: Paulist, 1993); Adams, ed., *Ecofeminism and the Sacred;* and MacKinnon and McIntyre, eds., *Readings in Ecology and Feminist Theology.*

19. Delores Williams, "Sin, Nature, and Black Women's Bodies," in *Ecofeminism and the Sacred,* ed. Adams, 24–29; see also Shamara Shantu Riley, "Ecology Is a Sistah's Issue Too," in *Readings in Ecology and Feminist Theology,* eds. MacKinnon and McIntyre, 214–29.

20. Aruna Gnanadason, "Towards a Feminist Eco-Theology for India," in *A Reader in Feminist Theology,* ed. Prasanna Kumari (Madras, India: Gurukul Lutheran Theological College, 1993) 95–105.

21. Annie Dillard, *Pilgrim at Tinker Creek: A Mystical Excursion into the Natural World* (New York: Harper & Row, 1974) 124.

22. McFague, *The Body of God,* 210. I am indebted to this author for her discovery and use of this passage.

23. For what follows, see Aquinas, *Summa theologiae* I, questions 4 (a. 3), 8, 13, 15 (a. 2), 18, 44, 45 (a. 7), and 104; and *Summa contra gentiles* III, chs. 17–21, 65–70.

24. *ST* I, q. 8, a. 1, 2, 3; and *SCG* 3.66, par. 7.

25. See Peter Steinfels, "Fifty Years of Catholic Talk," *New York Times,* 20 June 1995, A12, on the fiftieth anniversary convention.

4

REVERENCE FOR
HUMAN LIFE

JAMES J. McCARTNEY

Villanova University

In the book of Deuteronomy, Moses tells the Israelites "Choose life!" This motif has been a central vision of both Judaism and Christianity for millennia, and the values that spring from this vision have been consistently articulated and enriched over the centuries by adherents of both of these monotheistic faiths. In John's Gospel, Jesus of Nazareth is seen as the source of all life (as the Word of God made flesh) and especially the spiritual life of humans ("I have come that they might have life . . . "). Reverence for human life in all of its dimensions—biological, psychosocial, ethical, and spiritual—is one of the hallmarks of Christian life and practice, and the dignity and sanctity of human life, especially the lives of the poor, marginalized, disabled, or oppressed, is one of the constant holdings of Christian ethics.

In this chapter, I hope to highlight many activities of the Christian churches that encourage and support reverence for human life. I also wish to discuss some of the obstacles spawned by our contemporary "culture of death" and some Christian ethical responses to these contemporary challenges.

Christian Activities That Support Reverence for Human Life

In his letter to all the Roman Catholic bishops throughout the world, *Evangelium Vitae* (The Gospel of Life), Pope John Paul II emphasizes that the Gospel (Good News) of Life is at the heart of Jesus' message. If this is true, we should be able to observe reverence for life manifested by Jesus' followers in the contemporary world, since the church sees itself as the sacramental instrument of Jesus' saving activity extended through space and time. What are some these "works of life" that the church, the people of God, now perform? I believe they can be divided into three broad areas: health and healing, concern for the public or common good, and developing culture and improving the quality of life.

Health and Healing

Concern for health and healing is rooted in the Gospels' description of Jesus' life and ministry. One of the first things that attracted people to this prophet from Galilee was his ability to heal, which Jesus always used as a sign of God's saving power in our lives. As the 1994 *Ethical and Religious Directives for Catholic Health Care Services* point out, Jesus "cleansed a man with leprosy, gave sight to two people who were blind, enabled one who was mute to speak, cured a woman who was hemorrhaging, and brought a young girl back to life. Indeed, the Gospels are replete with examples of how the Lord cured every kind of ailment and disease." But "Jesus' healing mission went further than caring only for physical affliction. He touched people at the deepest level of their existence; he sought their physical, mental and spiritual healing."[1]

Christian concern with health and healing is embodied in such church-sponsored activities as missionary clinics, rural and urban community health centers, home health programs, long-term care, rehabilitation centers, acute care facilities, and hospice care. These health care ministries are generally collaborative efforts of women and men, non-ordained Christians and ordained Christian ministers, all committed to the "goals of healing, the maintenance of health, and the compassionate care of the dying."[2]

What are the moral or ethical grounds for such activity? First of all, Christians are committed to promote and defend human dignity. The Book of Genesis declares that we are created in God's image, and one interpretation of this passage is that as humans we share in the dignity of the Divine. This concern with human dignity is the foundation of the reverence that Christians have for the sacredness of every human life. In turn, this attitude of reverence entails a right to adequate health care necessary for the proper development of life.

The Good Samaritan is one of the best known and most deeply moving of Jesus' stories. In response to the question, "Who is my neighbor?" Jesus shows, by means of this parable, that the neighbor is anyone who helps those who are in need. The Jew left for dead on the roadside is helped by a foreigner whom the Jews considered an outcast. Responding to this Gospel mandate to be compassionate toward those in difficulty, Christian health care services are almost always committed by their mission to serve the poor and those who cannot afford to pay for health care.

The Common Good

One of the most important responsibilities of government at every level is concern for the public or common good. This concern entails building and maintaining bridges and highways and providing other aspects of the infrastructure of society, as well as providing adequate social safety nets, for vulnerable members of the society (e.g., decent, low-cost housing and access to health care for the poor and elderly).

In our libertarian and individualistic society, we easily forget that concern for the common good is rooted in our social nature as well as in the religious value of reverence for life. When the common good is put before our own interests, not only are others helped, but we ourselves share the benefits of the bonds of human solidarity. When we pay taxes and support other civic and religious organizations either financially or through volunteerism, not only are we reaching out to others in need, but we ourselves can experience the human growth that such concern for the common good generally effects. Finally, commitment to the public good not only benefits society as a whole, but its promotion and support by Christians is another way of enhancing human dignity and respect for human life.

Development of Culture and the Quality of Life

Reverence for human life also entails activities that promote the development of culture and the improvement of the quality of life for all members of society. Although periods, movements, and individuals in Christian history have understood the Church as essentially countercultural, Christians have generally tried to use the "leaven" of the Gospel to Christianize various human societies and cultural traditions. By saying, "In the same way, let your light shine before others, so that they may see your good works and give glory to your Father in heaven" (Mt 5:16), the Gospel has been instructive in this regard. Development of culture and improvement of the quality of life are manifested by such Christian activities as liberal arts education, Christian involvement in telecommunications and computer networking, support for scientific research, ministry to those in prison, provision of food and shelter for the homeless, concern for runaway children and adolescents, care for the disabled, and establishment of orphanages, foster care, and homes for unwed women to bear children in dignity.

In Matthew's Gospel (chapter 25), Jesus commends the just by saying, "Come, you who are blessed by my Abba God! Inherit the kingdom prepared for you from the creation of the world. For I was hungry and you fed me, I was thirsty and you gave me drink, a stranger and you welcomed me, naked and you clothed me, I was ill and you comforted me, in prison and you came to visit me." The just ask Jesus, "When did we see you hungry and feed you, or see you thirsty and give you drink? When did we see you as a stranger and invite you in, or clothe you in your nakedness? When did we see you ill or in prison, and come to visit you?" He responds, "The truth is, every time you did this for the least of my sisters or brothers, you did it for me" (Mt 25:40).

Seeing the face of God in the other is, for the Christian, the most important ethical motivation leading towards the development of culture and the improvement of the quality of life. Other's cultural and human needs are always experienced existentially, and response to the "wholly other" cannot be reduced to an objective algorithm of cultural duty or a formulaic response to human need. True reverence for life entails respect for the radical difference of others and the unique demands their otherness makes upon us. Thus, enhancing culture through education, improving communication, or supporting cultural diversity cannot and should not attempt to predict the outcomes of these activities in advance; attempting to improve the quality of life must be open to manifold interpretations of what a good quality of life might be. This stance means that a truly Christian reverence for life is not reducible to Western European or American cultural visions and values, no matter how important these are in our own lived experience or in those of our family, friends, and local community. As we experience the shrinking of the world through enhanced telecommunications and travel, we must be more wary than ever of cultural and social imperialism mistakenly exercised in the name of the Gospel of Jesus Christ.

Obstacles to Reverence for Life and Christian Ethical Responses

In the *Gospel of Life,* John Paul II suggest that the Western world at the end of this millennium is embracing a "culture of death." When we consider the continuing controversies over reproductive technologies, genetic engineering, abortion, research involving human subjects, assisted suicide and euthanasia, random violence, genocide, and the acceptance of capital punishment in the United States, the Pope certainly has a point. It is not too difficult in our times to be a "prophet of doom." Yet, when we consider every other epoch of human history, we will find that the pervasiveness of sin in the world has always resulted in bloodshed, violence, exploitation, and cruelty, sometimes in the name of the truth, justice, and God. But the best of the Christian ethical tradition has always responded to these and other obstacles to reverence for life not just with condemnation, but with a sense of positive vision and authentic values. The Christian ethical tradition has arguably increased and improved understanding of human dignity and reverence for life, notwithstanding the many obstacles still left to be overcome. In the following sections, I will outline some of these contemporary obstacles to reverence for life as they manifest themselves in the debates over abortion, assisted suicide, and euthanasia, and then suggest ethical responses drawn from the Christian tradition that lead to a more positive approach.

Abortion

The problem of abortion continues to be one of the most vexing in American society. Christians stand on both sides of the abortion divide, with most

Catholics and evangelical Christians taking a stance that sees the fetus as a vulnerable person to be protected, while many Jews, mainline Protestants, and a few Catholics see the fetus either as an aggressor in some situations, or else as part of the woman's body that can be removed as desired, much like extra adipose tissue can be removed by liposuction. Originally argued as a private choice between a woman and her doctor, abortion is now understood and debated as a much more broadly construed social issue.

A decision to terminate a pregnancy has many ramifications. In addition to the obvious religious and ethical quandaries and the debates over when personhood begins, an intention to abort has significant social implications that are often passed over or ignored. Additionally, the issue of abortion can be analyzed and debated from the perspectives of the various social theories of ethics and law that compete for the hearts and minds of people today.

It is truly ironic that the United States Supreme Court in *Roe v. Wade* made it possible for states, if they so choose, to legalize abortion on demand until birth and did so on the grounds of protecting personal privacy (the privacy of the relationship between the woman and her doctor). Given the web of relationships and responsibilities the pregnant woman has with her unborn offspring—with the father of the child, with her family, with her peers, and with her education and career, as well as with her doctor—it would seem that the decision whether or not to terminate a pregnancy, however it is resolved ethically, is an inherently social decision and hardly "private" at all. It is true that the choice to abort or not is the pregnant woman's to make, but the rationale for that choice ought not be grounded on individualistic preference (privacy in a narrow sense), but on a mature consideration of what reverence for life entails regarding social relationships and demands that situate each human life in its concrete specificity and context.

Robert N. Bellah and his coauthors have masterfully shown in their book *Habits of the Heart* that this tendency to individualize inherently social decisions is a characteristic of American culture. And Larry R. Churchill in *Rationing Health Care in America* has demonstrated how the negative ramifications of this one-dimensional individualism continue to influence contemporary attitudes towards health care in the United States. Our modern emphasis on individualism and privacy has pushed to the background of awareness our relatedness and responsibility to others and theirs to us, leading to a diminished sense of the "common good." Nowhere is this emphasis on extreme individualism more rampant than in the rhetoric of those "pro-choice" on the issue of abortion who are not willing to consider any restrictions of that choice no matter what social good may be accomplished by reasonable procedures and limits, as the recent debate on partial birth abortions clearly demonstrated. This American emphasis on the rights of decontextualized individuals in abortion and divorce law has been accurately portrayed by Mary Ann Glendon in her important study, *Abortion and Divorce in Western Law.*

This overemphasis on privacy and the subsequent downplaying of the social implications of the abortion decision has been acknowledged by the United States Supreme Court. In its decision on *Planned Parenthood of Southeastern Pennsylvania v. Casey,* the Court, although retaining and once again reaffirming what it understands to be the essential holding of *Roe v. Wade* (that a woman has a constitutionally protected right to choose to have an abortion before viability and to obtain it without undue interference from the state), believes that "the ability of women to participate equally in the economic and social life of the nation has been facilitated by their ability to control their reproductive lives." This reason is surely a social one, but it moves the Court away from *Roe* emphasis on privacy and leads the plurality—sensitive to other social dimensions of the decision to terminate a pregnancy—to assert what is implied in the *Roe* holding that "the State has legitimate interests from the outset of the pregnancy in protecting the health of the woman and the life of the fetus that may become a child." In a later section of this decision, the justices emphasize that this part of the *Roe* holding "has been given too little acknowledgment and implementation by the Court in its subsequent cases." This emphasis can be interpreted as the Court's acknowledgment that some negative social dimensions of abortion relating directly to the issue of reverence for life should properly and constitutionally be regulated by statutory law.

Many Americans, although agreeing that a woman has the right to procure an abortion, are comfortable with some restrictions of this right because of the social implications of the abortion decision. For example, most are opposed to the use of abortion as a means of sex selection or career enhancement, even though many of these same people would support a termination of pregnancy in other situations. Many are also comfortable with parental notification laws for minors and laws providing a time and

context for truly informed decision-making to take place. Some are opposed to public funding of abortion because they believe that the government should have other spending priorities, and there are those who are
opposed to using public facilities or those who work in them for the
procurement of abortions because of the State's legitimate interest in the
protection of fetal life. Others, of course, would be opposed to almost all
abortions because of what our casual acceptance of the termination of
pregnancy says of our attitude as a society about the dignity of human life.
All of these critiques are based primarily on a value-weighted analysis of the
social implications of abortion, rather than primarily or exclusively on the
moral judgment that the murder of an innocent person is taking place.

Christian Ethical Teaching and Abortion

Over the centuries, Catholic theology has made significant contributions to
the development of profoundly Christian ethical teaching. In this section,
some values or operating assumptions characteristic of Catholic ethical
thought will be analyzed and applied to the abortion debate.

The first value that Catholic ethical theory has consistently emphasized
is the dignity of the human individual. Human dignity is rooted in the
biblical belief that humans are created in God's image and that personal life,
since it reflects the Spirit of God in its own spirituality, is intrinsically
valuable and to be considered as an end in itself and not merely as a means
to some other end. However, this stress on the dignity of the individual
should not be misinterpreted as a focus on individual autonomy; rather,
human persons are understood in the Catholic tradition as essentially social
beings whose personhood has both a private and a relational dimension
insofar as our concrete actions and experiences both influence and are
influenced by the world of persons around us as well as the subjects we
ourselves are continuing to become. John Paul II describes these phenomena as the transitive and intransitive (reflexive) dimensions of human actions and experiences.

The Church's emphasis on the dignity of the person, especially the
personhood of the unborn, is what has motivated its opposition to almost
all abortions and its emphasis on the importance of reverence for life.
However, it is becoming increasingly clear that the social, gender, and
economic injustices that often force women to an abortion decision are also

significant affronts to human dignity and reverence. This reality has led many Church leaders to emphasize what is called a "seamless garment" approach to life issues, which holds that reverence for life demands that human life, at all its stages and in every context, be protected and that its quality be enhanced and improved. In fact, many "pro-life" organizations take this holistic approach and are trying to change some of the injustices that motivate decisions to terminate pregnancies. They are also providing realistic alternatives for women who believe they must make this decision, and are establishing "Project Rachel" programs to provide support and counseling for women who have already procured abortions.

The interpersonal dimension of reverence for life is the basis for the Catholic ethical tradition's continuing emphasis on the notion of the common good. This operating assumption is empirically grounded, since experience demonstrates that we are not isolated individuals, but are profoundly related to one another in most dimensions of our lives. Indeed, as the world itself continues to shrink through improvements in telecommunications and travel, this coming millennium promises to be the most interconnected in the history of humankind. While grounded in empirical observation, Catholic social thought also emphasizes the value and obligation of societal responsibility. This responsibility is valuable insofar as it benefits, at least indirectly, the individual person himself or herself; it is an obligation insofar as individuals cannot exist or flourish without belonging to at least one community of shared values and goals. Human participation and solidarity, as understood by John Paul II, is the virtue that motivates us to transform the existential fact of human interrelatedness into collaborative and purposeful social activity for the common good.

Although its conclusions can and should be contested, it was just such a "common good" motivation that prompted the plurality in the *Planned Parenthood* decision of the United States Supreme Court to uphold the basic provisions of the *Roe* holding as described above. These justices worried that, if they were to overturn *Roe,* reliance on the stability of law and the societal benefits this provides would be radically undermined and possibly destroyed. Thus they decided that the common good demanded that *Roe* be upheld, even though as individuals some of them are opposed to abortion. Perhaps the "common good" would be more emphatically protected and enhanced if the Court were to have taken a "seamless garment" approach to life issues, providing the constitutional right to life to the unborn, outlawing capital punishment and euthanasia, and providing constitutional grounds for the improvement of access to affordable housing and to quality education and health care.

Seeking to imitate Jesus of Nazareth, whose teaching it proclaims, the Church, in its social teaching, emphasizes that Christians must have a fundamental commitment to improving the lot of the poor and the marginalized just as Jesus himself did. Actualization of this commitment, of course, can take many forms, but Catholic social teaching—whether supporting the rights of workers to organize, condemning racism and sexism, or decrying the structural injustices of nations and institutions—has had as one of its central values the empowerment of the disenfranchised and dispossessed.

This concern for biblical justice has special relevance to the abortion debate. Unborn persons are radically marginalized in our society, and for this reason alone the Church must constantly be holding up their plight before our eyes. Not only are unborn persons vulnerable, but many people of color are convinced that abortion is being promoted in order to bring about genocide for reasons of race and ethnicity under the guise of concern about population control. Others who have been marginalized in decisions to terminate a pregnancy include the father of the unborn, the family of the pregnant woman, and even the pregnant woman herself. Even well intentioned ecclesial sanctions (e.g., excommunication) have had the unintended side effect of alienating and spiritually dispossessing the very people the Church should be most concerned about helping. These penalties should be reconsidered in light of the Church's fundamental commitment to the marginalized, something many bishops have already begun to do.

Assisted Suicide and Euthanasia

The most vivid symbol of America's "culture of death" is the antics of Dr. Jack Kavorkian, the pathologist turned thanatopractor who has assisted in the suicide of dozens of people to this point. Kavorkian's actions have prompted a societal debate about assisted suicide and euthanasia with mixed results. At the present time, several states have explicitly outlawed assisted suicide and euthanasia, while one state, Oregon, has legalized assisted suicide by voter referendum. Two different federal appeals courts recently held that the laws prohibiting assisted suicide in the states of

Washington and New york are unconstitutional, but the United States Supreme Court, in a unanimous affirmation of the reverence due to human life, has reversed these holdings at the end of the 1996–97 term (*Washington v. Glucksberg* and *Vacco v. Quill*). In these cases, the Court did not "discover" a right to die in our legal texts and traditions that would invalidate statutes prohibiting assisted suicide (in fact, it discovered just the opposite), but neither did it proclaim a Constitutional "right to life," which would invalidate Oregon's law although it really couldn't, because Oregon's law was not under review. It does, however, hold that these types of public policy questions are best decided by the states. Florida's supreme court, also resisting the "culture of death", recently held that the right of privacy guaranteed in its state constitution does not include a right of assisted suicide.

At the present time, all the states and the District of Columbia allow the refusal of life-prolonging procedures. This refusal can be effected either by the person actually receiving the procedures, by a proxy or surrogate, or by an advance directive (living will). In both federal appeals rulings, the judges declared that there was no legal distinction between intending to refuse life-prolonging procedures and intending suicide, a position refuted and reversed by Chief Justice Rehnquist's majority opinion in the two Supreme Court decisions referred to above. Thus the Court establishes in constitutional law an ethical distinction that we will see is very important for the Catholic tradition. I believe that, if assisted suicide is eventually legalized, active euthanasia must be legalized as well, because, if it is legally acceptable to kill yourself (with assistance from a physician), it must also be legal (for the same alleged reasons) for another (the physician) to kill you when you cannot do it yourself because you are paralyzed, incapacitated, etc. I am not advocating this legalization of active euthanasia (in fact, it is one of the reasons I am opposed to assisted suicide), but I think both logic and equal protection under the law would make this slippery slope both possible and necessary, a point of view supported by Justice Souter in his concurring Opinion in the cases mentioned above.

Christian Ethical Teaching Regarding the End of Biological Life

The U.S. bishops assert the following: "The health care professional has the knowledge and experience to pursue the goals of healing, the maintenance

of health, and the compassionate care of the dying . . ." [3] In the Catholic
tradition, compassionate care of the dying does include the provision of
adequate palliative care and support, presence, touch, and spiritual com-
fort, as well as the right to refuse burdensome or useless treatments. It does
not include assisted suicide and euthanasia.

It should not come as a surprise that death and dying are of major
theological interest for the Christian tradition. Christians believe that it is
precisely through the redemptive death and resurrection of Jesus of Nazareth that God's saving self-disclosure in human history has taken place.
Christians participate in this divine redemptive activity through baptism,
wherein the believer promises to *die* to sin and live in Christ. Indeed, part
of the symbolism of baptism by immersion is the figurative entering into
the tomb (dying to the power of sin) and emerging from the tomb clothed
in the radiant innocence of Jesus' resurrection and glorification.

Emphasis upon sacramental activity is a hallmark of Roman Catholic
piety and spirituality. Catholics believe that God's saving power is mediated
through earthly signs and symbols that touch us at special graced moments
of our lives. And at least four of the sacraments—baptism, reconciliation,
Eucharist, and anointing—are seen as appropriate in the situation of death
and dying, since this particular time is best spent preparing to enter into the
fullness of God's kingdom.

Thus the notion of Christian death has always meant for Catholics a
time of refocusing energies away from earthly survival and biological life
towards spiritual realities and life with God in Christ whose Spirit we share.
Death with dignity in the Catholic tradition means the ability to prepare
oneself spiritually for the life to come, since Catholics believe that when the
body dies "life is changed, not ended," as the *Preface for the Dead* proclaims
so well. Yet at the same time the Catholic ethical tradition has emphasized
that we should take reasonable means to preserve our biological life and
health, since we are stewards, not masters, of our own bodies. Oftentimes
Catholics are confronted with whether they should try to focus their energies on staying alive, possibly at great burden or expense to themselves or
others, or on preparing for Christian death.

Since the Catholic tradition has always seen the sacrament of the
anointing of the sick as appropriate while the person is dying, but inappropriate after the person has already died, Catholic philosophers and theologians have often explored the meaning and determination of personal

death. When does death take place? How do we determine this? When does care of body cease to become reasonable and yield to the importance of preparing for death? All these questions and others that focus on death with dignity within the Catholic tradition have been reflected upon and will be discussed below.

Brain Death

Religious descriptions of death generally tend to be rather abstract. The Catholic tradition has described death as "the separation of the soul from the body," "the emergence of the spirit from the flesh," "the return of the disembodied spirit back to God," or some other similar formulation. Generally, the determination of when death takes place has been left up to the competency of the medical profession and is not seen as a theological issue in itself. Thus, until recent times, the Catholic Church accepted the medical community's criterion of total and irreversible heart/lung cessation as appropriate for determining death. But with the advent of technologies for sustaining the biological activity of organs and organ systems, including the heart and lungs, cessation of the function of the total brain including the brain stem is now accepted by physicians as an adequate criterion for determining death. The Church has generally seen this determination of brain death as an acceptable way of judging that the person in question is actually deceased.

Brain death is simply the declaration that the person has died because the total brain, including the brain stem, has irreversibly ceased functioning. This method of determination of death was needed because of the possibility of maintaining some organs and organ systems for a fairly long time with the help of artificial procedures for prolonging biological activity, and also because people wished to donate these organs and organ systems for beneficent purposes once they were deceased. However, using the traditional heart/lung cessation criteria for determining health would have rendered these organs useless because of oxygen deprivation. Physicians, knowing that the heart and lungs will not function spontaneously when true brain death has taken place, now generally accept the diagnosis of brain death as adequate for declaring the person dead.

It should be emphasized that brain death is not a halfway house between life and death. It is a declaration that the person has indeed passed from this life and that all that remains is a corpse or a cadaver, with some life systems being kept functional artificially. The determination of brain death is a clinical decision based on valid medical and conceptual criteria, and it is difficult to understand and accept how some states (e.g., New Jersey) allow these standards to be overriden by the values and preferences of non-clinicians, especially when the public good demands prompt interment and discontinuation of expensive medical resources for the deceased. Brain death statutes generally allow physicians, once the family has been informed of the diagnosis, to remove all life-supporting technologies with or without the family's consent, since treatment of a corpse is a medical impossibility. In fact, many states require that the death certificate be written immediately after the brain death diagnosis, *before* life-prolonging technologies are discontinued.

Since the Catholic tradition generally leaves the diagnosis and determination of death to physicians, there can be no principled disagreement against the stance of most members of this profession that a person is dead when the total brain, including the brain stem, has irrevocably ceased functioning. However, because of the significant ontological and legal implications of the diagnosis, the Church can and should encourage Catholic health care professionals to exercise the greatest prudence in making these determinations. Nonetheless, nothing in current brain death diagnoses or public policy would be opposed to Catholic teaching or reverence for life as such.

Generally, brain death determinations are made because of a desire to transplant one or more of the organs of the brain dead cadaver into the body of another person in order to save life or improve health. Organ donation of cadaveric organs, even the heart and lungs, so that another might live is clearly a corporal work of mercy of the greatest magnitude because of its emphasis on the reverence for life, and so it is generally encouraged within the Christian tradition.

Suicide and Euthanasia

In the Roman Catholic tradition, suicide, whether assisted by another or not, has usually been seen as a usurpation of the divine prerogative of deciding life and death and a direct affront to the reverence due to human life. While some Christian theologians argue that, in some rare cases, the person or those who assist the person may be acting as God's agents in effecting a suicide, general Christian consensus is that suicide is incompatible with gospel values.

When the Catholic tradition uses the word euthanasia, it has an ethical, rather than a descriptive, meaning. That is, the word *euthanasia* as used by Catholic moral theologians and the Church, is comparable to words like *murder* and *lying* (as opposed to killing and telling a falsehood). For Catholics, euthanasia is always wrong by *definition* because it is the *unjustified* intention to end someone's life for supposedly beneficent reasons, just as murder is always evil, and lying is always an ethical disvalue, precisely because we define murder as the *unjustified* taking of human life and lying as the *unjustified* telling of a falsehood. And just as killing and telling a falsehood can sometimes be justified, so allowing to die for beneficent reasons is also ethically acceptable. However, just as justified killing is not called murder and the justified telling of a falsehood is not lying, so the justified allowing of someone to die for beneficent reasons is not, strictly speaking, euthanasia.

The Catholic tradition sees suicide and euthanasia as unjustified and therefore wrong. However, this position sometimes causes great confusion since society often uses the word euthanasia in a descriptive—and not in an ethical—sense. For example, many philosophers consider active euthanasia as any overt action that causes death for a beneficent reason and passive euthanasia as any omission that either causes death or allows it to take place for a beneficent reason. In contrast, Catholic teaching holds that any action or omission done with the *direct* intention of ending or shortening life for a beneficent reason is unjustified and therefore euthanasia. But this tradition also understands that allowing someone to die is not necessarily to intend to kill the person; in fact, it does *not* hold that we must do everything possible to stave off death. For the Catholic tradition, allowing to die for some beneficent reason is not always considered euthanasia precisely because allowing to die for some beneficent reason may sometimes be justified. Finally, Catholic teaching accepts that some overt actions, such as providing effective relief from pain, have the foreseen side effect of shortening life or removing consciousness. These actions also can be justified and are not considered euthanasia. The Supreme Court in its *Washington v. Glucksberg* and *Vacco v. Quill* decisions emphasizes the importance of doing everything possible to alleviate pain and suffering for those in terminal situations, even if aggressive pain management shortens life. This decision is exactly what the "compassionate care of the dying" advocated by America's Catholic bishops entails.

To sum up, the Catholic tradition is always opposed to euthanasia and assisted suicide, just as it is always opposed to murder or lying, but the church allows some actions that society would consider passive euthanasia and sometimes even encourages them precisely because they can be justified as rendering effective care to the whole person by helping him or her prepare more adequately for the life to come.

Legitimate Refusal of Medical Treatment

The Catholic tradition puts high value on the promotion and preservation of life and health. It believes that biological life is a gift from God and that we are stewards and conservators of this gift and must take those means generally available to preserve our lives and enhance our well being. However, biological life is not considered an absolute value by the Catholic tradition; it is in fact a relative good, because its purpose is to support and enable the possibility of spiritual life. Nevertheless, biological life is a most basic value and, in fact, is the source of all other human values and goods.

Catholic teaching sees the responsibility to care for one's life and health as a positive command, part of the affirmative natural law. Unlike some negative commands that, in principle, can bind absolutely (e.g., the command against directly taking the life of the innocent), affirmative commands may always, in principle, admit exceptions. Thus the command to worship on Sunday by attending mass does not bind absolutely, but allows for exception when sickness or other serious obstacles stand in the way. The responsibility to care for life and health, being an affirmative command, also does not bind absolutely. In fact, the Church, acknowledging human limitation and finitude, stresses that not everything possible need be done to preserve life and health because this would be a moral impossibility in some situations.

The Catholic Church has always honored the profession of medicine, seeing physicians as possessing certain skills and knowledge to enhance biological health, cure disease, and treat illness. Nonetheless, the Church has always seen the promotion of life and health as a personal responsibility, and has allowed people great discretion regarding the means they consider necessary to accomplish these laudable goals. Therefore, physicians must always get the informed consent of the patient in order to treat, and it is ultimately up to the patient, not the physician, to determine what treatment options will best meet the obligations of stewardship the patient has before God. This decision about treatment options, however, is not totally subjective and discretionary. Catholic teaching has suggested several standards in order to help people decide whether a given medical intervention is mandatory or not.

Ordinary vs. Extraordinary

Unless another standard contravenes, Catholic teaching maintains that those medical interventions that would be customary or usual, given the lifestyle of the person in relation with his or her society, should be considered ethically mandatory. Those interventions that would not be customary or that would be unusual within a given culture would be considered extraordinary and medically optional. Perhaps better wording for this standard would be "usual vs. unusual," since oftentimes "ordinary" has been interpreted as "standard medical treatment" and "extraordinary" as "experimental" treatment, clearly a misunderstanding of the Church's emphasis regarding these items.

An excellent example of the use of this criterion is provided by Gary Atkinson[4] when he discusses the sixteenth century moralist Francisco De Vitoria. Vitoria believes that, if a person uses foods that people commonly use and in the quantity that customarily suffices for the conservation of strength, then the person is acting morally, even if by acting in this way one's life is notably shortened. In addition, an individual would not be required to use the best, most delicate, most expensive foods, even if they were the most healthful. Vitoria says that, if the doctor were to advise the person to eat chicken and partridges, the individual could still choose to eat eggs and other common items instead, even though the person knew for certain that life could be extended another twenty years by eating such foods. Abbots of monasteries often followed this advice when monks became ill, since they were worried that, if monks grew accustomed to more nutritious foods during times of sickness, perhaps when they got well they would not be able to return to their more simple manner of life.

In deciding whether a given medical intervention is ordinary or extraordinary, we should consider whether its use, *for this particular person,* would be perceived as usual/customary or not. Medical interventions that would generally be considered ordinary and usual would include medicine taken by mouth, injections, minor surgery, and most commonly used diagnostic interventions. Also included would be temporary intravenous feeding and medications as well as temporary modifications of diet and lifestyle. These all could become extraordinary and unusual if the person could honestly say that, for some weighty reason, they were not the customary means to health as far as they were concerned or because this was not the customary way of treatment within their culture or society. Obviously, the criterion of ordinary vs. extraordinary, even if helpful at times, is a very ambiguous one.

Burden vs. Benefit

Another standard often proposed and discussed within the Catholic tradition for determining whether or not a medical intervention is morally obligatory is the standard of burdensomeness. Often this criterion is coupled and contrasted with the notion of benefit, and it is held that a medical intervention is truly burdensome when the difficulties of treatment outweigh any possible benefits to be gained. However, many times it is difficult to assign moral weight to the interventions suggested and the results anticipated. This uncertainty can cause the person to become genuinely confused as to whether an anticipated course of action will be more beneficial than burdensome or vice-versa. Using a benefit/burden calculus to determine the extent of the burden greatly constricts and limits the notion of burden as traditionally understood by Catholic scholars and the Church.

Examples of burdensome interventions (as construed by the patient) have been provided by Catholic moralists through the years. These include moving to a more healthful climate (in the case, for example, of respiratory distress) if by moving one would have to uproot oneself from job, family, and other relationships; amputation surgery, when it is believed that the disfigurement, pain, or crippling effect of the amputation will be too difficult to bear either physically or psychologically; chemotherapy for cancer, when it is anticipated that the side effects of the drugs will be gravely debilitating; and major surgery, when great expense is involved or when the risk is very high. Notice that some of these examples clearly relate to how

the person assesses his or her quality of life after the intervention. Therefore, to hold that decisions involving an increased burden must only focus
on the burdensomeness of intervention and not on the (anticipated) burdens of life after the intervention is a clear misinterpretation of the doctrine
of burdensomeness as it has been historically construed. We may, and
indeed should, make quality of life judgments about ourselves when deciding which contemporary medical or surgical interventions we wish to accept or refuse. What we ought not to do is decide that another person's life
is not worth living, because this directly contradicts the reverence for life
that Christians should have. We may, however, make treatment refusals on
behalf of another when that person has told us that he or she does not want
continued treatment under certain specific circumstances because he or she
would consider the situation too difficult and burdensome in these circumstances. We are also sometimes legally and ethically empowered to make
decisions about another when that other has not told us what he or she
would have wanted in that situation. In these cases, decision-making is very
difficult because what must be considered is the best interests of all involved
in the decision, including the patient and the caregivers alike. A colleague
of mine and I have tried to deal with this issue by developing a decision-
making grid that might be helpful in decisions with newborns, children, or
anyone who has not expressed his or her wishes regarding treatment options in the situation of terminal illness or catastrophic injury.[5]

Generally, the assessment of whether or not a given treatment option
is a grave burden should be made by the patient or at least by his or her
designated health care proxy. However, if an appointment of a proxy has
not been made and the wishes of the patient are not known, the Catholic
tradition suggests considering the burden that the proposed intervention
places on the family itself before deciding whether to continue. Pope Pius
XII expresses this clearly with regard to resuscitation in the allocution "'Le
Dr. Bruno Haid'": "Consequently, if it appears that the attempt at resuscitation constitutes such a burden for the family that one cannot in all
conscience impose it upon them, they can lawfully insist that the doctor
should discontinue these attempts, and the doctor can lawfully comply. . . .
The rights and duties of the family depend in general upon the presumed
will of the unconscious patient if he or she is of age and *"sui juris."* Where
the proper and independent duty of the family is concerned, they are
usually bound only to the use of ordinary means."[6] And, although Pius XII

in this allocution does relate ordinary means to the notion of burden, I believe that in this passage his notion of "ordinary" can best be construed as saying that the family must provide for the unconscious person what is customary and usual care, and not feel bound to medical interventions that are needlessly prolonging the process of dying, or are not restoring the person to health. In secular terms this choice is often referred to as the "best interest" principle.

Burdensome treatment options are those that the patient believes are jeopardizing his or her higher goals, that are not offset by comparable benefits, or that cause great anxiety to the patient, either because of the intervention itself (anticipated pain, suffering, depression, financial ruin) or because of the poor quality of life rendered by the intervention (isolation or separation from significant others, disfigurement, economic burden to others).

As Pius XII stated in the allocution cited above: "normally one is held to use only . . . means that do not involve any grave burden for oneself or another. A more strict obligation would be too heavy for most people to bear and would render the attainment of the higher, more important good too difficult. Life, health, and all temporal activities are in fact subordinated to spiritual ends."[7] In this passage, the Pope seems to be focusing on burdensomeness in and of itself without consideration of any countervailing benefit.

Thus, if a person perceives any medical intervention as being too burdensome because of the pain or suffering involved, because the intervention will be disfiguring or crippling, because it will cause the family too much grief and hardship, or even because it will cause the person or the family financial difficulties (although society has the responsibility to provide a level of health care that should make this type of burden less significant ethically), then this person is free to reject the intervention. I wish to emphasize that the determination of a grave burden should be made by the patient or at least by those who know and respect the values and beliefs of the patient. In addition, burdens are not only determined by considering physical interventions, but also by assessing the psychological, economic, or spiritual harms as perceived by the patient or patient surrogate.

A good example of this kind of assessment of burdensomeness is provided by Jehovah's Witnesses, who, for religious reasons, believe that the acceptance of blood transfusions causes expulsion from their religious community and possibly condemnation by God. Jehovah's Witnesses construe the spiritual burden of expulsion and possible condemnation as weighty enough to refuse blood and blood products in almost all situations. Although Catholics do not share this interpretation of Biblical revelation, Catholic health care facilities must, on the ground of religious freedom, respect the Witnesses refusal of transfusions as an ethically optional choice because for them accepting transfusion constitutes a grave burden.

It is clear that the Catholic tradition, when considering burden as a reason for refusing a treatment option, does so in a broad and inclusive manner and not in a narrow and strict way.

Useful vs. Useless

The useful/useless distinction made by Catholic authors is of rather recent vintage and was developed most extensively by Gerald Kelly in the United States.[8] Simply stated, this distinction holds that even medical interventions considered as usual and not generally burdensome are not morally obligatory when they are medically useless, that is, when they do not offer a reasonable hope of benefit. In fact, Kelly would want to designate these interventions as ethically *extraordinary* precisely because of their uselessness. However, I mentioned before that this approach strips away the conceptual fullness of the original understanding of *ordinary*, which, as we have seen, really meant usual or customary when it was first used in ethical discourse. Thus I would prefer to understand uselessness not as a criterion in itself, but as an instantiation of the burden/benefit distinction discussed in the previous section. There the burden/benefit calculus was accepted even though it is very important psychologically to consider the burden (present or anticipated) in and of itself. In the case of a useless medical intervention, we are confronted with a situation in which there is some burden without any reasonable hope of benefit (as Kelly himself describes his notion of useless). Thus there is always a net effect of burdensomeness, since there is in these situations no reasonable anticipated benefit to offset the burden, however slight. I would hold that useless medical interventions are ethically objectionable because they provide a burden (possibly minimal) that is not offset by a reasonable hope of benefit.

One significant problem that arises within the context of discussing useless interventions is exactly what constitutes them. For example, is the provision of artificial sustenance and hydration to a person in a persistent

vegetative state (PVS) *useless,* since it is not providing the benefit of restoration of health, or *useful,* since it is keeping the individual alive (sometimes
for long periods of time)? It seems that Kelly introduced the distinction
precisely because he was concerned about the use of intravenous feeding for
people who are not going to recover. Thus, he holds some restoration of
health necessary in order to consider a medical intervention useful. I will
discuss my own approach to the sustenance issue in a later section in which
I will try to show that the artificial provision of sustenance for individuals
in a PVS is ethically optional for several reasons, all of which relate to the
criteria I have discussed here.

Proportionate vs. Disproportionate

Treatment options can be ordinary or extraordinary, burdensome or beneficial, useless or useful, or some combination of any or all of these criteria.
To determine whether a proposed treatment option is ethically mandatory
in a given case, one would have to take all the relevant criteria into consideration. When one decides that a treatment option is morally obligatory, it
is generally described as proportionate, since there is a favorable proportion
among all the values involved, indicating that the proposed intervention
ought to be chosen and accepted. When this weighing of values helps the
person decide that a treatment is ethically optional since it involves an
unusual, burdensome, or useless intervention, the treatment option is said
to be disproportionate, since the disvalues outweigh the values in this
particular case. Thus the terms proportionate or disproportionate are really
used as an ethical shorthand to indicate when a proposed intervention is
ethically mandatory in a given case or not. It is important to stress that this
weighing of values must be done for each individual case and that often
evaluation must be continued while treatment is being given. Some treatment options that initially seem promising and do not appear to have much
burden attached to them are transformed into very burdensome and/or
ineffective procedures as the disease progresses. The Catholic tradition has
always allowed for the possibility that a treatment option construed as
proportionate at the beginning of the intervention may become disproportionate because of a change of circumstances. Just because a treatment
option has been accepted as ethically mandatory and initiated does not
mean that it must be continued. As the circumstances of the case change,

the ethical evaluation of medical interventions also may change, and these may be discontinued once they are experienced as disproportionate and ethically optional.

Artificial Delivery of Nutrition and Hydration

It is my conviction that the artificial provision of nutrition and hydration by feeding tube (either through the nose or directly into the stomach) or by intravenous infusion is a medical treatment (and not basic care). I am supported in this conviction by the supreme courts of several states and of the United States, and also by the American Medical Association and other health care organizations. I believe that a person could decide, on the basis of the criteria presented above, that the artificial delivery of nutrition and hydration is morally disproportionate and therefore ethically optional and able to be refused. When persons make this evaluation and decide that they wish to refuse artificial nutrition and hydration if they should be terminally ill or in a PVS—and especially when they indicate this desire in writing in some sort of advance directive for health care—their wishes and values should be respected and followed. Pius XII states this conviction explicitly in the allocution cited above: "The rights and duties of the doctor are correlative to those of the patient. The doctor, in fact, has no separate or independent right where the patient is concerned. In general, the doctor can take action only if the patient explicitly or implicitly, directly or indirectly, gives permission."[9]

How do the standards discussed earlier apply in the situation of the acceptance or refusal of the artificial delivery of nutrition or hydration? First of all, people are not generally fed through a feeding tube or an intravenous line. And while these interventions have short-term benefits for some patients and it has become customary or usual to use them in these circumstances, it is not customary or usual (ordinary, as I understand the term) to receive sustenance and hydration in this way for a long period time. Certainly this situation is true in less well developed countries that have trouble providing enough food for their citizens to eat by mouth, but I believe that even here (in the United States) one could construe this procedure as not customary and usual and thus refuse it on the grounds that it is an extraordinary means of delivering nutrition and hydration and therefore able to be forgone.

I also hold that the artificial provision of nutrition and hydration could be seen as a grave burden. In the first place, this treatment is often accompanied by diarrhea and other discomforts and irritations that of themselves could be gravely burdensome, especially when the person is conscious. But, additionally, persons might rightly decide that continuing this treatment (especially if they were in a PVS) might place heavy psychological or economic burdens on other family members that the patient would not want them to bear. Although a comparison of benefits and burdens is difficult here because some will point to the benefit of continuing biological life as resolving the issue of continuing the provision once and for all, while others might point out that prolonging biological life without restoring conscious awareness is not really a benefit but actually a burden. Nevertheless, the other burdens of providing sustenance that I have considered are ample justification for considering it ethically optional, no matter how beneficial one considers it to be.

A consideration of usefulness, unless the patient is terminally ill with little time to live, encounters the same sort of conceptual difficulty as a consideration of benefit and is not helpful in this discussion. What I mean is that those who see continued biological life as a great good will assess this intervention as very useful, while those who see continued biological life without the restoration of consciousness as a grave burden will consider the provision of sustenance and hydration as useless. Usefulness comes into play in this discussion when, for those patients who are in a borderline PVS and who may perceive pain, provision of sustenance and hydration is considered as a palliative treatment. If the evidence in a particular case is that it is useful in this regard, then it should be provided, unless the patient has specifically indicated refusal even with the knowledge that it might have a palliative application in his or her specific case.

Regarding the assessment of the provision of sustenance and hydration for incompetent patients who have not made their wishes known, I recommend caution and prudence as well as statutory safeguards to prevent abuse. But I also recognize that there are situations in which families have the right to make decisions that will allow loved ones to die, either because they have a sense that this is what the person would have wanted in this situation even though the person has never told them so explicitly, or even because the total care and treatment of a family member is causing the family grave psychological, economic, or spiritual hardship. I repeat the words of Pius XII in this regard: "Where the proper and independent duty of the family is concerned, they are bound only to the use of ordinary means." Regarding nutrition and hydration, a useful rule of thumb is provided in the *Ethical and Religious Directives for Catholic Health Care Services* in Directive 58, which states: "There should be a presumption in favor of providing nutrition and hydration to all patients, including patients who require medically assisted nutrition and hydration, as long as this is of sufficient benefit to outweigh the burdens involved to the patient."[10]

Care for the Terminally Ill

Care for the terminally ill within the Catholic tradition is an extremely important religious, as well as social, activity. Reverence for life requires that dying people be treated with dignity and helped to prepare themselves spiritually for death. They should be given palliative medical treatments that will significantly reduce pain and suffering while at the same time allowing as much conscious activity as possible. And they should be helped to work through the various emotions of dying such as denial, bargaining, depression, anger, and acceptance. Respect for the person's dignity generally entails that, when dying is clearly in its last stages, it is not prolonged by the use of inappropriate medical technologies, such as respirators or cardiac resuscitation techniques. During this time, medical interventions are often inappropriate, while basic care is of the greatest importance.

Two general goals of medicine are healing and maintaining health, i.e., a state of life in which the patient may be reasonably expected to pursue the purpose of life, whatever that may be. Palliative medicine focuses on the third goal of health care, which is the compassionate care of the dying. Practitioners of palliative care seek to manage pain or discomfort caused by a disease or pathology, by the effects of the illness, or even by the interventions used to treat the illness in the first place. Delivery of palliative treatments requires special skills and training and possibly some invasive procedures.

Developing an understanding of terminal illness that is conceptually clear and rigorous has proven most difficult for legislators; nonetheless, most clinicians are able to determine with reasonable accuracy when various diseases and illnesses have reached their end stage, rendering the person who suffers from them terminally ill. It is at this time that the focus of medical interventions must shift from therapeutic to palliative and that care becomes a more important activity for the person than cure. It is precisely in this context that the hospice movement works so effectively.

The philosophy of hospice care was begun in the United Kingdom several decades ago. The name "hospice" originates from the medieval way stations—hospices—where travelers were able to rest overnight while they were on pilgrimage. The contemporary notion of "hospice" is a setting wherein people can find respite on their journey from this world to the next.

Hospice care can be delivered in the home, in a nursing home, or in a hospital. Generally, hospice organizers prefer the home setting because patients feel most comfortable there. Whenever hospice care is delivered, the philosophy is the same: to provide holistic care to the terminally ill patient and the family and to provide the necessary palliative medical interventions necessary to keep the patient as comfortable as possible, but also as alert as possible. Generally, hospice teams are composed of nurses, counselors, social workers, clergy, and a hospice physician who is specially trained in the pharmacology of palliative treatment. Usually a nurse coordinates this team, since the basic focus of hospice is care, not cure. The hospice team works with the family as well as with the terminally ill patient and provides bereavement counseling to the family after the sick person has passed away.

The hospice model is a paradigm for the care of the terminally ill within the Catholic tradition because it attempts to provide all the important social and religious values that can make the process of dying as dignified as possible. Catholics concerned with reverence for life could not do better than to enroll a dying loved one in a hospice program.

Regarding the pain and suffering often experienced by those terminally ill, the Catholic tradition encourages those suffering to view this through spiritual eyes as participation in the passion of the Lord. At the same time, it accepts pain and suffering as the negativities they are and encourages palliative care and treatment when such is possible. It recognizes that pain and suffering can be for some an occasion for despair and thus justifies palliative interventions for removing pain even when it is foreseen that the patient's consciousness or life itself will be shortened by their employment.

If one reflects on the values and attitudes of the Catholic tradition presented in this section, one can easily perceive how balanced it is in the face of death. Although Catholic teaching sees the gift of life as precious, given by God and not to be directly ended by human agency, it also views the negativity of death with the eyes of faith and holds that the process of dying should be as dignified and natural as possible. Thus the Catholic tradition does not hold that biological life should be prolonged at all costs and has developed many standards for determining when lifesaving medical interventions are ethically optional. It does stress, however, the importance of holistic care for the dying person and enjoins all Catholic Christians, on the basis of the corporal and spiritual works of mercy, to provide such care when they have the opportunity to do so. If this care is "death with dignity", then the Catholic tradition, because of its emphasis on the reverence for life, supports this concept as in accord with the mind of Christ.

Summary

This chapter began with the exhortation "Choose Life!" We have reflected on the many Christian activities that support reverence for human life, especially activities involving health and healing, promoting the common good, and enhancing culture and the quality of life. We then considered some of the obstacles to reverence for life, especially those that relate to the 'culture of death'—abortion, assisted suicide, and euthanasia—and have suggested Christian ethical responses to these obstacles derived from the moral tradition of Catholicism. The ethical principles discussed in this chapter provide the springboard for discussing other issues dealing with reverence for life—for example, genetic testing and research, cloning, spousal and child abuse, and capital punishment, which are certainly subjects for further reflection and study.

Endnotes

1. National Conference of Catholic Bishops (1994), *Ethical and Religious Directives for Catholic Health Care Services* (Washington, DC: United States Catholic Conference) 3.
2. Ibid. 13.
3. Ibid.
4. G. M. Atkinson, "Theological History of Catholic Teaching on Prolong-

ing Life," in *Moral Responsibility in Prolonging Life Decisions* (St. Louis: Pope John Center, 1981) 95–115.

5. J. M. Trau and J. J. McCartney, "In the Interest of the Patient; Its Meaning and Application Today," in *Health Progress* (April 1993) 50–56.

6. Pope Pius XII, "Allocution 'Le Dr. Bruno Haid'," *Acta Apostolicae Sedis* (Nov. 24, 1957) 1031–1032.

7. Ibid.

8. G. Kelly, "The Duty to Preserve Life," in *Theological Studies* XII (1951) 550–556.

9. Pope Pius XII

10. National Conference of Catholic Bishops (1994), 23.

5

THE PROPHETIC ROLE OF FEMINIST BIOETHICS *

MARIE J. GIBLIN
Xavier University

Health care in the United States is in a period of profound and tumultuous change. There is a need to address critically a multitude of issues including: the lack of health insurance of forty-three million Americans and the underinsurance of twenty-five million more, the possibility that a right to physician-assisted suicide may be endorsed while a right to health care is not, the changing environment of health care in a highly competitive market model, the lack of social supports for families dealing with chronic illness, and the challenge of developing more holistic views of health that better unify body, mind, spirit, and environment.

At present, contemporary mainstream bioethics fails to face the depth of injustice in our health care system. The issues that bioethics does acknowledge, it often approaches with only thin conceptions of human dignity, justice, and community. Health care ethics needs infusion with a critical social ethics. I propose that health care ethics from a Christian perspective can benefit from consideration of feminist bioethics because of its strong social ethical critique. Feminist bioethics is not univocal but diverse. In what follows I lift up aspects of this work that can lead us to a more prophetic reading of health care issues than current mainstream bioethics provides. I point to two important tasks for feminist health care ethics before concluding.

Feminist Bioethics

Biblical prophets gain our attention today less for any foretelling of the future than for their acute perception of their context in light of the community's relationship to God and to one another. The prophets called into question the religious and social status quo whenever it tolerated or fostered oppression of the vulnerable and complacency among those in power. Urging the community to understand events in the context of covenantal relationships, the prophets challenged the community to face the fears, pains, and injustices that were being denied and to move toward integrity and faithfulness.[1]

Most feminist bioethicists are thinking in secular frameworks, without reference to prophecy or convenantal duties. A few Christian feminist ethicists have done some of their writing in bioethics and are explicit in their reference to religious tradition.[2] Yet many secular feminist bioethicists bring a sense of community and mutual obligations that are akin to prophetic sensibilities. Even in their secular form feminist perspectives produce powerful prophetic criticism of social inequities in health care and open the field to new considerations of virtue, self, and community.

While one layer of diversity in feminist bioethics has to do with a secular or religious perspective, another relates to the philosophical and political. The categories of liberal, radical, and cultural feminist perspectives have relevance to many health care issues.[3] The broader feminist discussion of a "care"-oriented ethic[4] in tension with a "justice"-oriented ethic[5] also carries over to bioethics.[6] The problem with using such categories and divisions is that they present positions as rigidified rather than in conversation with each other and learning from each other.[7]

Instead of reading bioethics in light of those categories and divisions, I will consider what is emerging from the conversation informed by the best of the various feminist approaches. I look in particular for the aspects that are the most conducive to a prophetic reading of health care issues in our time. The following six characteristics appear to me as the most promising:

1. *Feminist bioethics centers on concern for the oppression of women and for the concrete forms of injustice that they suffer in the U.S. health care system.* Susan Wolf defines feminist bioethics as "a bioethics that sees oppression based on gender as a serious wrong and critically investigates the workings of power and gender."[8] This perspective on the discipline does not just raise

gender as an analytical category but opposes harm to women. Furthermore, a feminist bioethics recognizes the differences among women and encourages priority of attention to "those historically least served and most harmed,"[9] including African American women, Hispanic women, and disabled women.[10] Feminist ethics fosters sensitivity and concern for various kinds of differences beyond gender, including race, ethnicity, age, social class, sexual orientation, and disability.

Questions about power, dominance, and oppression are essential dimensions of feminist ethical analysis. Since the 1970s feminists have been highly critical of the medical system's power over women, especially in obstetrics, gynecology, and mental health. Practices in these areas were the first to be seen as reinforcing women's oppression and legitimizing women's limited social roles.[11] The women's health movement represents contemporary efforts to give power back to women. Giving women agency over their own health is a goal of feminist bioethicists as well. This approach seeks to redistribute medical knowledge more widely and to reduce the hierarchical structure of medical relationships and the power of medical authority.[12] Greater mutuality between the physician and the embodied person/patient is understood as a means to enhance their respective expertise.

2. *Feminist bioethics is critical of ethical notions of impartiality and posits a view of knowledge as always "situated."* Many modern moral philosophers and bioethicists have maintained that impartiality and universalizability are essential to ethical judgment. Such an approach often means that the group claiming the impartial standpoint (usually the dominant group) assumes the universalizability of their vision and imposes it on others. In contrast, feminist philosophers stress "the particularity and embodiment of all vision" and argue that human knowledge is drawn from situated perspectives.[13] This makes all knowledge partial. Only through considering a patchwork of partial perspectives can we approach objectivity.[14] The standpoints of subjugated groups stand the best chance of providing a corrective lens to the myopia of the dominant groups. Standpoint theory (or a theory of partial perspectives) can also be extended to individuals as well as groups so as to take into account differences at both levels.[15] Standpoint theory is not a relativistic stance. Feminist philosopher Donna J. Haraway writes:

the alternative to relativism is not totalization and single vision. . . . The alternative to relativism is partial, locatable, critical knowledges sustaining the possibility of webs of connections called solidarity in politics and shared conversations in epistemology. Relativism is a way of being no-where while claiming to be everywhere equally. The "equality" of position-ing is a denial of responsibility and critical enquiry. Relativism is the perfect mirror twin of totalization in the ideologies of objectivity; both deny the stakes in location, embodiment, and partial perspective; both make it impossible to see well.[16]

Feminist bioethicists, while affirming the partiality of knowledge, tend to use the more totalizing language to express norms and to fend off charges of relativism. For example, Mary Mahowald writes that feminism in its diverse forms insists on gender equality as an objective, universalizable ethical norm.[17] Susan Sherwin expresses the dilemma she sees: "[A]bsolutist principles are often oppressive, but relativist ones seem to undermine the strength of moral arguments against oppression."[18] Sherwin argues for an absolutist stance against oppression but a more relativist stance on "other moral matters" so as to incorporate feminist moral sensibilities.[19] This seems unsatisfactory—what is to be counted as oppression and what as "other moral matters"? More work in this area lies ahead.

Despite these difficulties, feminist epistemologies that examine the re-lationships between power, gender, and the means of producing authorita-tive knowledge are very important to the expansion of democracy in knowledge production and to the development of feminist bioethics.[20]

The understanding of all knowledge as situated has practical implica-tions. The ethicist and others come to each problematic setting with their own basic beliefs and ways of selecting and interpreting facts that may conflict with those of others. None of us is impartial—not the ethicists, not the patient, not the caregivers, not the family, not the health care adminis-trator, not the insurance executive, nor the legislator. Each of us comes with our ethical lenses already honed by our own particular experience, back-ground, values, and interests (acknowledged or not).

3. *Recognizing that all knowledge is "situated" and perspectives are partial, feminist bioethics calls for a diverse community of reflection that goes beyond the experts (bioethicists, physicians, scientists, and governmental authorities) and includes patients, nurses, families and others.* Particularly important to the conversation are those who are at risk of disadvantage—women, people of color, and those who lack insurance. The "subjugated," for too long excluded from the conversation, must be invited and welcomed. Any delib-

eration must include those who will be affected by its outcome, especially those who may be disadvantaged by it or bear its burden.[21] Indeed, those who have in various ways suffered the effects of our health care "system" have enhanced ability to indicate what is wrong and what needs to be changed. Their input can help to produce new mutual learning.

In much of bioethics, patients and research subjects have been the objects of concern rather than full members of the conversation.[22] This is inappropriate if we look upon the process of bioethics as a mutual search for moral knowledge that calls upon and respects the insight of those who have experience of the health care system or who are marginalized from it. Many ordinary people have searched deeply their own hearts and with their families and friends for ways to deal with suffering, disability, and death. This is an area in which many people have concrete experience which can be enormously beneficial to ethical discernment and its expression of the moral wisdom of the community. Local churches and support groups might be forums for sharing insight and bewilderment that can build up a compassionate and ethically sensitive community.

4. *Feminist bioethics takes a critical view regarding the standard principles of bioethics—autonomy, beneficence, nonmaleficence, and justice.*[23] Like others, feminist ethicists criticize "principlism": the deductive use of theories and principles, mechanically applied. More particularly, feminist criticism points to the systematic erasure of the person's gender, class, race, and insurance status that takes place when universal moral rules or principles posit an abstract, generic person. Overlooked are the relevance of context, partiality, and relational ties.[24]

Despite the criticism of the dominance of principles and their mechanistic application, most feminist bioethicists do not wish to abandon principles. In particular, most make clear that they do not make a choice of a "caring ethics" that emphasizes relational bonds over an ethics of principles.[25] The caring model (considered more a feminine model than a feminist one) may illuminate American women's care-giving experience, but it may also reinforce society's expectation of this virtue from women while continuing to allow men to focus on abstractions that protect their rights and autonomy. Caring itself is certainly important, but it is not sufficient for a feminist ethic. What is also required is a commitment to the pursuit of social justice, a justice that is explicitly sensitive to the injustice in its concrete forms.[26]

A number of feminist bioethicists have suggested supplementing the four classical principles (autonomy, beneficence, nonmaleficence, and justice) with others: embodiment, attentiveness, mutuality, community, and a truly inclusive common good. A recognition and appreciation of the principle of embodiment is basic: seeing the human person as "co-extensive with, and inevitably influenced by, the particularities of one's human body."[27] This principle of embodiment carries implications for respect for bodies, responsibility to care for them, and greater sensitivity to our connections with the rest of nature.[28]

Attentiveness to the particularity of the moral situation can be viewed as a principle that calls for joining the other principles with the careful examination of the real situations of those at risk so that ethicists can bring about necessary modifications of the body of principles and their interpretation.[29] To consider the impact of action on relationships and community, not just on individuals, is also required.[30] Reflection on mutuality and community are very significant for a feminist perspective on health care. Gudorf submits this principle: "[P]romotion of the common good includes the good of *all* persons in the community."[31] A health care system is to be tested "not only against abstract principles such as justice, individual integrity, community, mutuality, and embodiment but also against the concrete and comprehensive well-being of the least powerful, most marginalized members of society.[32] Feminist liberation theologians like Gudorf name this a preferential option for the poor and the marginalized. They call for justice in terms of "the welfare of those at the bottom of the sociopolitical and economic ladder."[33]

Feminist bioethics supports a qualified form of bioethical principlism.[34] Principles are valued, but seen as needing to be coupled with complex reality in ways that allow social relationships to be taken into account. Susan Wolf, for example, takes the approach of "principled caring" in her critique of physician-assisted suicide. For Wolf, "[t]he mandates of caring fail to bless killing the person for whom one cares"[35] and the mandates of justice indicate that in the real society in which we live there are compelling reasons not to allow doctors to kill. Among these reasons are the systematic biases of classism, racism, and sexism within health care and American society.[36]

5. *Feminist bioethics is critical of liberal individualism and its privileged status in mainstream bioethics.* There is a great deal of allegiance to Kant and

to John Stuart Mill in bioethics. This has its advantage—the individual is seen as an end, not a means, and as entitled to self-rule. Beauchamp and Childress take as essential to autonomy "personal rule of the self that is free from both controlling interferences by others and from personal limitations that prevent meaningful choice, such as inadequate understanding."[37] Unfortunately, the interpretation of autonomy in health care ethics has taken an almost libertarian direction that emphasizes non-interference. As medical sociologist Reneé C. Fox has argued, the focus on individual autonomy in bioethics has left only secondary status to more socially oriented values and ethical questions. Even concern with just and fair distribution of scarce and expensive resources, which arose in the 1980s, is structured around an individual, rights-oriented conception of the common good.[38]

It is the privileged status of individualism that has so elevated the principle of autonomy. While the principle of benevolence (to do good and avoid harm to others) is important, the cultural emphasis on individualism limits benevolence and circumscribes it in respectful deference to individual rights, interests, and autonomy of others.[39] Noninterference ranks higher than neighbor love.

The emphasis on individualism explains at least partially why bioethics has avoided involvement in social problems. An example of this can be seen in bioethicists' deep immersion in the questions of the justifiability of nontreatment decisions in neonatal intensive care. At the center of the problems are individual (abstract) babies. Not considered are the deprived conditions out of which many premature and very low birth-weight infants and their mothers come. Such considerations are defined as social rather than ethical problems and not included in the realm of moral scrutiny and concern.[40] In adult medicine also, mainstream bioethics deals with the "generic" person. Feminists question the usefulness of the concept of the abstract individual as the basic unit of society and morality because it leaves out highly significant data of personal and social histories and contexts.[41] It leads to a bioethics of the privileged, because it has assumed that the person is one "with access to health care and with a doctor likely to listen to, understand, and respect that person."[42]

Giving highest place to abstract individuals turns communities into problems to be accounted for, ignoring how much our very selves are shaped by these communities. Individuals are seen as independent and self-directed, "somehow prior to and independent of their social circumstances."[43] There is little room for consideration of the interdependence of persons and the role of reciprocity, solidarity, and community. Emphasizing persons as independent rational individuals has led bioethicists to downplay virtues that depend upon feeling, connection, and relatedness: qualities of kindness, generosity, service, empathy, and caring.[44]

6. *Feminist bioethics is critical of the discipline's loyalties and social location.* It asks the question: whom does bioethics serve? The field of bioethics serves particular clients. The questions come from physicians, other health professionals, administrators of health care institutions, and governmental bodies.[45] Feminists raise to light the embeddedness of the discipline in institutional relationships: "The overarching question is whether we bioethicists retain enough independence and distance from the very institutions that often employ and house us to do genuinely critical work."[46]

One of the disturbing results of these arrangements is the narrowing down of the questions within acceptable parameters.[47] Both the professional and class interests of the actors tend to suppress radical questioning. As Sherwin explains,

> most bioethicists choose to define their role locally: they evaluate or criticize very specific aspects of health care practices and refrain from analyzing the overall social effects of the organization of health care in society. They present their examination of particular features of health practitioner behavior within an implicit acceptance of the basic organization of health services, avoiding the sorts of evaluations of the health care system as a whole that feminist and other social critics present.[48]

If feminist bioethics intends to deal with the just structuring of power as well as the just distribution of health care,[49] then the system and its impact demands critique. The lack of real access to health care services for many groups of people (and women's particular vulnerability) is one area that receives little attention by mainstream bioethics, despite the relatively large number of uninsured Americans. This social issue of health is even larger, however, than the problem of health care access in a market-based system. Sherwin contends:

> Health is a product not only of health care, but also of social and economic position, and protection from violent attack and environmental toxins. Homelessness, addictions, violence, and lack of adequate food and clothing are increasing problems in the United States and they carry with them

extraordinary costs in terms of illness and death. Yet while highly expensive technological health care services are being expanded to meet the needs of the privileged, resources to meet basic human needs for the most disadvantaged segments of the population are being withdrawn.[50]

Feminist bioethics asks why medical services alone are made the measure of society's responsibility to the health needs of the population. "Feminism directs us to examine the role of medicine in our society and to ask why it has assumed dominance in health matters."[51] Such questions have been raised by public health practitioners, but not by health care ethicists.

Two Important Tasks

The six characteristics above describe what some feminist bioethicists are already doing and the strong social critique that they bring to mainstream bioethics. I would like to propose two further tasks for feminist bioethics. The first concerns an area for research; the second task is a methodological one.

The current metamorphosis of health care in the marketplace deserves special attention. Health care has become a market commodity rather than a service that responds to human needs and human dignity. While the need for efficiency and cost containment are real, the logic of the market being brought to bear on health care can be callous. The power of business is leading down a path that marginalizes increasing numbers and groups of people from adequate and caring health care services. Government response has been minimal.[52] Moral sensibility should enable ethicists to bring hermeneutic suspicion to what can be a whitewashing rhetoric of cost containment and efficiency. Huge issues are at stake—the closing of public hospitals that have historically served the poor, the growth and increasing power of investor-owned health care corporations with their profit-driven dynamics (not only in hospital and other health care services but in insurance/managed care), and the cooptation of non-profit health care systems in the increasingly competitive atmosphere. This is a formidable area that neither mainstream nor feminist bioethics has begun to address adequately. Neither of the dominant paradigms—a medical ethics that focuses on physician/patient interactions nor corporate business ethics—is adequate to the current task.[53] Christian social justice traditions in economic matters have an important role here that can be enhanced and supplemented by feminist sensitivities for seeking the well being of women and of the whole community.

The second task is methodological. I would suggest that feminist bioethicists consider more contact with grassroot struggles by women over health care issues and more reflection on those struggles within their writing. The discipline of bioethics has encouraged abstraction. A feminist response could counter this through the use of stories. Feminist bioethics exists because of the real-life circumstances, struggles, and creativity of women in meeting health care challenges. It is women's stories that are hidden deep below the surface of most feminist ethics writings. These stories need to be brought to the surface and highlighted by writers who have themselves heard the stories directly and in all their concreteness.[54] Debbie Ward, for example, in an article on "Women and the Work of Caring" tells the story of chronically ill Miss B, an 82-year-old woman living alone and tended by a combination of caregivers organized by Miss B's niece—the niece herself, home health aides, a visiting nurse, and great-nieces.[55] Such stories can enrich and energize health care ethics and enable feminist ethicists to do more effectively what they intend: to construct theory from life experience instead of imposing theory on life. Stories alone are not sufficient for ethical analysis or as a source of norms,[56] but bringing forward such stories encourages all of us to respect the complexity of our judgments. The discipline of bioethics has only begun to open itself to the richness of stories (rather than the bare facts of "cases"). Hearing real stories requires coming into contact with those who suffer and placing their individual suffering in its social context. This is a challenge to the current, more academic, methodology of feminist bioethics.

Conclusion

Feminist bioethics brings a social ethics critique to the discipline of bioethics. Not all feminist writers in health care ethics are equally critical. This may be due to pressures within the field to limit questions to specific quandries and to leave the system as a whole unquestioned. It may also be due to the sheer difficulty of casting off our cultural blinders of liberal individualism and capitalist assumptions. It is possible to address women's issues while retaining these blinders and staying within the expected parameters, but the result is inadequate because of the failure to assess seriously enough women's social context.

What may strike the reader about the six characteristics above are the echoes of liberation theology: the starting point of oppression, the criticism of liberal individualism, the approach to issues and the discipline itself with a "hermeneutic of suspicion," the highlighting of particularity rather than universality, and the desire to give voice to the voiceless. Feminist bioethics shows one entry to a liberation approach to health care ethics. Focusing on gender as their starting point, many feminist writers attempt to raise issues of class and racial barriers to women's well being and to lift up considerations of insurance, disability, age, etc. They provide a partial perspective that is open to others and welcoming to the insights of the undeserved.

While much of the feminist criticism of bioethics is a cry for justice, it is more. It is also an affirmation of community ties and obligations (critically perceived), of the centrality of just relationships, and of the mystery and dignity of every human person. These elements could be more effectively communicated by letting the stories of women struggling for justice and care have a more prominent place. Even in its secular forms, feminist bioethics can provide a prophetic lens with which to see more clearly the injustices of health care in our times and the possibilities for more caring and just communities.

Endnotes

*This essay first appeared in *Horizons*, 24/1 (1997), and is used with permission.

1. Walter Brueggeman, *The Prophetic Imagination* (Philadelphia: Fortress, 1978) 49–50.

2. Among these Christian feminists, part of whose writing is in bioethics, are: Lisa Sowle Cahill, Margaret A. Farley, Christine E. Gudorf, Beverly Wildung Harrison, and Karen Lebacqz.

3. For a specific example of the diversity of these perspectives, see Rosemarie Tong, "Feminist Bioethics: Developing a 'Feminist' Answer to the Surrogate Motherhood Question," *Kennedy Institute of Ethics Journal* 6/1 (1996) 37–52.

4. See Carol Gilligan, *In a Different Voice: Psychological Theory and Women's Development* (Cambridge: Harvard University, 1982); and Nel Noddings, *Caring: A Feminine Approach to Ethics and Moral Education* (Berkeley: University of California, 1984).

5. See Susan Moller Okin, *Justice, Gender, and the Family* (New York: Basic

Books, 1989); Beverly Wildung Harrison, *Making the Connections: Essays in Feminist Social Ethics*, Carol S. Robb, ed. (Boston: Beacon, 1985); and Karen Lebacqz, *Six Theories of Justice* (Minneapolis, MN: Augsburg, 1986).

   6. Helen Bequaert Holmes and Laura M. Purdy, eds., *Feminist Perspectives in Medical Ethics* (Bloomington: Indiana University, 1992).

   7. For bibliographies of feminist bioethics see Karen Lebacqz, "Feminism" in Warren T. Reich, ed., "Encyclopedia of Bioethics" 2 (New York: Simon and Schuster/Macmillan, 1995) 808–18; Pat Milmoe McCarrick and Martina Darragh, "Feminist Perspectives on Bioethics" (Scope Note 30) in *Kennedy Institute of Ethics Journal* 6/1 (1996) 85–103; and Pat Milmoe McCarrick, "Gender Issues in Health Care" (Scope Note 27) in *Kennedy Institute of Ethics Journal* 5/1 (1995) 61–82.

   8. Susan M. Wolf, "Introduction: Gender and Feminism in Bioethics" in Susan M. Wolf, ed., *Feminism and Bioethics: Beyond Reproduction* (New York: Oxford University, 1996) 8. I am indebted to Susan Wolf for her delineation of many of the issues discussed here.

   9. Ibid. 21.

   10. Ibid. 23.

   11. See Lebacqz, "Feminism" 812; Phyllis Chesler, *Women and Madness* (New York: Harcourt Brace Jovanovich, 1972); and Barbara Ehrenreich and Deirdre English, *The Sexual Politics of Sickness* (Old Westbury, NY: Feminist, 1973).

   12. Susan Sherwin, "Feminist and Medical Ethics: Two Different Approaches to Contextual Ethics" in Holmes and Purdy, eds., *Feminist Perspectives* 28.

   13. Donna J. Haraway, *Simians, Cyborgs, and Women: The Reinvention of Nature* (New York: Routledge, 1991) 189; also see Mary B. Mahowald, "On Treatment of Myopia: Feminist Standpoint Theory and Bioethics" in Wolf, ed., *Feminism and Bioethics* 95–101.

   14. See Ibid. 99; Haraway, *Simians, Cyborgs, and Women* 180ff.; and Carol S. Robb, "Introduction" in Robb, ed., *Making the Connections* xv.

   15. Mahowald, "On Treatment of Myopia" 101. Haraway notes that there is a danger in romanticizing the vision of the less powerful and in considering their standpoints as "innocent" positions without critical interpretation. However, she sees their standpoints as preferred because they seem to promise more adequate, transforming accounts of the world (see Haraway, *Simians, Cyborgs, and Women*, 181).

   16. Ibid.

   17. Mahowald, "On Treatment of Myopia" 99.

   18. Susan Sherwin, *No Longer Patient: Feminist Ethics and Health Care* (Philadelphia: Temple University, 1992) 59.

   19. Ibid. 75. Sherwin uses Marilyn Frye's definition of oppression as "an interlocking series of restrictions and barriers that reduce the options available to people on the basis of their membership in a group" (13).

   20. Wolf, "Introduction" 25. Wolf notes the work of Helen Longino as distinct from standpoint theory but also indicating a need for a diverse community

and a process of dialogue rather than exclusion. See Helen Longino, "Subjects, Power, and Knowledge: Description and Prescription in Feminist Philosophies of Science" in Linda Alcoff and Elizabeth Potter, eds., *Feminist Epistemologies* (New York: Routledge, 1993) 101–20.

21. Wolf, "Introduction" 25 and Robb, "Introduction" xv.

22. Wolf, "Introduction" 25.

23. The classical text outlining these principles is Tom L. Beauchamp and James F. Childress, *Principles of Biomedical Ethics* 4th ed. (New York: Oxford University, 1994). Feminist ethicists are not the only critics, as can be seen in Edwin R. DuBose, Ronald P. Hamel, and Laurence J. O'Connell, eds., *A Matter of Principles? Ferment in U.S. Bioethics* (Valley Forge, PA: Trinity Press International, 1994). In that book a number of different perspectives (European, Latin American, Buddhist, African American, feminist, religious) and a number of different ethical methodological approaches (phenomenological, narrative, hermeneutical, as well as virtue and casuistry approaches) take a critical view of what they call "principlism."

24. See Wolf, "Introduction" 15, and Susan M. Wolf, "Gender, Feminism, and Death: Physician Assisted Suicide and Euthanasia" in Wolf, ed. *Feminism and Bioethics* 296–97, 282.

25. See Laura M. Purdy, "A Call to Heal Ethics" in Holmes and Purdy, eds. *Feminist Perspectives* 10–11; Wolf, "Introduction" 8–9; Sherwin, *No Longer Patient* chap. 2; and Christine Gudorf, "A Feminist Critique of Biomedical Principlism" in Dubose, Hamel and O'Connell, eds., *A Matter of Principles?* 168.

26. See Sherwin, *No Longer Patient* 50–52, and Susan Sherwin, "Feminism and Bioethics" in Wolf, ed., *Feminism and Bioethics* 54.

27. Gudorf, "A Feminist Critique" 175.

28. Ibid. 175–76.

29. Wolf, "Introduction" 28, and Gudorf, "A Feminist Critique" 168.

30. Wolf, "Introduction" 28.

31. Gudorf, "A Feminist Critique" 171.

32. Ibid. 177.

33. Ibid. 172.

34. Ibid. 177.

35. Wolf, "Gender, Feminism, and Death" 307.

36. Ibid. 304, 306–7.

37. Beauchamp and Childress, *Principles of Biomedical Ethics* 121; on allegiance to Kant and Mill, see Wolf, "Introduction" 16.

38. Reneé C. Fox, "The Evolution of American Bioethics: A Sociological Perspective" in George Weisz, ed., *Social Science Perspectives on Medical Ethics* (Philadelphia: University of Pennsylvania, 1990) 206.

39. Ibid.

40. Ibid. 208.

41. Sherwin, "Feminism and Bioethics" 52.

42. Wolf, "Introduction" 18.

43. Sherwin, "Feminism and Bioethics" 52, 53.

44. Fox, "The Evolution of American Bioethics" 207.

45. Wolf, "Introduction" 18.

46. Ibid. 19.

47. A few male bioethicists have already worried publicly that bioethics has stopped asking the larger questions. See Daniel Callahan, *What Kind of Life* (New York: Simon and Schuster, 1990), and Leon R. Kass, "Practicing Ethics: Where's the Action," *Hastings Center Report* 20 (January–February 1990) 5–12. However, they do not link the narrowing of the questions to the social location of the discipline. Wolf, "Introduction" 19.

48. Sherwin, "Feminism and Bioethics" 55.

49. Hilde Lindemann Nelson and James Lindemann Nelson, "Justice in the Allocation of Health Care Resources: A Feminist Account" in Wolf, ed., *Feminism and Bioethics* 364.

50. Sherwin, "Feminism and Bioethics" 56.

51. Ibid.

52. The *Kennedy-Kassebaum Act,* while positive, does little to make insurance affordable, even if it makes it available to those changing jobs. The difference between having a policy offered and having it offered *and* affordable has to be kept in mind regarding discussions of "health care access." An example of government acquiescence to managed care organizations is the July 1996 shelving of rules issued in March 1996 that restricted the ability of health maintenance organizations to pay bonuses and other financial rewards to doctors as inducements to limit services provided to elderly and poor patients under Medicare and Medicaid (Robert Pear, "Federal Rules Seek to Keep H.M.O's from Putting Profits Ahead of Patient Needs," *New York Times* [National Edition], March 27, 1996, A11, and Robert Pear, "U.S. Shelves Plan to Limit Rewards to H.M.O. Doctors," *New York Times,* July 8, 1996, A1).

53. See Wendy K. Mariner, "Business vs. Medical Ethics: Conflicting Standards for Managed Care," *Journal of Law, Medicine & Ethics* 23 (1995) 236–46.

54. Good examples of case stories can be found in *Second Opinion,* a journal from the Parkridge Center. Christian feminist ethicist Karen Lebacqz effectively uses stories that she obtained from other published sources in two articles: "Feminism and Bioethics: An Overview," *Second Opinion* 17/2 (October 1991) 11–25; and "The 'Fridge': Health Care and the Disembodiment of Women" in Lisa Sowle Cahill and Margaret A. Farley, eds., *Embodiment, Morality, and Medicine* (Boston: Kluwer Academic, 1995) 155–67.

55. Debbie Ward, "Women and the Work of Caring" in *Second Opinion* 19/2 (October 1993) 11–25.

56. Wolf, "Introduction" 27; for a perspective that appreciates the richness of stories yet points to their limitations, see Kathryn Montgomery Hunter, "Overview: 'The Whole Story,'" *Second Opinion* 19/2 (October 1993) 97–103.

6

SEXUALITY
AND INTIMACY

WILLIAM WERPEHOWSKI
Villanova University

Moral reflection about sexual intimacy and sexual intercourse often proceeds from and advances toward understandings of the kinds of human relationship that may or should include these activities. We begin with a general and seemingly straightforward case—sexual relations within heterosexual marriage—and ask questions about the features of marriage that morally justify or authorize "sex." These features should tell us what makes human sexual life more, rather than less, fully human and what advances, rather than impedes or opposes, our flourishing as the sexual creatures we are and ought to be. The answers to the questions can vary. Some persons may focus on the "love" the sexual partners have for each other, while others might stress their mutually realized and respected freedom in lovemaking. Still others will fasten onto the significance of the marital vow or will say that marriage is the proper context within which to have and raise children (should they be conceived). Our thinking can then move toward a normative idea of what goods specifically humanize sexual relationships. At least for the purposes of critical understanding, one may not want to rule out *in advance* that other bonds besides marriage contain and can realize these goods.

Falling in Love and Being Together

In order to help us think about approaches to sexual ethics within the Christian tradition, I am going to start with another sort of relationship. We refer to it when we talk about people (including ourselves) "falling in love" and wanting "to be together." We can call this connection "erotic" or "romantic" love. My description of it will be a basepoint for comprehending and assessing "traditional" and "revisionist" Christian sexual ethics.

Let us consider Robert Nozick's portrayal of being "in love" or infatuation, which he describes as an early form of "romantic love." Being in love involves:

> . . . almost always thinking of the person, wanting constantly to touch and be together; excitement in the other's presence; losing sleep; . . . feeling that short separations are long; smiling foolishly when remembering actions and remarks of the other; feeling that the other's minor foibles are delightful; experiencing joy at having found the other and at being found by the other; and . . . finding *everyone* charming and nice, and thinking they all must sense one's happiness.[1]

Should infatuation transform itself into "continuing romantic love," it becomes a matter of wanting to unite with the beloved "to form and constitute a new entity in the world, what might be called a *we*."[2]

This sort of desire transforms one's personal *need* for the beloved into "appreciation," or a regard for the beloved "as a thing admirable in herself, important far beyond her relation to the lover's need."[3] Appreciation, however, does not *eradicate* the erotic "wanting to form a *we* with that particular person . . . and also wanting the other to feel the same way about you."[4] The desire that your well-being be bound up with the well-being of your beloved in this way calls for a *sharing of identity*. Each person in an erotic "we" seeks to "possess" the other; "yet each also needs the other to be an independent and nonsubservient person." Thus the wish to "possess" is fulfilled in *mutual giving and receiving*, a mutuality vividly described throughout the *Song of Songs*: "My lover is mine and I am his" (Sg 2:16). Desire "can only nourish a love that is freely given and returned, a partnership that acknowledges the joy of being possessed as well as the need to possess."[5] In this light, *marriage* marks the point at which lovers identify *fully* with the "we," which hereafter "lives their life together."[6]

From a Christian point of view, erotic love should be understood to be a good gift of God the Creator. It expresses a unique kind of caring and intimacy. It honors our vulnerability and need for others, our respect for loved ones as being valuable in themselves, and the intense fulfillment of love that comes with mutually cherishing one another and the bond we have forged together. Human beings living in the image of God ought to celebrate and not be ashamed of a loving desire for peaceful communion of this sort with another person. At the same time, we also must admit that "the possibility of injustice increases with the closeness of our relations. For such closeness makes us at once more vulnerable and heightens and orders our expectations."[7] The depths of erotic love remain, sad to say, as opportunities for selfish betrayals that hurt all the more because they take place within circumstances of realized and hoped-for intimacy.

Eros is a gift and a blessing, but it is also perilous in the hands and hearts of flawed, sinful human creatures. As such, what does Eros have to do with sex? In what follows, I present two approaches to sexual ethics that give contrasting responses to this question.

The Two Shall Become One Flesh

The title of this section refers to a passage in the Book of Genesis that describes the covenant of man and woman who, as God's creation, find one another to be fit helpmates (Gn 2:24: "Therefore a man leaves his father and his mother and clings to his wife, and they become one flesh.") Note how the language of the title *could* be seen to fit my discussion of erotic love. One can ask, "Since such love involves a desire for 'mutual possession' and the sharing of identity with the beloved, then why not mark, celebrate, and enhance love through passionate and embodied sexual relations? Lovers coming together, desired and desiring, becoming one flesh—isn't that what sex is all about?"

For what we might call the "traditional" approach to Christian sexual ethics, this reading is an instance of (as it is said in other connections) "moving too fast." One version of the approach goes like this. The good of human sexuality and human sexual relations has really to do with *two inseparably connected moral values or meanings* that may be realized by a man and a woman in sexual intercourse. There is, on the one hand, the way sexual intercourse expresses and enriches a community of love between the partners. Call this the *unitive meaning*. There is, on the other hand, the *procreative meaning*, the way that heterosexual intercourse may tend toward the generation of human life. The permanent and faithful bond of *marriage* is the proper human undertaking within which intercourse should take place. The *promise* of a man and a woman to take one another as spouses establishes a covenant of fidelity. The nurturing of love and openness to new life is held together inseparably within that covenant and with the spouse you have married.[8] "Therefore a man . . . clings to his wife, and they become one flesh."

How do adherents of this view justify it? First, it is argued that only conditions of permanence and fidelity can enable the sort of mutual presence and self-giving that the unitive aspect of sexual relations promises and demands. When they "make love," lovers present and give themselves to one another, and "this presentation carries with it not all that they are, but some aspect of everything they are. They are present as living beings filled with sensations, feelings, thoughts, images, desires, intentions."[9] Sexual "being-present-to" and "receiving-the-presence-of" the other make up so deep and concrete an exchange for these *unique* and *particular* human beings that their union may and must presuppose an unbounded and exclusive commitment to share a life together. The unconditional vow of marriage is *not* taken with and for a *particular sort* of person (smart, attractive, athletic, witty, "the kind who makes me happy," etc.); rather, it is taken with and for *this particular person* ("I take *you* . . . for better or worse, for richer or poorer, in sickness and in health, until death do us part."). Marriage rightly frames and disposes the full intimacy of loving sexual union; moreover, since this intimacy does *not* merely "come naturally," but is rather a moral *achievement,* the commitment to continuity enables a kind of education in virtue through which lovers learn over time the meaning of self-giving and response to the gift of the other.

Second, defenders of the traditional perspective claim that permanence and fidelity also *protect* sexual relationships from our selfish tendencies to deceive and to dominate. The possibilities for exploitation for the sake of our immediate desires and fantasies are considerable, and they are compounded by the special favor we invariably give to our own projects and problems. Factually true or not, the story of the professional football player who justified his adultery with the claim that "God wants me to be happy" speaks a lesson to all of us who would find a way to make similarly vicious proposals. The human capacity to be faithful may make marriage possible, but the human propensity to be faithless (and faithless in sexual relationships) makes marriage necessary.[10]

Third, we should think about the procreative meaning of sexual intercourse and what it indicates about "responsible parenthood." Should new human life come forth from sexual intercourse, that life ideally ought to be welcomed and honored; marriage enables welcoming children as the fruit of spouses' love for each other—as "flesh of their separate flesh made one."[11] It also would secure a lasting familial basis for the care and instruction of those children over the years of their growth and development.

Both meanings of human sexual relations point in the one direction. In marriage, lovers may truly become "one flesh." In accepting children, they embody out of their separate bodies "one flesh" who is rooted in their histories and the shared history of their life together. For some commentators, the inseparability of deep personal love and generativity images and testifies to the love of God, whose creative will is at one with God's love as it is revealed in Jesus Christ.[12]

The version of sexual ethics just presented is representative of recent Protestant thought on "traditional" lines. Roman Catholic "traditionalists" can, I think, accept much of this analysis. Yet a very important difference remains regarding the meaning of "inseparability." The Catholic stance is that the inseparable connection between unitive and procreative meanings must, for married couples, be respected in every act of sexual intercourse. Neither spouse may turn directly against either or both of these two values in any such act. On the one hand, one may not pursue the love-building meaning of sexuality through an act that disavows sexuality's procreative meaning, but this is what is said to be done whenever spouses freely employ artificial contraceptives to prevent conception. On the other hand, spouses ought not to seek to have their own biological children in a manner that separates the generation of new life from the specific act of sexual intercourse through which conception ought to take place, but this is what is done, the Catholic argument goes, when married couples participate in *in vitro* fertilization to circumvent their "infertility." The "traditional" view we covered earlier would morally question third party–assisted reproduction involving donation of sperm or ovum from a person outside the specific marital relation and/or maternal "surrogacy" arrangements. The idea is that there would be a violation of "one flesh unity" in the full sense, according to which the nurture and procreation of children is not to be separated in principle from the marital bond. But for Protestants, typically, contraception and exclusively marital forms of artificial fertilization are not opposed for reasons that have to do with inseparability.[13]

The Catholic position should not be misunderstood. Its claim is not that married couples are morally forbidden to intend to delay having children, even for an indefinite time. "Responsible parenthood" includes making judgments about parental "readiness" on economic, social, psychological, and other grounds. Nor does the position rule out the use of all means to achieve this purpose. "Natural family planning" or "periodic continence, that is, the methods of birth regulation based on self-observation and the use of infertile periods," is permissible.[14] Finally, in principle, the position does not hold that sexual intercourse is only or even primarily fully human because of its procreative significance; rather, that meaning is to be respected in its inseparable connection with the love-embodying significance of this uniquely conjugal act. In this light, contraception may be judged immoral on the grounds that it expresses a withholding and not a total giving unto one's spouse, a withholding of one's very generativity. But contraception is also wrong because it amounts to a positive refusal to be open to new life, to an *anti-procreative* aim or intention. "Periodic continence" is *non-procreative* in that what is done involves no disavowal of sexual generativity at all. Of course, our motivations affect the moral quality of our acts. A couple using "natural family planning" because they like charts and hate children and want to go on living utterly selfish lives together would be an example of serious moral deficiency. But what is wrong about their choices stems from their motives and not from the aim, embodied in their contraceptive act, of directly turning against procreativity. Or so traditional Catholic ethics seems to hold.

Along the same lines, for a married couple to affirm human generativity apart from its connection with the value of building and expressing loving communion in and through the act of martial intercourse embodies the will that that couple's child *not* be the fruit of such a loving act. To that extent, the exclusively marital pursuit of *in vitro* fertilization or of artificial insemination using the husband's sperm subjects procreation to the terms of the technical manufacture of a product by *replacing* sexual intercourse with medical technique.[15]

Traditionalist *critics* of this version of traditional sexual ethics argue that inseparability can be maintained across a shared marital life. They think, for example, that a couple who has lovingly raised their four children and now chooses for good reasons to say "no more kids" has preserved their openness to life and love in their marriage and through their covenant with each other within the history of their sexual sharing; their use of contraception at this point hardly nullifies or jeopardizes their "one flesh unity." And a couple unable to have biological children as a direct consequence of sexual intercourse may nevertheless affirm that the marital love nurtured in their lovemaking is thoroughly bound up with their openness to new life that is flesh of their flesh.

Whatever we are to make of these challenges, we need to face up to a central general response from the traditional Catholic perspective. It is the simple but rigorously defended view that our free acts make up our character. A wrongful act freely performed does orient us to the evil that we have chosen, and to some extent it readies us for future choices of this sort. It appears to be morally evasive to say that, "for the most part" or "throughout our lives together," we have honored the moral integrity of married sexual intercourse while engaging in individual acts that violate the moral norm properly understood. One would have to *repent* of the evil actually done to right oneself and *not just do other things* that come closer to the mark.[16] Contraceptive acts enact and contribute socially to a "contraceptive mentality" that more and more orders sex to merely individual desire. Participation in forms of artificial fertilization that replace conjugal sex as the decisive procreative event enact and contribute to a "product mentality" that treats nascent human life as an object to be designed as much as possible to fit the desires and dreams of parents. Sexuality is about mutually cherishing one another and honoring generativity; having children is about showing unconditional love to needy beings we receive as gifts, not as commodities we are owed. Traditional Catholics believe that their single-act approach to sexual ethics protects and advances these human purposes as they are or are not done in the actions we freely choose. Opponents often answer that this approach imprisons the moral meanings of sexual intercourse exclusively within the terms of its physical structure and biological tendencies.[17]

Both versions of the traditional ethic can be comprehended more fully, perhaps, by referring them to the kinds of practices and virtues that Christians hope to realize and enact in their common life together in and for the world. In marriage, spouses may, in their fidelity to one another, give living testimony to God's fidelity to Israel, the Church, and humanity at large. In their most intimate union with and service to one another, they would be an image of the permanent and unconditional bond of love promised to continue between Jesus Christ and the Christian community. From the source of their covenanting love, the readiness of husband and wife to welcome children into the world is itself a sign of hope in the covenanting God, who will not give up on sinful human creatures and who wills "nevertheless" to make the world a place in which children may live with the promise of fellowship and peace. Finally, marriage is a form of self-giving and mortification of the self-serving ego, as spouses learn by the light of Christ to nourish themselves in their communion with one another. In short, marriage may witness to the character of God's kingdom. Sex becomes intelligible, the case goes, through these practices as a reality that contributes to faithful intimacy, loving union, the receiving of children as gifts, and a life that replaces selfishness with self-giving.[18]

For a traditional or conservative ethic, erotic love in and of itself is not yet the fitting relation with which sexual intercourse may be fully human. In the absence of a vow of permanent and exclusive mutual loyalty, such love cannot bear the real promise of sexual intimacy in its "unitive" and "procreative" aspects. It also cannot withstand the perils that our sinfulness presents through the medium of our sexual desire. Saying this is not to deny the real human good attained in this relationship. But it is to insist that "the relation in question, no matter what good it may involve, is nonetheless wrong; it is part of the broad rather than the narrow way in which Christ calls his disciples to follow."[19]

Love and Respect in Sexual Ethics

Like "traditionalism," not all Christian "revisionist" sexual ethics are the same. Some approaches depart from traditional perspectives more than others do. The point of view that I will develop below should not be taken to establish exclusively the conditions for membership in the revisionist camp. I have chosen to present this version because of its continuing influence and for the sake of sharper contrast with the competing account.[20]

Revisionism, as embodied in the work of Christian thinkers such as Marvin Ellison, Beverly Harrison, James Nelson, and Christine Gudorf, holds that all forms of sexual relationship ought to express a measure of loving commitment and should be a means to mutual growth and community between sexual partners. The norm of *justice,* or "right relation," is often taken to be paramount. Justice requires that partners be empowered by one another responsibly "to assert one's own desires and needs while respecting others' integrity." From this perspective, according to Marvin Ellison, "it is entirely fitting not to grant special status or moral privilege to heterosexual marriage, but rather to celebrate *all* sexual relations of moral substance whenever they deepen human intimacy and love"; these criteria, moreover, countenance the possibility that "some marriages may make room for additional sexual partners while others will thrive only by maintaining genital sexual exclusivity. Although justice requires relational fidelity—honoring and responding fairly to the demands of a relationship—the precise requirements for maintaining faithfulness cannot be predetermined in advance."[21]

Revisionist sexual ethics requires *respect* for a person's freedom, lived choices, and basic needs; that rules out *"relations in which persons are abused, exploited, and violated."*[22] Carelessness, cruelty, selfishness, or any hint of coercion are also condemned accordingly. Sexual relations should contribute to another's emotional well-being, self-worth, and human wholeness. Various virtues are ordered to this end, such as honesty, which expresses "as truthfully as possible the meaning of the relationship that actually exists between the partners," and fidelity, an "ongoing commitment to this relationship . . . without crippling possessiveness."[23]

The "procreative meaning" of human sexuality for these revisionists seems not simply to be subordinated to the conditions of active love and respect; for subordination might still be compatible with the requirements of one-flesh unity and exclusive claims regarding marriage. Instead, the move involves *dividing* the meanings, so that the moral importance (or unimportance) of procreativity for would-be sexual partners is established relative to the degree and purposes of loving commitment. Procreativity appears to possess no essential or constitutive moral weight. From this angle, "the same [moral] considerations apply equally to male and female, aged and young, able-bodied and disabled, homosexual and heterosexual."[24]

Now if the word "revisionist" has any significance in the sexual ethics I have just described, we should expect that it is formulated partly in critical response to traditional sexual ethics. What are some of the criticisms? First, revisionists challenge traditionalists for not really understanding or taking seriously enough how sexual *pleasure* is itself a good gift of God; the latter all too often remain shackled by judgments or feelings to the effect that pleasure is irredeemably associated with selfish and uncontrollable lust, on the one hand, or with our merely animal nature, on the other.[25] Yet sexual pleasure satisfies deeply felt human needs "for touch, for excitement, for physical release, for companionship," and for intimate community. It is a "premoral good," which means that "it is ordinarily a good, and should be understood as one aspect of the general social good." Of course, this does not mean that attaining such pleasure always rules in the moral sphere; its value may well be "outweighed by conflicting, premoral goods within the process of moral discernment."[26] The critical point remains, however, that constant suspicion and shame about our human enjoyment of sexual touching are unjustified.

Second, revisionists point to persisting connections between traditional sexual ethics and a patriarchal culture "built on gender inequality and the legitimacy of men's control over women, children, and men of lesser power."[27] All these victims tend to be treated in conformity with stereotypes of feminine passivity and weakness. The high regard given to procreation, especially in the traditional Roman Catholic view, has the effect of limiting women's human prospects by giving pride of place to their past, present, and future motherhood within heterosexual marriage. Motherhood locates women primarily within the "private" home; there, it is supposed, they can fully realize their "caring" and "nurturant" natures for their own sake and for the common good. But their life in the "private sphere" may also tend to impose upon women a dangerous condition of economic and social dependence upon men, who are themselves taught in patriarchal culture to be "the boss." Traditional sexual ethics, the critics complain, typically foster inequity, disrespect, and contempt for women. The problems of injustice are exacerbated in vicious attitudes towards homosexuals that derive from the perception that homoerotic men are "failed men, no better than females."[28] Misogyny and homophobia are linked: one hatred makes another possible, and the "compulsory heterosexuality" of traditional sexual ethics too readily supports these patterns of domination.

Third, a revisionist sexual ethic may presume that our sexuality is both intrinsic to our relation with God and is a reality to be redeemed in salvation. If we understand "sin" to be not simply wrong kinds of sexual acts that violate strict rules, but rather alienation from our sexuality as God intends it to be, then the *recovery* of who we ought to be as sexual beings is part of our sanctification before God. Our sexual embodiment should be reintegrated with our personal selves and not objectified and alienated from ourselves because of crippling shame or the unchecked desire for pleasure. The idea of sanctification also suggests coming to sexual wholeness that transcends gender stereotypes, "with males fearful of tenderness, emotion, and vulnerability, and females fearful of (or kept from) claiming their strength, assertiveness, and intellect." The gracious and accepting love of God permits growth in self-acceptance, "the kind that "personalizes" the body, making me more vitally aware that I can celebrate the body which I am and thus affirm the ways in which my body-self relates to the world."[29] Proponents of this vision claim directly to challenge traditional theology and ethics insofar as they work only with abstract norms and not with the stuff of lived experience, and to the extent that they view our sexual selves as incidental or detrimental to the realization of communion with God and neighbor. Revisionist correction includes an active recognition that our bodily being in its fullness is called to a life of love of God and neighbor. To reserve that life for our "spiritual" selves, set apart from or in opposition to our sexual embodiment, is a mistake.

For the purpose of presenting a revisionist response to the question of whether the mutuality of erotic love *per se* justifies sexual relations, let us consider a specific theological proposal regarding a sexual ethic for *single persons*. Believing that the rule prescribing "celibacy in singleness, fidelity in marriage" is inadequate and that the traditional specification of unitive and procreative purposes in sexual life is incomplete, Christian ethicist Karen Lebacqz argues that the created goodness of sexuality has very much to do with the appropriate expression of *vulnerability*. The passionate desire for union with another contains within itself a responsive openness to human relationships as well as the capacity for being wounded.

> Vulnerability may be the condition for both union and procreation: without a willingness to be vulnerable, to be exposed, to be wounded, there can be no union. To be "known," as Scripture so often describes the sexual encounter, is to be vulnerable, exposed, open.
>
> Sexuality is therefore a form of vulnerability and is to be valued as such. Sex, eros, passion are antidotes to the human sin of wanting to be in control or have power over another. "Appropriate vulnerability" may describe the basic intention for human life—which may be expressed in part through the gift of sexuality.[30]

If sexual relations violate one's own or one's partner's vulnerability, they are

morally deficient. It is wrong to exploit another's exposure to hurt, self-pro-
tectively guard one's own power, or fail to pursue a proper equality in which
sexual vulnerability may be safely given and received. A sexual ethic for
single men and women must call this viciousness by its proper name and
also develop social and relational contexts that "heighten or protect vulnerability."

On the one hand, the norm of appropriate vulnerability seems to be
satisfied *in principle* within the terms of the erotic bond described at the
beginning of this essay. Premarital unions, gay and lesbian unions, and
others that engage the project of the "we," a *sharing of identity,* might conform marvelously to this ideal, just as unloving, rote-like, and coercive sex in
marriage can fail miserably to even approach it. On the other hand, Lebacqz
worries that single persons (who might be in love in this sense) often lack "a
supportive context for vulnerable expressions of the self." In theory the
covenant of faithful, monogamous marriage does provide such a context,
but with single life "no covenant of fidelity ensures that my vulnerability will
not lead to my being hurt, foolish, exposed, wounded. In short, in singleness
the vulnerability that naturally accompanies sexuality is also coupled with a
vulnerability of context"[31] that calls for vigilant attention to matters having to
do with the age, maturity, levels of commitment, and relative social power of
single persons. *In fact,* then, Lebacquz's revisionism sounds a note of caution.

Debate

One way a traditionalist could respond to a revisionist like Lebacqz is to argue
that, even at its best, the norm of appropriate vulnerability invites commen-
dation of merely "limited engagements." However one might wish to stress
the virtues of care, commitment, openness, trust, and so on, as such these
bonds exist for limited purposes (e.g., sharing pleasure, warmth, and mutually affirming companionship). They are "for the time being," or for some
undetermined but not permanent extent and duration. But then these bonds
appear to promote tendencies that do not easily fit the norm of appropriate
vulnerability itself. Limited engagements readily become calculating regarding the comparative benefits and burdens of a relationship; they can involve
practices of *testing* the sincerity of feelings and assessing whether our love is
or is not "here to stay." The question for the revisionist, then, is whether the
limited commitment that "appropriate vulnerability" permits "is the expres-

sion of a soul that at its deepest level blows neither hot nor cold." Is the dedication to testing the quality of the loving, sexual relationship "a virtue for the tentative, one that calls to mind the image of someone testing the water of a bath by sticking their toe in?"[32] If this description is accurate, then "appropriate vulnerability" in nonmarital sexual relations includes a guardedness and a distance that may contradict the norm itself.

The revisionist can disagree with this critical interpretation, but he or she might also concede the point and proceed to argue for the full humanity of sexual relations that reflect some functional equivalent of marital commitment. For example, gay and lesbian unions emerge as candidates for such a nonlimited engagement. Of course, at this point the traditionalist may need to counter with the criticism that sexual bonds like these are antiprocreative. Should the revisionist pose the scenario of gay and lesbian couples building a family and raising children through practices of adoption or forms of artificial fertilization, the debate would have to move toward an appraisal of these arrangements in light of one or another traditional ideal of "becoming one flesh."[33]

The critical exchange can continue along another line. Revisionists understand human sexuality and bodily sexual pleasures as divine gifts. They can ask whether the persisting "procreationism" of traditional sexual ethics reflects a dominant and destructive *dualism*. Do not traditionalists *really believe after all* that the procreative good of sex *is* paramount, and do not they hold this because of their fear or contempt of the body and bodily desire? The body and its enjoyments are viewed as evil, or as an impediment to being more fully human, and in any case are divided from and against the world of the spirit in which God is sought and real love is thought to be enacted. In contrast, the revisionist could appeal to philosopher Sara Ruddick's powerful description of "complete sex," when "two persons embodied by sexual desire actively desire and respond to each others' active desire."[34] Here the description of mutual personal presence captures how each one of us is, as God's good creature, the soul of his or her body and the body of his or her soul. The traditionalist needs, perhaps, thoroughly to accept this description and to display its proper place in sexual ethics.

However, the traditionalist may make a parallel argument by claiming that, in truth, revisionist sexual ethics are dualistic. "On this understanding the most important thing is that human beings of reproductive age, whether male or female, are *persons,* and by *persons* [revisionists] mean conscious subjects aware of themselves as selves and capable of entering into meaningful relationships with other persons or selves . . . a person is a *conscious subject of experiences that possesses a body,* that is, a human being who happens to be either a male or a female."[35] The body, it is claimed, is viewed as a *tool* to be used for realizing fulfilling human relationships, rather than as something essential to our identity as *male or female generative human beings.* Nothing other than this dualism, traditionalists would hold, can explain the splitting away of the procreative meaning of sexual intercourse from its unitive significance.

We want our ethics to apply to, make sense of, and help us to see better the world we inhabit. That is, we want ethics to be realistic. Each of the positions we have surveyed has a case for realism. The revisionist, we suppose, thinks it unrealistic in this day and age to expect folks to adhere to the norm of "fidelity in (solely heterosexual) marriage, celibacy in singleness." Given the expectation that people have been and are going to continue to be sexually active outside marriage, it makes sense to come up with a sexual ethic that is humanely supportive and protective of persons "where the action is." This effort is not a matter of "caving in" or "accepting second best"; it embodies a positive vision of human well-being that is more closely connected to legitimate human needs and desires than is its rival. Or so the argument goes. The traditional view, in contrast, would attest to its even deeper "realism" by reiterating how the most intimate form of being personally present to one another requires a context of fidelity and permanence. The truth proposed is that sexual relations promise gifts, including the gift of new life, which can be received fully and integrally in the midst of lifelong partnership. Apart from such partnership, we are all too vulnerable to the exploitation of others and to our own selfishness. If this latter case is to be convincing, traditional sexual ethics must especially heed and respond to the criticisms that it belittles the good of sexual pleasure and perpetuates patterns of misogynist and homophobic domination.

Endnotes

1. Robert Nozick, *The Examined Life: Philosophical Meditations* (New York: Simon and Schuster, 1989) 69.

2. Ibid. 70.

3. C. S. Lewis, *The Four Loves* (New York: Harcourt, Brace, Jovanovich, 1960) 136.

4. Nozick, *The Examined Life* 70.

5. Roland E. Murphy, *A Commentary on the Book of Canticles or the Songs of Songs* (Minneapolis, MN: Fortress, 1990) 102.

6. Nozick, *The Examined Life* 85.

7. Gene Outka, "Universal Love and Impartiality," in Edmund N. Santurri and William Werpehowski, eds., *The Love Commandments* (Washington, DC: Georgetown University, 1992) 91.

8. Compare Paul Ramsey, *The Essential Paul Ramsey* (New Haven: Yale University, 1994) 137–46.

9. Philip Turner, *Sex, Money and Power* (Cambridge, MA: Cowley, 1985) 56. See also William E. May, *Sex, Marriage, and Chastity* (Chicago: Franciscan Herald, 1981).

10. Paul Ramsey, *One Flesh* (Bramcote, Nottingham: Grove, 1975). Ramsey here adapts Reinhold Niebuhr's famous formulation that "Man's capacity for justice makes democracy possible; man's inclination for injustice makes democracy necessary." Reinhold Niebuhr, *The Children of Light and the Children of Darkness* (New York: Scribner's, 1944) xiii.

11. Leon Kass, *Toward a More Natural Science* (New York: Free, 1985) 110.

12. Ramsey, *The Essential Paul Ramsey* 141–42. Cf. Vatican II's *Pastoral Constitution on the Church in the Modern World,* par. 50: "the true practice of conjugal love, and the whole meaning of the family life which results from it, have this aim: that the couple be ready with stout hearts to cooperate with the love of the Creator and the Saviour, who through them will enlarge and enrich His own family day by day." In Walter M. Abbott, S.J., The Documents of Vatican II (Amercia Press, 1966) 254.

13. For an example of opposition to *in vitro* fertilization that is not based on inseparability, see Paul Ramsey, "The Issues Facing Mankind," in *The Question of In Vitro Fertilization* (London: Society for the Protection of Unborn Children Educational Trust, 1984) 1945.

14. *Catechism of the Roman Catholic Church* (Liguori, MO: Liguori, 1994) par. 2370. Cf. Paul VI, *Humane Vitae,* in Robert Baker and Frederick Elliston, *Philosophy and Sex* (Buffalo, NY: Prometheus, 1975) 131–49.

15. Congregation for the Doctrine of the Faith, *Instruction on Respect for Human Life and on the Dignity of Procreation. Replies to Certain Question of Our Day* (Washington, DC: United States Catholic Conference, 1987).

16. See John Finnis, *Moral Absolutes* (Washington, DC: Georgetown University, 1991) 58ff.

17. For discussions that apply this kind of criticism to both contraception and *in vitro* fertilization, see Thomas Shannon and Lisa Cahill, *Religion and Artificial Reproduction* (New York: Crossroad, 1988), and Oliver O'Donovan, *Begotten or Made* (Oxford: Clarendon, 1984). Cahill describes herself as a Catholic "revisionist,"

and her general views are well presented in "Can We Get Real About Sex?" *Commonweal* 117:15 (September 14, 1990) 497–503.

18. Vigen Guroian, "An Ethic of Marriage and Family," in Wayne Boulton et al., eds., *From Christ to the World* (Grand Rapids, MI: Eerdmans, 1994) 322–30; Stanley Hauerwas, *A Community of Character* (Notre Dame, IN: Notre Dame University, 1981) 155–95.

19. Philip Turner, "Limited Engagements," in Philip Turner, ed., *Men and Women* (Cambridge, MA: Coweley, 1989) 79.

20. For example, Lisa Cahill—a self-styled Catholic "revisionist" who affirms presumptively, if not absolutely, the unity of sex, love, and parenthood—would certainly not agree with everything that follows. But she would be sympathetic to revisionist critiques of patriarchy and traditionalist suspicions about sexual pleasure. See footnote 17, *supra*.

21. Marvin M. Ellison, "Common Decency: A New Christian Sexual Ethics," in Paul T. Jersild and Dale A. Johnson, eds., *Moral Issues and Christian Response,* fifth edition (New York: Harcourt, Brace, Jovanovich, 1993) 44–45.

22. Ibid. 47. Author's emphasis.

23. James B. Nelson, "The Liberal Approach to Sexual Ethics," in *From Christ to the World* 358.

24. Ibid.

25. See Christine E. Gudorf, *Body, Sex, and Pleasure* (Cleveland, OH: Pilgrim, 1994) 82–89. Gudorf argues that "the most salient characteristic of, and chief motivation for, sex is sexual pleasure," and that a "Christian sexual ethic should make mutuality in sexual pleasure normative." Ibid. 139.

26. Ibid. 90.

27. Ellison, "Common Decency" 43.

28. Beverly Wildung Harrison, *Making the Connections* (Boston: Beacon, 1985) 140.

29. Nelson, "The Liberal Approach to Sexual Ethics" 358.

30. Karen Lebacqz, "Appropriate Vulnerability," in James B. Nelson and Sandra P. Longfellow, eds., *Sexuality and the Sacred* (Louisville, KY: Westminster/John Knox, 1994) 259.

31. Ibid. 260. Cf. Cahill, "Can We Get Real About Sex?" 211–12.

32. Turner, "Limited Engagements" 75.

33. For a controversial critique of "homogenital acts," see The Ramsey Colloquium, "The Homosexual Movement," *First Things* (March 1994) 15–20.

34. Sara Ruddick, "Better Sex," in Baker and Elliston, eds., *Philosophy and Sex* 90. Ruddick's description is indebted to the work of Jean Paul Sartre.

35. May, *Sex, Marriage, and Chastity* 7–8. Cf. Turner, *Money, Sex and Power* 40–42. Cahill is sensitive to this issue and explicitly rejects this sort of "dualism" in "Can We Get Real About Sex?" 212–13.

7

RESPONSIBILITIES WITHIN THE FAMILY

SARAH-VAUGHAN BRAKMAN

Villanova University

When we talk about "ethics," the discussion is about how we should treat others or what we are morally bound to do for others. For instance, do I have a duty to save a drowning person? Do I have a (moral) duty to stop and help a stranded motorist? Ethics is about what attitudes, principles, or guidelines ought to guide our conduct. While it is important to think about the respect and dignity we owe others in general, such discussions often overlook thinking about how we should treat those in our family. Indeed, when it focuses on what duties or responsibilities we have to our friends and family, ethical theory often refers to these duties as "special obligations," or obligations that we have due to specific roles that we either chose or find ourselves occupying in relation to particular others. However, the irony of calling these responsibilities "special" is that many of the moral dilemmas that most of us face on a daily basis concern these types of obligations more so than dilemmas concerning strangers in a moral sense. So, in a way, there is really nothing "special" about these obligations at all.[1]

For most of us, the family is the first time we experience community and relationship; it is also the place where individuals learn how to treat others. The question then of what responsibilities individuals in a family have to one another is a crucial one. While there are many types of family relationships, each with important and unique concerns, a question that is gaining increasing importance in this regard concerns the issue of what adult children owe to parents. This question takes on central prominence in today's world, where, as a result of increased technology, healthier life-styles, and medical advances, people are living longer and living longer with chronic illnesses. Those over the age of 65 make up the largest age cohort in the population. Additionally, on average, married couples are having fewer children. Women, who were traditionally relied upon as a source of unpaid care giving, are no longer available for this role due to their presence in the workforce. This all results in more elders who need care and assistance for many more years than previous generations had and fewer family members who are available to help care for these elders. Many still consider place-ment in any skilled care facility (nursing home) to be a moral failing. Parents and grandparents do not want to be a burden to their children and grandchildren; yet all of us believe that something is owed between genera-tions in families. Why? We will examine the issue in this chapter, but to answer the question, we need a moral framework from which to address it.

Catholic moral teaching speaks to family responsibilities and has a rich ethical tradition through which we can understand familial obligations. This chapter focuses attention on the vision of the family in the Catholic tradition and on the foundations of morality as each of these addresses the question of what obligations adult children have to parents. We will show that such obligations are grounded in the Christian conception of the roles of the family and on the virtues of love, compassion, charity, self-sacrifice, and gratitude. Finally, we will consider the practical implications of these answers for families today, as well as discuss how an ethics informed by Catholic social and moral teaching is, in important ways, countercultural to prevailing societal norms and attitudes.

Before turning to this discussion though, we need to address two concerns that are often voiced about "obligations" in families. The first one goes something like this: we are "good" to our family members because we love them, because of the affective ties that bind, because "blood is thicker than water." Questions about "obligations," "duties,"[2] and responsibilities are out of place in relationships characterized by love and trust. The re-sponse to this concern is that love and affection may be why in fact some people act in ways we consider good and virtuous to their family members, but it does not illuminate the situations in which, for whatever reason, such affective ties are not present. If a person does not "feel" love for her parents, sisters, grandparents, then is there no responsibility? This situation brings up the moral aspects of love, which we will also consider in this chapter.

The second concern follows the line of thought with which we began this chapter: many might believe that morality is not really about how we treat our families, but how we treat the stranger. This thinking suggests that "your family is your family, and they have to love you and put up with you," but others do not, so you have to be "nice" to others, but not to your family. This view rests on the notion that intimacy and familiarity somehow replace or lessen respect and responsibilities. However, this kind of thinking does not work if we see the family as a microcosm of society, a central belief of the Catholic tradition. It is contradictory to claim that the family is the basic unit of society and also to claim that we need only worry about "ethics" when dealing with strangers.

With this background in mind, let us turn to our first topic; the vision of the family in the Christian tradition.

The Family

The vision of the family in the Catholic tradition is characterized by four interrelated and rich roles: (a) forming a community of persons, (b) serving life, (c) participating in the development of society, and (d) sharing in the life and mission of the Church.[3] We will consider all but (b) here, since other chapters in this volume discuss important aspects of this role of family life, such as reverence for human life (McCartney), and intimacy and sexuality (Werpehowski).

Let us begin with (a) the concept of "forming a community of persons." In *Famililaris Consortio*, Pope John Paul II says:

> The family, which is founded and given life by love, is a community of persons: of husband and wife, or parents, and children, of relatives. Its first task is to live with fidelity the reality of communion in a constant effort to develop an authentic community of persons.
>
> The inner principle of that task, its permanent power and its final goal is love: without love the family is not a community of persons and, in the same way, *without love the family cannot live, grow and perfect itself as a community of persons.*[4]

This passage demonstrates that the moral, psychological, and physical basis of a family is rooted in love and that the "first task" of a family is to truly be persons joined in love. But what does "love" mean in this context?

Central to Christianity is the belief that God is love and that the foundation of Christianity is God's love for his people. God's love is known as "agape"—unconditional, undeserved love. The love of God for humankind is first manifested in creation and consists in God giving people what they need, not what they deserve.[5] "If God is love, the Christian reality is a share in that love, through which the Spirit transmits to us Christ's life, by which we become God's children."[6] Hence, people become "brother and sisters in Christ" when they accept God as their father and Jesus as His Son and their Lord. Christians are called and are bound by duty to love each other as God loves them.

The family rooted in God, instituted by God, is a community of persons relating and living with others in an attitude of agape love. Those in such a community support each other and give to each other what each needs. This relationship means that those in a family need to work towards a communion with each other on all levels.

> All members of the family, each according to his or her own gift, have the grace and responsibility of building, day by day, the communion of persons, . . . this happens where there is care and love for the little ones, the sick, *the aged;* where there is mutual service every day; when there is a sharing of goods, of joys, and of sorrows.[7]

Let us turn next to the role of the family that involves (c) "participating in the development of society." The family is known as the first cell of human society,[8] which means that the family is the first and smallest social unit. "It is from the family that citizens come to birth and it is within the family that they find the first school of the social virtues that are the animating principle of the existence and development of society itself."[9] The family has the social role of procreation and education, but its social and political roles do not stop there. The family should not be turned inward on itself, focusing only on these worthy goals, but it must also be turned outward to others as part of both recognizing its participation in the greater family of nation and humanity and also to heeding the call to hospitality of opening heart and home to those in need.

The Christian family is thus called upon to offer everyone a witness of generous and disinterested dedication to social matters, through a "preferential option" for the poor and disadvantaged. Therefore, advancing in its following of the Lord by special love for all the poor, it must have special concern for the hungry, the poor, *the old,* the sick, drug victims and those who have no family.[10]

The third role means that, among others, the family is called to protect and defend the right of the elderly to a worthy life and a worthy death.[11]

Just as the intimate connection between the family and society demands that the family be open to and participate in society and its development, so also it requires that society should never fail in its fundamental task of respecting and fostering the family. The family and society have complementary functions in defending and fostering the good of each and every human being. But society—more specifically the State—must recognize that the family is a society in its own original right.[12]

Finally, we will discuss the role of the family that involves (d) "sharing in the life and mission of the Church." This ecclesial task of the Christian family means that we understand the family as the "domestic church" or the "Church in miniature." Each family is a community, like each parish is a community of the Church. Each family is a place where God is experienced and worshipped. The family as a concept is so important because it is both "a living reflection of and a real sharing in God's love for humanity and the love of Christ the Lord for the Church."[13]

The Christian family also builds up the Kingdom of God in history through the everyday realities that concern and distinguish *its state of life.* It is thus in *the love between husband and wife and between the members of the family*—a love lived out in all its extraordinary richness of values and demands: totality, oneness, fidelity and fruitfulness—that the Christian family's participation in the prophetic, priestly and kingly mission of Jesus Christ and His Church finds expression and realization. Therefore, love and life constitute the nucleus of the saving mission of the Christian family in the Church and for the Church.[14]

This role means services of love, prayer, and protecting the vulnerability of the elderly in one's family.

Therefore, it is important to see that the family must be a community of persons that fosters life and love, that it is the first and vital cell of society, and that it is the domestic church. Through these roles, we understand that those in a family have responsibilities to the other members, especially the elderly and elderly parents. We will now look more closely at the grounding for how we should treat parents and about what the tradition and faith specifically have to say about filial obligations.

The Tradition, Virtues, and Filial Obligation

The argument for filial obligations for the Christian tradition is an extension of the general Christian call to love one another as Christ loves his people. This call makes sense if we understand that the two commandments given to Christians are to love God with one's whole heart, soul, mind, and strength, and to love one's neighbor as one loves oneself.[15] Who could be considered more of a neighbor than the members of our own family? If we turn to agape as the attitude that should direct our actions and our feelings, we find embedded in it the fundamental Christian virtues of charity, compassion, and self-sacrifice. To love one's neighbor in the way commanded entails a willingness to be a servant to others. But there is more. How we should treat family members must also be informed by the special nature of the family as a community of love and life and the commitment that members of a family ought to have to one another. The Catholic tradition understands filial virtue as piety that is part of the general virtue of charity and benevolence. Thomas Aquinas argues that there is a specific virtue known as piety that is the worship of parents: "Piety is a protestation of the charity we bear towards our parents and country."[16]

Our parents are also the people who have met our needs and, at times, sacrificed for us. Thus, especially for filial obligations, there is also the obligation of gratitude. The Christian tradition's understanding of filial obligations rests on the virtues of gratitude and compassion. Later we shall say more about what gratitude is and to what it obliges us.

Jesus demands that the treatment of parents and family be set apart. Christian respect for filial obligations are rooted in the arguments and traditions found in the Old Testament and the Judaic tradition.

The Biblical commandment to 'Honor your father and mother' (D5:16) reminds us that, above all else, the family ought to be a place of love, respect and caring for the aging members of society.[17]

Regarding the obligation of children to their parents, the documents of Vatican II state:

As living members of the family, children contribute in their own way to making their parents holy. For they will respond to the kindness of their parents *with sentiments of gratitude, with love and trust.* They still stand by them as children should when hardships overtake their parents and old age *brings its loneliness.*[18]

In 1940, Pope Pius XII said:

The old people! . . . Toward, these, regardless of your own age, you are bound, as you know, by the precept of the Decalogue. "Honor thy father and thy mother" (Ex 20:12). You will not be of the number of those ungrateful children who neglect their old parents, and who in turn will, often enough, find themselves abandoned when age renders them in need of assistance.[19]

Thomas Aquinas[20] says that parents are due reverence and service from a child. His reason is that the parents are the "principle of his being."[21] This argument, based in the thought of Aristotle, states that the parents are essentially connected to the child because they gave her biological being.[22] Since the child would not exist if it were not for the parents, Aquinas argues that the child was benefited by those who are called parents. Further, he says that God is the most excellent and most good thing that exists and that God is the ultimate creator of humans—our first "principle" of being. He says:

I answer that, Man becomes a debtor to other men in various ways, according to their various excellence and the various benefits received from them. On both counts God holds first place, for He is supremely excellent, and is for us the first principle of being and government. In the second place, the principles of our being and government are our parents and our country, that have given us birth and nourishment. Consequently *man is debtor chiefly to his parents and his country, after God.* Wherefore just as it belongs to piety, in the second place, to give worship to one's parents and one's country.[23]

In this passage, Aquinas also shows us that the virtue of religion, or wor-shiping God, is greater than the virtue of piety, or the "worship" of one's parents, because God is the most excellent and supreme creator and care-taker. Pope John Paul II concurs with Aquinas when he states:

> "Honor your father and your mother, that your days may be long in the land which the Lord your God gives to you" (Ex 20:12). This command-ment comes after the three basic precepts which concern the relation of the individual and the people of Israel with God. . . . It is significant that the fourth commandment is placed in this particular context. "Honor your father and your mother," because for you they are in a certain sense representatives of the Lord; they are the ones who gave you life, who introduced you to human existence in a particular family line, nation, and culture. After God, they are your first benefactors. While God alone is good, indeed the Good itself, parents participate in this supreme goodness in a unique way. And so, honor your parents! There is a certain analogy here with the worship owed to God.[24]

At least four occasions are reported in the Gospels in which Jesus places the obligation to God's call before filial piety. In the Gospel of Matthew, Jesus says:

> I have come to set a man at odds with his father, a daughter with her mother, a daughter-in-law with her mother-in-law: in short, to make a man's enemies those of his own household. Whoever loves father or mother, son or daughter, more than me is not worthy of me. He who seeks only himself brings himself to ruin, whereas he who brings himself to naught for me discovers who he is.[25]

And again, when Jesus was addressing a crowd of people, his mother came to see him:

> The crowd seated around him told him, "Your mother and your brothers and sisters are outside asking for you." He said in reply, "Who are my mother and my brothers?" And gazing around him at those seated in the circle he continued, "These are my mother and my brothers. Whoever does the will of God is brother and sister and mother to me."[26]

Third, when Jesus was calling disciples, he said, "'Come after me.' The man replied, 'Let me burn my father first.' Jesus said to him, 'Let the dead bury their dead; come away and proclaim the kingdom of God.'"[27] The fourth example is from Paul who says that "Children should not save up for their parents, but parents for children."[28]

These passages, while seeming to de-emphasize filial obligations, may be understood as actually emphasizing the supreme obligation to follow Jesus and to love all God's people as one would love members of one's family. Christianity holds that, to be a follower of Christ, one must understand that the only obligation more encompassing than those of the virtue of piety is the virtue of religion. Aquinas says:

> Now, as stated above (I-Ii, Q.7, A.2; Q.18, A.3), the act of every virtue is limited by the circumstances due thereto, and if it overstep them it will be an act no longer of virtue but of vice. Hence it belongs to piety to pay duty and homage to one's parents according to the due mode. But it is not the due mode that man should tend to worship his father rather than God, but, as Ambrose says in Luke 12:52, *the piety of divine religion takes precedence of the claims of kindred.*[29]

In addition, Aquinas goes on to say that, if the worship of parents prevents or diminishes the worship of God, such worship of parents would no longer count as an act of piety.[30] Aquinas says that it is important to realize that the reason that Jesus told the disciple not to bury his father (in one of the examples given above) could have been either—as was Chrysostom's view—that he wanted to spare the man that sorrow and there were others who were also bound by the duties of kinship to take care of it, or—as was Cyril's view—that the father was yet living and that the request was really that he might stay to support him until he should have to bury him, and this again could be taken care of by others who were bound to take care of him.[31] However, because the "worship to God includes the worship due to our parents as a particular"[32] and because taking care of our parents is also like taking care of our neighbors, which God commands us to do, it is usually the case that, if parents are in need of our assistance, there is no one else to help them, and they do not "incite us to nothing against God, we must not abandon them for the sake of religion."[33]

In the New Testament, Jesus rejected some of the traditions of the elders, such as the washing of hands before meals, saying to the pharisees:

> "You disregard God's commandment and cling to what is human tradition." He went on to say: "You have made a fine art of setting aside God's commandment in the interests of keeping your traditions! For example,

Moses said, 'Honor your father and your mother'; and in another place, 'Whoever curses father or mother shall be put to death.' Yet you declare, 'If a person says to his father or mother, any support you might have had from me is korban' (that is, dedicated to God), you allow him to do nothing more for his father or mother. That is the way to nullify God's word in favor of the traditions you have handed on."[34]

The apostles state that good children provide for parents[35] and widows.[36] Disobedience to parents is censured; it is grouped with being selfish, greedy, licentious, and profane.[37] In addition, there is one reference to treating the old in general as one would treat a father[38] and to providing for any of one's relatives: "If anyone does not provide for his own relatives and especially for members of his immediate family, he has denied the faith; he is worse than an unbeliever."[39]

Gratitude and Filial Obligation

In addition to what the tradition says children owe parents, Aquinas supports a conception of filial piety that relies heavily upon gratitude to parents for having given the child existence. The premise of this argument is as follows: to bring a person into existence is to benefit her.[40] The person benefited then owes the benefactor. However, as Aristotle said, how can children pay back to parents more than what parents gave them? Aquinas says that this is possible if we consider the "will of the giver and of the repayer."

> As stated above ([Q.106] A.3, and 5, A.5), in repaying favors we must consider the disposition rather than the deed. Accordingly, if we consider the effect of beneficence, which a son receives from his parents, namely, to be and to live, the son cannot make an equal repayment (Aristotle *Ethics* 8.14). But if we consider the will of the giver and the repayer, then it is possible for the son to pay back something greater to his father, as Seneca declares (*De Benefit* iii). If, however, he were unable to do so, the will to pay back would be sufficient for gratitude.[41]

We see here that an important component of what adult children owe to their parents is their disposition, their will towards their parents in this regard—the fact that they recognize all that the parent has done and their will to repay the parents. On Aquinas's view, grown children do not, strictly speaking, owe obedience, but they do owe piety. The nature of piety seems to be very similar to that of gratitude. Blustein rightly notes that while Aquinas appears at one point to make a distinction between gratitude and piety, piety can be conceived of in his view as "a higher form of gratitude."[42] Blustein says:

> Gratitude does not obligate us to respond to all our benefactors in the same manner, with the same degree of devotion. On the contrary, "the nature of the case requires that a recipient respond to his benefactor in a way that reflects their relationship" (question 106, article 3), and since our relationship with our parents is so closely bound up with who and what we are, more is required to demonstrate our gratitude and appreciation to them than to any other benefactor, with the exception of God. Just what is required of children cannot be determined with the precision that would be possible if filial obligation were a matter justice, *for gratitude looks to the nature of the particular family and of the particular relationships within it, and not, as in the case of justice, to an "equality . . . of external objects."*[43]

Part of what gratitude includes is the spontaneity and the freedom to choose the ways in which gratitude will take shape in our lives, as well as considering the appropriate response in light of the particular nature of the particular family. Meilaender, another philosopher who wrote about virtues and gratitude, says a life characterized by gratitude is stamped at least as deeply by freedom as by obligation. According to him, gratitude as an obligation leaves us free to fulfill it in countless ways—that our way need be no one else's and no one else's way need be ours. Once we see that at least some gifts can never be repaid, we may recognize that gratitude is something more than just a duty; it is a way of life.[44] Gratitude admits a freedom of response, it is not "tit for tat," like reciprocity. A person is free to choose the particular way her response meets the obligation. We have here then a discussion of filial obligations that says that adult children owe parents gratitude, which is primarily an attitude or disposition of the will, but that also leads to certain actions. However, the specifics of such acts cannot be set out because there is latitude to the gratitude response. However, we can lay out some general guidelines for actions and then discuss what kinds of acts are more likely to show gratitude.

We see that what follows from the notion of "to benefit," is that beneficiaries are morally bound a) to give thanks for their benefactors, and/or b) to provide help to their benefactors if the benefactors are in need. Aquinas states that children owe assistance and support to parents when the parents are in need of temporary assistance. If the parent is ill, the child should visit, if poor, the child should support. The child, according to Aquinas, should respect and honor his or her father.[45] But what is "honor"?

> Honor denotes a witnessing to a person's excellence. Therefore men who wish to be honored seek a witnessing to their excellence (Aristotle *Ethics* i. 5, viii.8). Now witness is borne either before God or before man. Before God, who is the searcher of hearts, the witness of one's conscience suffices; wherefore honor, so far as God is concerned, may consist of the mere internal movement of the heart, for instance when a man acknowledges either God's excellence or another man's excellence before God. But, as regards men, one cannot bear witness, save by means of signs either by words, as when one proclaims another's excellence by word of mouth, or by deeds, for instance by bowing, saluting, and so forth, or by external things as by offering gifts, erecting statues, and the like. Accordingly honor consist of signs, external and corporal.[46]

It seems that at the least, we may say that children owe parents the following:

1. Not to harm parents or to act contrary to their interests. This charge may include such things as not competing with or gossiping about parents. We can call such a violation the "Patti Davis Syndrome."[47]
2. Help the parents when they are in need and if the adult child can do so at no great cost to him or herself. Surely those who have benefited us so much in the past ought to be able to count on us in times of need.
3. Accede to the reasonable requests of the parents. The presence of sacrifice on the parent's part also increases the strength of the obligation. What counts as reasonable is also context dependent. For example, one distinction that we may make is that a request may be one of two kinds: either a request whose nature intrinsically concerns the parent and his or her fundamental well-being or a request whose nature does not intrinsically concern the parent and his or

her fundamental well-being, such as a request involving the personal life and behavior of the adult child.

The film, *Like Water for Chocolate*,[48] portrays a particular family in Mexico in which the tradition in the family was that the youngest daughter in any generation would not marry and would take care of her mother until her mother's death. This sacrifice was considered obligatory on the daughter by the mother. The mother in the film treated her youngest daughter in a callous manner and even in an emotionally cruel way. But what if the mother had treated the girl well? Would gratitude obligations be owed? According to this analysis, the answer is yes. And in that case, because of the context of this tradition, should the girl not marry and take care of the mother in old age? The answer to this is no. The youngest daughter had a right to pursue her own projects, to exercise her personal freedom, and to live by her integrity.[49] The broader culture of Mexico, moreover, accepted that young women should be able to marry if they wished, that children should take care of their parents and that the two are not mutually exclusive. In fact, the demands placed on this daughter would generally be considered unreasonable in the broader Mexican culture. The girl may have an obligation to care for her mother, but it does override all other obligations, like those to self and others. Additionally, any other child in this family may have gratitude obligations as well. This daughter may have had some obligation to care for her mother, but not any obligation that her parent demanded.

Counter-Cultural Morality and Implications for Today's Families

We have discussed the roles of family in the Catholic tradition and what this means for filial responsibilities, and we have discussed what specifically the tradition, as seen through the sources of scripture and moral philosophers, has had to say about such responsibilities and obligations. We have seen that filial piety is rooted in charity, compassion, gratitude, and self-sacrifice, and we have discussed briefly the kinds of actions that these virtues compel. This last section will discuss how the connection between the emphasis on the roles of the family and the description of filial piety lead us to a morality for family relations that is in many important respects countercultural. This connection in large measure is due to the family's function as the basic unit of society. The family, not the individual, is the first cell of society. The responsibilities and obligations that individuals have within families are stronger on such an account than the obligation that might be generated on an account that does not recognize the fundamental importance of the family. This position does not mean that individual rights are not supported. In fact:

> The rights of the family are closely linked to the rights of the person: if in fact the family is a communion of persons, its self-realization will depend in large part on the correct application of the rights of its members. . . . But the rights of the family are not simply the sum total of the rights of the person, since the family is much more than the sum total of the rights of the person, since the family is much more than the sum of its individual members. It is a community of parents and children, and at times a community of several generations.[50]

The Catholic tradition in particular emphasizes that the virtues of gratitude and compassion cannot be totally discharged by substitutes. The provision of basic physical needs, obtained through personal service or purchases, is not enough. One must give of oneself in providing emotional support and companionship. The notion of self-sacrifice comes into play at this point.

> Should elderly family members require a form of institutionalization, the obligations of the family remain. Responsibility for their well being cannot be left to health care professionals and social service agencies alone. Often, only relatives and friends can provide the love and personal attention that humanize the sometimes lonely experience of institutional care.[51]

However, what about parents who have not been good to their children? These children should also be good to their parents if only under the general appeal to love others, even those who have done harm or wronged the individual. Jesus tells us:

> If you do good to those who do good to you, how can you claim any credit? Sinners do as much. If you lend to those from whom you expect repayment, what merit is there in it for you? Even sinners lend to sinners, expecting to be repaid in full. . . . Be compassionate, as your Father is compassionate. Do not judge, and you will not be judged. Do not condemn, and you will not be condemned. Pardon, and you shall be pardoned. Give, and it shall be given to you.[52]

In response to the "bad" or absent parents, Christianity calls its followers to exhibit the highest form of love and caring, love of the enemy and of the downtrodden.

There are many who do tremendous amounts for their parents and their children and are finding themselves caught in the middle, sometimes having to choose whose needs ought to be served when limited resources are available. The psychological and sociological literature present numerous cases of women, in particular, who have both young children and elderly parents who need help (mostly elderly mothers) and who believe, quite often, that a choice must be made between meeting obligations to the very young and meeting obligations to the very old within the family.[53]

As in the discussion above concerning competing obligations of gratitude, this analogous case is one of competing special obligations. In cases like these, obligations are thought to flow forward.[54] In other words, when filial obligations and obligations to children are both present, the obligations to the younger generations are thought to override those of filial obligations. Societal opinion as well as philosophical argument supports this line of thought. This judgment does not mean that, if one has an obligation to a young child, that person no longer has obligations to his or her parents. It means, rather, that at that particular moment, when only one of the obligations may be met, the filial obligation is overridden until such time as the obligation to the young is met. We must also specify that the situation envisioned above included the additional assumption that the required actions for both obligations were roughly equivalent in proportionate need. Certainly, needs outweigh requests, and so, even though obligations are forward flowing, a parent who has basic life-threatening needs may have a greater claim on the adult child for help than the young child has on his or her parent when the young child requires a minimal life-enhancing "need" or perhaps even a more minimal life-threatening need.

Aquinas, however, argues that scripture tells us that a son should support his parents if they need it, but the son should not plan or expect to support the parents because "naturally parents are not the successors of their children, but children of their parents."[55]

Wherefore since our father is related to us as principle, even as God is, it belongs properly to the father to receive honor from his children, and to the children to be provided by their parents with what is good for them. *Nevertheless in cases of necessity the child is bound out of the favors received to provide for his parents before all.*[56]

And again, he states that "in a case of extreme urgency, it would be lawful to abandon one's children rather than one's parents, to abandon whom it is by no means lawful, on account of the obligation we lie under towards them for the benefits we have received from them."[57]

In Question 26, Article 9, Aquinas argues that individuals are more closely connected with their children than with their parents. Aquinas argues that people should love parents more than they love their child because parents are more like God than the child is, for the father is a more exalted good. The better a thing is, the more like God it is and therefore the more it should be loved. In these ways, when viewed from the Catholic perspective, we see a difference in emphasis and importance between filial obligations and obligations to children, as opposed to society's views (hence, the label, "countercultural").

Let us also consider competing obligations between filial obligations and obligations to oneself. One's own projects and integrity matter.[58] We need to return to the concept of sacrifice. Self-sacrifice is not qualified by whether a person "deserves" another's sacrifice. The only relevant consideration is whether another needs your service or attention. If the need exists, then according to agape, you should try to fill it. If this action requires personal or self-sacrifice, that makes the action even more laudable. The Catholic tradition holds that humanity did not deserve the sacrifice of Jesus' life, but that we needed it. Therefore, if we are to act Christ-like, we must remember this ultimate sacrifice. Implicity appealed to in this Christian understanding of filial duties and the virtues that underlie them are the context of the family and the concept of self-sacrifice. As seen above, the Catholic tradition holds that the family as the primary community in which a person lives is the most important basis of the community. It is here that the important human relations nourish and strengthen a person.

The family is the basic unit of any community and is itself an expression of love. We cannot emphasize enough the critical role of the family in caring for their aging loved ones and keeping them in their midst as valuable, contributing members. The family is where the elderly feel most comfortable and accepted. We call on each family to weigh carefully its obligation to care for an elderly father or mother, uncle or aunt.[59]

Conclusion

This chapter has shown that, in fact, there are responsibilities and obligations that adult children have to their parents and that these are based on the virtues of charity, compassion, gratitude, and self-sacrifice. The emphasis on the family as the first cell of society and as the domestic church also leads us to see that, in fact, such obligations are primary and that there is indeed nothing "special" about them.

Endnotes

1. A point made clear to me in discussion with Stephen Post many years ago.

2. Strictly speaking, there is a philosophical difference between obligations and duties, but we will treat them as synonymous here.

3. Pope John Paul II, *The Role of the Christian Family in the Modern World (Familiaris Consortio)* (Boston: St. Paul's Editions, 1981).

4. Ibid 32.

5. The Bible, Revised Standard Version, Genesis 1–2.

6. *New World Dictionary Concordance to the New American Bible* s.v. "Love."

7. *Familiaris Consortio* 67. Emphasis added.

8. Ibid. 67.

9. Ibid. 67–68.

10. Ibid. 73. Emphasis added.

11. Ibid. 72.

12. Ibid. 70.

13. Ibid. 32.

14. Ibid. 76.

15. Mark 12:28–31.

16. Aquinas. Question 101, Article 3, 1627.

17. Catholic Bishops of the United States, *Society and the Aged: Toward Reconciliation* (Washington, DC: USCC, May 5, 1976) part I, paragraph 6.

18. Vatican Council, *The Documents of Vatican II* (New York: Herder, 1966) part II, chapter 1, section 48. Emphasis added.

19. Pius XII, "Scritte e Discorsi, II: The Holy Father Speaks to Newlyweds," in A. Werth and C. S. Mihanovich, eds., *Papal Pronouncements on Marriage and the Family* (Milwaukee: Bruce, 1955) 139.

20. Aquinas is one of the major influences on the tradition of Catholic moral theology and is a principal commentator (along with Augustine, Ambrose, and Peter Lombard) on scriptural interpretation. He applied the natural moral philosophy of Aristotle to Christian teachings and Revelation.

21. Aquinas. Question 101, Article 2.

22. Though it is possible to interpret this passage to mean that the parents essentially and uniquely contributed to the type or kind of person that the child had become, we can assume that this is not what Aquinas meant here, since in another section he defines what he means: "For father and mother are loved as principles of our natural origin. Now the father is principle in a more excellent way than the mother, because he is the active principle, while the mother is a passive and material principle. . . . In the begetting of man, the mother supplies the formless matter of the body; and the latter receives its form through the formative power that is in the semen of the father. And though this power cannot create the rational soul, yet it disposes the matter of the body to receive that form." [Question 26, Article 10, 1296].

23. Saint Thomas Aquinas, *Summa Theologica,* translated by Fathers of the English Dominican Province (Westminster, MD: Christian Classics, 1981) Question 101, Article 1, 1626. Emphasis added.

24. Pope John Paul II, *Letter to Families from Pope John Paul II* (Boston: St. Paul Books and Media, 1994) 49.

25. Matthew 10:34–39; cf. Luke 12:52.

26. Mark 3:31–35.

27. Luke 9:59–60.

28. 2 Corinthians 12:14.

29. Aquinas. Question 101, Article 4, 1628.

30. Ibid.

31. Ibid.

32. Ibid.

33. Ibid.

34. Mark 7:8–14; cf. Matthew 15:3–6.

35. Acts 7:14.

36. 1 Timothy 5:4.

37. 2 Timothy 3:2.

38. 1 Timothy 5:1–2.

39. 1 Timothy 5:8.

40. Aquinas. Question 31, Article 3; Question 106, Article 3.

41. Ibid. Question 106, Article 6.

42. J. Blustein, *Parents and Children: The Ethics of the Family* (Oxford: Oxford University, 1982) 61.

43. Aquinas. Question 106, Article 6, cited by Blustein, 61–62. Emphasis added.

44. G. C. Meilaender, *The Theory and Practice of Virtue* (Notre Dame, IN: University of Notre Dame, 1984) 168.

45. Aquinas. Question 26, Article 9.

46. Ibid. Question 103, Article 1.

47. Patti Davis is the daughter of the former President and Mrs. Ronald Reagan. Her virtually nonexistent literary career took off with a supposed work of fiction that closely resembled her life and revealed much that was embarrassing to her parents.

48. Based on the book in the Spanish by L. Esquivel, *Como Agua Por Chocolate*.

49. B. Williams, "A Critique of Utilitarianism," in J. J. C. Smart and B. Williams, eds., *Utilitarianism: For & Against* (Cambridge, England: Cambridge University, 1988) 108–118.

50. *Letter to Families from Pope John Paul II: 1994 Year of the Family* 61–62.

51. *Society and the Aged: Toward Reconciliation* Part III, section B, paragraph 40.

52. Luke 6:27–34, 36–38; cf Matthew 5:39, 5:45, 7:12.

53. E. M. Brody et al., "Women's Changing Roles and Help to Elderly Parents: Attitudes of Three Generations of Women," in *Journal of Gerontology* 38(5) (September 1983) 597–607; E. M. Brody et al., "What Should Adult Children do for Elderly Parents?" in *Journal of Gerontology* 39(6) (November 1984) 736–746; E. M. Brody, "Filial Care of the Elderly and Changing Roles of Women (and Men)" in *Journal of Geriatric Psychiatry* 19(2) (1986) 175–201; S. L. Hanson et al., "Racial and Cohort Variations in Filial Responsibility Norms," in *The Gerontologist* 23(6) (1983) 626–631; T. Premo, "A Blessing to our Declining Years: Feminine Response to Filial Duty in the New Republic," in *International Journal of Aging and Human Development* 20(1) (1984–5) 69–74.

54. H. Sidgwick, *The Methods of Ethics* (Chicago: University of Chicago, 1962).

55. Aquinas. Question 101, Article 2.

56. Ibid. Question 26, Article 9.

57. Ibid. Question 31, Article 3.

58. Williams, 108–118.

59. *Society and the Aged: Toward Reconciliation,* part III, section B, paragraph 39.

8

THE EVOLVING TEACHING ON PEACE WITHIN ROMAN CATHOLIC HIERARCHICAL THOUGHT*

JUDITH A. DWYER

University of St. Thomas

The quest for international peace is complex, one which engages many important themes in modern Catholic social teaching: reverence for creation, a sense of responsibility for the ecological health of the planet, the solidarity of the human family in terms of rights and duties, and the emerging sense of global interdependence. Catholic social teaching also recognizes that eschatological tension marks contemporary life: the grace of the Kingdom of God is already present, but the fullness of God's reign has not yet been realized. A certain tension therefore exists between the vision of God's reign and its concrete realization in history. Within this context, the Catholic Church situates its treatment of peace. A true peace, which is always more than the absence of war, flourishes in a social order founded on truth, built on justice, enlivened by love and refined in freedom.[1]

This essay attempts to trace some key developments in Catholic hierarchical teaching on peace as they have emerged over the past one hundred years, most notably since World War II.[2] It is a topic that necessarily involves many interlocking issues: just-war theory, pacifism, deterrence, disarmament, development, education, and the call for a "theology of peace."[3]

The Presumption Against the Use of Force

Maintaining peace in an exceptionally fragile international community has been a major challenge to humanity and a key theme in Catholic teaching, especially in this century. *That* all people of good will desire peace is assumed; how best to achieve this goal is where sharp disagreement emerges. Both just-war theory and pacifism share the presumption that binds all Christians: we should do no harm to our neighbor; how we treat our enemy reflects the degree to which we love our neighbor; the possibility of taking even one human life should be contemplated in fear and trembling.[4] Both just-war theory and pacifism, therefore, share a presumption against the use of force as a means to resolve conflict. The positions differ, of course, concerning the legitimacy of overriding this presumption against war.

Just-War Theory

Just-war theory holds that short of the fullness of the Kingdom of God, efforts to pursue both peace and justice can, at times, be in tension, given the reality of sin and the inordinate quest for power or material gain that result from sin. The struggle for justice, which is the foundation of a true peace, may therefore necessitate some restricted use of force in order to achieve a context in which human dignity and human rights may flourish.

The just-war criteria, which developed over centuries of thought, include the *jus ad bellum* principles of just cause, right intention, call to war by legitimate authority, reasonable hope of success, and war as last resort. The *jus in bello* principles of just-war theory include discrimination, which protects the innocent from direct attack in war, and proportionality, which holds that the "goods" one is trying to achieve in combat (protection of human life, restoration of political rights, and so forth) must outweigh the "evils" that will surely result from war (loss of human life, destruction of property, and so forth).

Modern Catholic hierarchical teaching notes three key developments in the evolution of just-war theory. In 1944, Pius XII restricted the "just cause" for taking up arms to that of *self-defense,* thereby removing the right to punish an offense and the right to recover something as justifiable reasons for going to war. The pontiff cited two reasons for this important revision: (1) the enormous violence of modern warfare itself, and (2) the fact that aggressive war blocks the progress of the international community by inhibiting the creativity and positive good that humanity might bring to conflict resolution.[5]

The second major development in Catholic social teaching is Vatican II's *The Church in the Modern World,* which takes up "the fostering of peace and the establishment of a community of nations" as one of its questions of special urgency.[6] While the Council does not explicitly use the just-war theory, the logic of that construct clearly underlies its teaching, as for example, when it recognizes the right of a nation to engage in legitimate defense, and reaffirms the role of legitimate authority to protect the people entrusted to its care. The Council notes, however, that not all use of force is necessarily just; it explicitly condemns total war, as well as "every act of war directed to the indiscriminate destruction of whole cities or vast areas with their inhabitants," as a crime against God and the human community.[7]

Finally, the very detailed use of just-war criteria in the United States bishops' 1983 *Challenge of Peace* represents an important contribution at efforts to restrict violence in the modern world. The bishops outrightly condemn indiscriminate nuclear or conventional warfare, determine that any "first use" of nuclear weapons is disproportionate, and remain highly skeptical about the possibility of fighting a retaliatory, "limited" nuclear war within the confines of justice.[8]

In sum, recent Catholic social teaching, while continuing to recognize the legitimacy of the just-war theory, employs that theory to restrict, ever more clearly, certain uses of force. The just-war principle of *last-resort,* for instance, increasingly points to the overriding emphasis in the teaching: nonviolent solutions ought to dominate the means by which the modern world resolves conflict. This emphasis is clearly evident in John Paul II's most recent encyclical, *The 100th Year (Centesimus Annus),* which presents a detailed analysis of the events of 1989, the year that witnessed dramatic and irrevocable shifts in the international landscape. These events prove "that the complex problems . . . can be resolved through dialogue and solidarity rather than by a struggle to destroy the enemy through war."[9] Similarly, the emphasis on nonviolent resolution of conflict was evident in the efforts by the United States bishops before the commencement of fighting in the Persian Gulf. Archbishop Daniel Pilarcyzk, president of the National Conference of Catholic Bishops, wrote to President George Bush, and

urged, "the moral imperative of persistent pursuit of nonviolent international pressure to halt and reverse Iraq's aggression without resort to war."[10]

Pacifism

One of the most remarkable developments in modern Catholic social teaching is the recognition of pacifism as a viable position for a Roman Catholic.
In 1956, Pius XII clearly taught that the right of a nation to defend itself
against aggression and the declaration of war by legitimate authority required that a Roman Catholic take up arms, if called to do so. A Catholic
could not in good conscience refuse to participate in such a war.[11] Vatican
II, however, argued that "laws should make humane provision for the case
of conscientious objectors who refuse to carry arms, provided they accept
some other form of community service."[12] This is the first time in official
Catholic teaching that the church argues for the rights of those who, in
conscience, refuse to engage in warfare. Note that the Church also recognizes the continued obligation of all citizens, including conscientious objectors, to contribute to the common good through some form of
community service. Implied here is the recognition that conscientious objectors, while removing themselves from direct engagement in fighting, do
not remove themselves from participation, through forms of public service,
in the political/social communities in which they live.

Challenge of Peace treated the issue of "the pacifist option" for the
Catholic more fully when it articulated the theological and moral rationale
that pacifists use to defend their position. The document went on to claim
just-war teaching and nonviolence as two distinct moral responses that
have a "complementary relationship," in the sense that both seek to serve
the common good, and both testify to the Christian conviction that peace
must be pursued and rights defended within moral restraints and in the
context of defining other basic human values. The bishops hasten to add,
however, that the "pacifist option" is open only to individuals, since a
government threatened by aggression must defend the people entrusted to
its care.[13] The document assumes that defense of the people might necessitate the use of force, provided just-war criteria are met.

Elsewhere, Challenge of Peace discusses just-war teaching and nonviolence "as distinct but interdependent methods of evaluating warfare. . . . We believe the two perspectives support and complement one

another, each preserving the other from distortion." Cited here are three links between the distinct positions: the shared presumption against the use of force, the shared Christian tradition, and the common opposition to methods of warfare that are indistinguishable from total warfare.[14] These developments regarding pacifism within Catholic teaching provide important areas for further reflection and research. For instance, the United States bishops' claim that just-war theory and pacifism have a "complementary relationship" certainly warrants more thorough analysis. Such a claim has generated more confusion than clarity.[15] Similarly, the relationship between pacifism and nonviolence needs more exploration, as does the entire issue of pluralism within Roman Catholicism.

Deterrence as a "Peace of a Sort"

The most complicated aspect of peace analysis is the question of deterrence. Is deterrence the best way to maintain peace in the nuclear age, as some theorists contend?[16] Does it provide humanity with a "peace of a sort," an argument that Vatican II admitted into its treatment of the question?[17] Recent Catholic social thought on the matter takes its cue from John Paul II's 1982 assessment that, given the precarious international situation, deterrence, not as an end in itself, but as a step on the way to progressive disarmament, may be judged to be morally acceptable. The pontiff warns, however, that in order to ensure peace, it is indispensable not to be satisfied with this minimum, which is always susceptible to the real danger of explosion.[18] John Paul II, however, neither analyzes the type of deterrence strategy at work, nor investigates the intention that lies behind the threat of deterrence.

Since the 1982 papal assessment, several major Catholic bishops' conferences have addressed the question of deterrence. In *The Challenge of Peace* (1983), the United States bishops rendered a "conditioned moral acceptance" to deterrence, although they insisted that the *raison d'etre* of the strategy must be to prevent use of nuclear weapons, that the quest for nuclear superiority must be rejected, and that deterrence should be used as a step toward progressive disarmament.[19] The bishops, however, still left many aspects of the morality of deterrence unresolved. This fact was not lost on the bishops, who raised a series of questions in *The Challenge of Peace*: May a nation threaten what it may never do? May it possess what it may never use? Who is involved in the threat each superpower makes: government officials or military personnel or the citizenry in whose defense the threat is made?[20] In *The Challenge of Peace,* the bishops recognized that threat is integral to the effectiveness of deterrence; they neither explored the legitimacy of such a threat, nor did they judge who is involved in the threat.

The French and West German Catholic bishops also explored the morality of deterrence in 1983.[21] The French bishops argued that "peace is still being served when an aggressor is discouraged and constrained to the beginning of wisdom as a result of an appropriate fear." Maintaining that the threat of force is not the use of force and that it is not evident whether the immorality of use renders the threat immoral, the French bishops therefore concluded that deterrence is the lesser of two evils, since abandonment of the deterrence could provoke nuclear blackmail or loss of national life, liberty, and identity. The West German bishops, asserting that nuclear deterrence is not a reliable instrument for preventing war in the long run, nevertheless interpreted John Paul II's 1982 assessment as toleration of deterrence, a position with which they agree, as long as deterrence demonstrably serves to prevent nuclear war.

Disarmament: The Road to Peace

Catholic social teaching has unwaveringly denounced the arms race as a grave threat to the establishment of a true global peace. Since Pius XII's 1951 condemnation of the arms race as a disproportionate drain of human and material resources,[22] papal and conciliar statements have labeled the arms race as a treacherous trap, an intolerable scandal, an insanity, a symptom of disorder, a diabolical capacity, a costly madness, a machine running mad, an act of aggression since its high cost starves the poor to death, a tragic contradiction. Queried John Paul II, "Are the children to receive the arms race from us as a necessary inheritance? How are we to explain this unbridled race?"[23] A clear call for an immediate halt to this technological runaway, therefore, has been the consistent position of the Catholic hierarchy on this pressing issue; the Church, moreover, has repeatedly argued for a bilateral, gradual, secure, and verifiable dismantlement of the stockpiled nuclear armaments and has supported negotiations aimed at reducing and limiting conventional forces.[24]

The hierarchy's position on nuclear disarmament disappoints some Catholic pacifists who endorse the call for unilateral disarmament; they argue that trust in weapons of such massive destruction violates the Christian's first priority, namely, to trust in God.[25] The hierarchical position, however, has placed the prevention of nuclear war as its overriding consideration, and has not wanted to risk the possibility that unilateral disarmament might provoke such a war, should an aggressor take advantage of a vulnerable opponent. The United States bishops have encouraged unilateral *initiatives* that might establish a more trusting political climate.[26]

The Catholic Church clearly sees disarmament as the road to global peace, though it realizes that such a path is long and complicated. The arms race, nuclear or conventional, is consistently envisioned as a strategy that only fosters distrust among nations and needlessly squanders human talents and resources—precious commodities desperately needed for human and social development.

Development: A New Name for Peace

Since Paul VI's 1967 encyclical, *On the Development of Peoples (Populorum Progressio)*, Catholic social teaching has emphasized the interlocking nature of authentic development and true peace.[27] Authentic development, a complete and integral development that promotes the good of the human person, of every human being, and society as a whole, eliminates excessive inequities, thereby providing a solid foundation upon which humanity can construct a true peace.

Subsequent papal encyclicals, especially John Paul II's 1987 encyclical, *On Social Concern (Sollicitudo Rei Socialis),* and the annual "World Day of Peace" messages have developed the insight of Paul VI by insisting that God has bestowed a precious dignity upon each human being and that grounded in this human nature are certain basic rights, the denial of which thwarts individual human fulfillment and the well-being of society as a whole. These include rights to the fulfillment of material needs (such as food, clothing, shelter), a guarantee of fundamental freedoms, and the protection of relationships that are essential to participation in the life of the society. In his writings, John Paul II consistently cites certain contemporary practices that prevent human solidarity and development: a xenophobia that closes nations in on themselves, ideologies that foster racial hatred or religious intolerance, and unjust or arbitrary border closings that separate families.[28]

On the international level, development includes the elimination of such problems as North-South inequalities, especially in the area of technology, the external debt of developing countries, the rise of insurgency and counterinsurgency warfare, and global terrorism.

Catholic social teaching evidences sharp awareness that the human community is interconnected and interdependent. Peace, a value without frontiers,[29] cannot be established in a just and lasting fashion except through broader cooperation at the regional, continental, and international levels.

World Peace and the Environment

In his "World Day of Peace" message for January 1, 1990, John Paul II makes a significant link between world peace and the environmental crisis. "In our day, there is a growing awareness that world peace is threatened not only by the arms race, regional conflicts and continued injustices among peoples and nations, but also by a lack of *due respect for nature,* by the plundering of natural resources and by a progressive decline in the quality of life."[30] The pontiff cites an indiscriminate application of advances in science and technology and the lack of respect for life itself as the root causes for the current environmental crisis. He calls for a renewed sense of our common heritage, a new moral solidarity among all people, and a more internationally coordinated approach to the management of the earth's goods.

This 1990 "World Day of Peace" message closely follows John Paul II's 1987 encyclical, *On Social Concern,* a document hailed as "a landmark in Catholic participation in the environment movement,"[31] and anticipates some of the ideas found in *The 100th Year.*[32] John Paul II insists that authentic development neither forgets the finitude of natural resources nor neglects the fragility of the environment. Global peace is threatened when humanity abuses the elements of nature and ignores the consequences of environmental pollution. Global peace is also threatened when consumer civilizations of the rich, highly developed societies absorb a disproportionate amount of the world's food and energy supplies, at the expense of the remaining societies, in which many people die each day from starvation or suffer from acute malnutrition.

Peacemaking and Education

The responsibility to foster peace is not limited to governments, however, but entails a conversion within each human heart. Education, through family activities, in the local parish, and at all levels of formal learning, is a practical yet key ingredient for changing hearts and opening minds.

Family life provides crucial opportunities to impart values that foster peace. The development of nonviolent, cooperative attitudes and skills in children in a home environment that supports affirmation, affection, cooperative chores and games, is an important responsibility that parents can exercise to offset the violence so often found in today's world. Creating time and space for family prayer, vacations, family meetings to resolve domestic conflicts, and corporate projects that engage the political/military establishment (for instance, letter writing to Congressional representatives) are concrete ways in which a family can learn about peace and justice. Parental example is especially crucial here, since a wife and husband who strive for martial harmony provide irreplaceable role models.[33]

The parish community is also an important locus in which creative peace education can take place. Perhaps the greatest challenge to parish ministers is to encourage the congregation to think of justice, the foundation of a true peace, as a "constitutive dimension of the preaching of the Gospel,"[34] and not as some marginal cause, relevant to only a few "activist" members of the parish. Within the parish setting, the study of Scripture, fasting and prayer as a congregation, workshops on nonviolent conflict resolution, and the liturgy itself are just a few of the many channels that are available to a parish community that seeks to become a living "sign of peace" to the wider community.

Formal education on peace, at all levels of learning, remains indispensable for the shaping of a more peaceful world. The classroom can teach younger children about the beauty of the world and the various peoples/culture within it; it can also impart to them the importance of resolving disputes through negotiation. Education can also introduce high school and college students, by the use of films and eyewitness accounts of war, to the realistic dimensions of combat. At this level, a reverence for life, a sense of responsibility for the ecological well-being of the planet, an awareness of global interdependence, and a challenge to develop imaginative solutions to conflict situations should permeate an interdisciplinary high school or university curriculum.[35]

Toward a "Theology of Peace"

Vatican II called for "a completely fresh reappraisal of war,"[36] when it examined the fostering of peace and establishment of a community of nations as one of its questions of special urgency. Since the Council, the political and economic shifts within the international community have been exceptionally dramatic; one almost has the sense that the human community is experiencing the final decade of this century as though it were participating in a "fast forward" global video. The movement toward more democratic structures within the Soviet Union, the stirring events of 1989 and their impact on Central and Eastern Europe, and the struggle in South Africa concerning apartheid are just a few of the major shifts occurring within the fragile international community. All point to the need for a new attitude toward conflict and to the development of a theology of peace.

Challenge of Peace provides key features that should characterize such a theology.[37] Drawing from biblical studies, systematic theology, moral theology, and the experience and insights of members of the church, a theology of peace must first ground the task of peacemaking solidly in the scriptural vision of God's Kingdom and indicate how such a task is central to the ministry of the church. This ecclesial question is key, since the Catholic Church has committed itself to the role of a "public church"; it therefore must resist a secretarian position on this question. A theology of peace must also incorporate the insights of social and political sciences, identify the specific contributions that a community of faith can make to peace efforts, and relate these to the wider work of peace pursued by other groups and institutions in society. Finally, a theology of peace must offer a message of hope to a fragmented world desperately in search of peace.

Conclusion

Peace is both gift and task, requiring the work of human hands and minds and hearts. Short of the fullness of the reign of God, the disciples of Jesus Christ, on pilgrimage in the modern world, work toward shaping a peaceful world that claims justice as its foundation. Working ecumenically, but also with all people of good will, the Catholic Church and its one hundred years of social teaching testify to a hope for a brighter future and to a belief in a

God who wills a time for us when the fullness of God's Kingdom is realized and justice and peace eternally embrace.

Endnotes

*This essay first appeared in *Journal for Peace & Justice Studies,* Volume 3, Number 2, 1991, and is used with permission.

1. John XXIII, "Peace on Earth (Pacem in Terris)" #37, as found in David J. O'Brien and Thomas A. Shannon, eds., *Renewing the Earth: Catholic Documents on Peace, Justice, and Liberation* (New York: Doubleday, 1977).

2. Although the post World War II era marks the most significant evolution in Catholic hierarchical teaching on peace, papal statements concerning international peace were issued throughout the century. For statements from Leo XIII, see Franziskus Stratmann, *The Church and War: A Catholic Study* (New York: P.J. Kennedy and Sons, 1928); Piux X, "Exhortation to All Catholics on the Outbreak of the Great War," August 2, 1914, as found in John Eppstein, *The Catholic Tradition of the Law of Nations* (London: Burns, Oates, and Washbourne, 1935)203; Benedict XV, "Exhortation to the Catholics of the Whole World," September 8, 1914, *Acta Apostolicae Sedis,* vol. 6 (1914) 201; *Ad Beatissimi, Acta Apostolicae Sedis* vol. 6 (1914) 565; *Pacem Dei munus pulcherrimum,* as found in *The Catholic Tradition of the Law of Nations* 236–42; Piux XI, "Letter to the Archbishop of Genoa," and "Apostolic Letter Nova Impendet," in *The Catholic Tradition of the Law of Nations* 177; Rene Coste, *Le probléme du droit de querre dans la pensée de Pie XII* (Paris: Aubier, 1962); Gustav Gundlach, "Die Lehre Pius XII vom modernen Krieg," in *Stimmim der Zeit* 164 (April, 1959) 1–14.

3. The call for the development of a "theology of peace" is found in National Conference of Catholic Bishops, *The Challenge of Peace: God's Promise and Our Response* (Washington, DC: United States Catholic Conference, 1983) #24–25. In this essay, I do not examine the biblical foundations for peace. See *The Challenge of Peace* #27–55.

4. *Challenge of Peace* #80.

5. Pius XII, "Christmas Message, 1944," in *Acta Apostolicae Sedis* 37 (1945) 18. See also, John Courtney Murray, "Remarks on the Moral Problems of War," in *Theological Studies* 20 (1959) 40–61.

6. *Pastoral Constitution on the Church in the Modern World (Gaudium et Spes)* #77–93 as found in Austin Flannery, ed., *Vatican Council II: The Conciliar and Post Conciliar Documents* (Grand Rapids, MI: Eerdmans, rev. ed., 1988).

7. *Church in the Modern World* #79–80.

8. *Challenge of Peace* #142–61.

9. John Paul II, *The 100th Year (Centesimus Annus)* in *Origins* vol. 21 no. 1 (May 16, 1991) with quote at #22.

10. See "Letter to President Bush," in *Origins* vol.20 no. 25 (November 29, 1990) 397, 399–400, with quote at 397.

11. Pius XII, "Christmas Radio Message," December 23, 1956, in *Peace and Disarmament* (Rome: Pontifical Commission Iustitia et Pax, 1982) 137.

12. *Church in the Modern World* #79.

13. *Challenge of Peace* #74–75.

14. *Challenge of Peace* #120–21.

15. See the thoughtful analysis of Kenneth R. Himes, "Pacifism and the Just War Tradition in Roman Catholic Social Teaching," in John A. Coleman, ed., *One Hundred Years of Catholic Social Thought: Celebration and Challenge* (Maryknoll: Orbis, 1991) 329–44.

16. See, for example, the writings of William V. O'Brien. Recent contributions from O'Brien include William V. O'Brien and John Langan, eds., *The Nuclear Dilemma and the Just War Tradition* (Lexington, MA: Lexington, 1986); and O'Brien, *The Conduct of Just and Limited War* (New York: Praeger, 1981).

17. *Church in the Modern World* #81.

18. John Paul II, "Message to United Nations Special Session 1982," #8, and quoted in *Challenge of Peace* #172–73.

19. *Challenge of Peace* #162–99. In 1988, the United States bishops re-evaluated and reaffirmed their position on "continued moral acceptance" of deterrence, as articulated in *The Challenge of Peace*. See "Building Peace: A Pastoral Reflection on the Response to *The Challenge of Peace*," in *Origins* vol. 18 no.9 (July 21, 1988) 129, 131–48.

20. *Challenge of Peace* #137.

21. Joint Pastoral Letter of the West German Bishops, *Out of Justice, Peace* and Joint Pastoral Letter of the French Bishops, *Winning the Peace*, as found in James V. Schall, ed. (San Francisco: Ignatius, 1984). Of course, many other national conferences have addressed questions related to international peace; for example, the Catholic bishops in Austria, Belgium, East Germany, Great Britain, Hungary, Ireland, Japan, the Netherlands, and Scotland have all issued statements concerning peace in the modern world.

22. Pius XII, "Address to Participants in the World Congress for the Universal Movement for World Federation," April, 1951, found in Vincent A. Yzermans, ed., *The Major Addresses of Pope Pius XII* vol. 1 (St. Paul: North Central, 1961) 143.

23. John Paul II, "The Dignity of the Human Person Is the Basis of Justice and Peace," Address to the United Nations, October 2, 1979, in *The Pope Speaks* 26 (1981) 310.

24. The recent U.S.A./U.S.S.R. decision to cut strategic weapons is one major sign of hope to the international community. See R. W. Apple, Jr., "Superpower Weapons Treaty First to Cut Strategic Bombs," in *New York Times* (July 18, 1991) 1, 10.

25. See, for instance, the thinking of Daniel Berrigan in *The Discipline of the Mountain: Dante's Purgatorio in a Nuclear World* (New York: Seabury, 1979).

26. *Challenge of Peace* #200–73.

27. Paul VI, *On the Development of Peoples* as found in *Renewing the Earth.*

28. See, for instance, John Paul II, *On Social Concern* (Boston: Daughters of S. Paul, 1988).

29. John Paul II, "World Day of Peace Message, 1986" in *Origins* vol. 15 (1986) 461–64.

30. John Paul II, *The Ecological Crisis: A Common Responsibility,* World Day of Peace Message, 1990 (Washington, DC: United States Catholic Conference, 1990) with quote at page 3, emphasis is original.

31. Drew Christiansen, "Ecology, Justice, and Development," in *Theological Studies* vol. 51 no. 1 (March, 1990) 64–81, with quote at 68.

32. John Paul II, *The 100th Year* #37.

33. *Challenge of Peace* #306. See also, James and Kathleen McGinnis, "The Social Mission of the Christian Family," in Judith A. Dwyer, ed., *Questions of Special Urgency: The Church in the Modern World Two Decades after Vatican II* (Washington, DC: Georgetown University, 1986) 37–52.

34. World Synod of Bishops, *Justice in the World,* introduction, as found in *Renewing the Earth.*

35. See my essay, "The Catholic Bishops' Peace Pastoral and Higher Education," in *Harvard Educational Review* vol. 54 no. 3 (August, 1984) 315–20.

36. *Church in the Modern World* #80.

37. *Challenge of Peace* #24–25.

9

THE DIGNITY OF WORK
AND ECONOMIC CONCERNS

SALLY J. SCHOLZ

Villanova University

A Christian ethic is one that grounds decision-making on the ethical teachings found in the New Testament and particularly in the gospel message of Christ. Among the primary components of a Christian ethic are the value of life, the uniqueness of each individual human person (Gn 1:27, Mt 10:30, Lk 12:7, 1 Cor 12:4–7), the interconnectedness of the global family, the importance of the community or common good (Acts 2:44, 4:32), and an obligation to the poor and suffering or those in need (Heb 3:12–14).

These principles of a Christian ethic allow us to discuss a number of issues, ranging from the value of life to social responsibility for the poor and oppressed. In what follows, I articulate a Christian ethical stance on the issue of work. After defining what counts as work, I address three main questions and several related issues: Does every person have a right to work? Does every person have an obligation to work? What other economic concerns need to be addressed in order to uphold the dignity of every human person?

First of all, what counts as work? Work is thought of as providing a service or skill in exchange for a wage. The service or skill may or may not be exercised in the production of something. Thus, skills exercised in the manufacture of goods are "work," as are skills that provide services such as medical assistance or education. In this chapter, I wish to expand this definition to also include work that does not receive a wage but is nonetheless valued. For example, our definition of work needs to include those traditionally uncompensated household tasks that are necessary for the running and maintenance of a family as well as other creative or valued tasks that may not always receive a wage. In addition, the skill or service ought to be determined by the individual performing it so as to best incorporate that person's talents as well as her or his current and future plans or projects. Work, then, is the freely chosen service or the exercise of a skill in the creation of a product that is valuable to society.

This definition of work highlights a number of important aspects of work within a Christian ethical framework. It entails a notion of a "unique capacity" used for or valued by society as whole. This unique capacity is a gift from God used by the individual to promote the good of the community and thus his or her own good. While we commonly think of work as a task performed to help care for oneself and one's family, it is also true that work may be done to lend care to those who cannot fully provide for themselves, or it may provide a specialized service for the community.

Thus far we have merely defined work. The next step in examining work from a Christian ethical perspective is to determine whether or not each human person has a right to work and what the nature of that right is.

What Is a Right?

Generally speaking, a right is something to which a person has a claim. This claim is grounded in what is morally correct or upholds standards of justice, that is, the right must be guaranteed so that an individual's claim to something is ensured. In other words, for every right there is a corresponding responsibility. The guarantor of a right enables the free exercise of that right or does not infringe in areas of the right holder's life that are protected by the right.

Two broad-based categories of rights are legal rights and moral rights. Legal rights are those guaranteed by law. An example of a legal right is the right to free practice of religion without state interference as guaranteed in the First Amendment of the United States Constitution. The right to private property is another example of a legal right. Moral rights are constructed more broadly and may include such things as a right not to go hungry, the right of people and innocent animals not to suffer, or, as some have argued, the right of the natural world not to be destroyed.

Legal rights are created by a state in order to ensure the proper functioning of that state and the protection of the individuals who reside under the state's jurisdiction. Any given legal right may or may not be informed by a specifically perceived moral right. Generally speaking, however, legal rights are based on some sort of morally permissible or morally prohibited action. Moral rights stem from a normative moral theory. Since the normative theory for our discussion of work is a Christian ethic, moral rights stem from our human perception or understanding of the will of God. God, then, is the ultimate guarantor of moral rights in this context. However, we as humans must serve as God's auxiliaries. We, as individuals and as a community, must strive to uphold the moral rights of each human person.

Do We Have a Right to Work?

Human rights is a category of moral rights that pertain to human beings, determined by the basic requirements for human dignity. For Christian ethics, human dignity entails a recognition of the unique powers and gifts of each individual as a creation of God and the responsibility to use these gifts to advance the common good of all. Since work allows the individual to strive to achieve his or her full potential while also emphasizing a sense of social responsibility, it is one of the criteria of human dignity and is thus a human right.

This argument deserves further explication. Since each human being is uniquely created by God, and is endowed with rationality, free choice, and creative capacity, to prohibit any individual from exercising these gifts is to act contrary to the will of God. It might be argued that work is only one of many possible ways in which an individual may exercise his or her creativity and autonomy. For example, one might spend his or her time creating a beautiful painting, writing a book, raising children, or planting a garden, that is, doing tasks for which he or she does not receive a wage. However, given the definition of work presented above, remuneration is not the criterion by which we judge some activity as "work." Thus, the objection only points out some activities that facilitate the flourishing of the individual through the exercise of creativity and autonomy. Indeed, one could argue that the activities listed in the above objection are freely chosen activities in service to the community (and the individual) and thus may be considered work. Insofar as each individual human person has the opportunity to perform a task in fulfillment of his or her human dignity and uniqueness, then that person's right to work has been upheld.

In 1948 the United Nations General Assembly adopted a statement called the Universal Declaration of Human Rights. This document is meant to apply to all members of humankind and was not explicitly grounded on any specific religious moral normative theory. However, the wisdom displayed in the document is in accordance with Christian ethical principles of the dignity of the person, the solidarity of all members of the global family, and the equality of persons. Articles 23 and 24 of this document pertain directly to the question of whether or not we have a right to work:

> Article 23. (1) Everyone has the right to work, to free choice of employment, to just and favourable conditions of work and to protection against unemployment. (2) Everyone, without any discrimination, has the right to equal pay for equal work. (3) Everyone who works has the right to just and favourable remuneration ensuring for himself [herself] and his [her] family an existence worthy of human dignity, and supplemented, if necessary, by other means of social protection. (4) Everyone has the right to form and to join trade unions for the protection of his [her] interests.
>
> Article 24. Everyone has the right to rest and leisure, including reasonable limitation of working hours and periodic holidays with pay.[1]

According to the United Nations, then, every human being has a right to work. That right is also protected by a number of additional rights to guarantee that other aspects of the worker's human dignity are not compromised.

The first point under Article 23 of the United Nations document asserts the right to work. The Declaration is not based on any particular political or religious system but is rather a general statement to which the signing countries can agree. It is an assertion of what the participating nations take to be the basic minimum standards of human dignity, that is, the basic standards under which an individual cannot only survive, but may also thrive.

Work, then, is just such a standard. But work must be freely chosen rather than coerced or enslaved labor. In addition, the conditions and/or environment within which a person works must not be harmful to the person's health or dignity. These conditions are in keeping with Christian ethical principles in that there is both a stress on the value and preservation of life and an emphasis on the dignity of that life.

Similarly, just as Christian ethics asserts the equality of all human beings, the United Nations statement of human rights asserts the equality of all persons in work. This equality is upheld, in part, through providing "equal pay for equal work," as the second point in Article 23 makes clear. Such a policy of equal pay for equal work would in part mean that the "natural" degradation of individuals is removed. By this I mean that, without such a standard, a community runs the risk of assigning its most degrading or difficult forms of work to those individuals perceived to be already degraded or inferior. Examples of this pairing of "natural degradation" with degrading or difficult work might be when a community requires its prisoners to sweep out sewers or quarry rock, or when society (whether consciously or unconsciously by means of coercive economic conditions) forces immigrants to perform sweat-shop labor.

Notice that the United Nations makes a strong statement in favor of the worker. According to the Declaration, workers have a right to a just wage. The just wage is determined according to a family existence worthy of human dignity, entailing such basic needs as clean drinking water, adequate health care, proper shelter and clothing, and substantial diet. If the wage is inadequate to provide such needs, then it is the responsibility of the state or the community to provide for its people. The Christian ethical perspective puts the dignity of each individual in a sort of symbolic relation with the good of the community, that is, every human person is integral to the community, and the state of affairs in the community affects the status of dignity for the individual. This being the case, any economic policy must be measured according to its impact on the community as a whole as well as on each and every individual person in that community.[2]

It is also worth noting that some wages are unjust not because of how small they are, but because of how large they are. When a wage exceeds the amount necessary for the maintenance of self and family, then it must be evaluated according to the Christian ethical principles listed above. For example, such a wage might be measured according to its effect on the community. Similarly, does the excessive wage lead the individual who receives it into a self-interested existence rather than an existence that emphasizes the common good? In other words, the excessively large wage may cause the individual to fail to see her or his responsibility to the community while it also directly and adversely affects that community. This is to say nothing of the overall harm to the community caused by competition for such wages.

The fourth point in Article 23 of the United Nations Declaration ensures that the individual is empowered to participate in the important decision-making procedures that affect her or his working conditions. The good of the individual human person and the good of the community are intertwined according to Christian ethics. This being the case, work ought to be measured not only according to the output of a service or product on behalf of a community, but also to the maintenance of the dignity of each participant in the process. Dignity in self and, by implication, dignity in work results from the exercise of one's unique talents and gifts. Having the ability to shape how those gifts are used in service to self and community means that each individual makes plans or sets projects and participates in the decisions that affect her or his ability to carry out those plans or projects.

Finally, it is important to limit work so that individuals may have time to develop other aspects of their human personality as well as spend time with family and friends. Thus, the United Nations *Declaration* like a Christian ethical response to the right to work, includes a statement about the need for leisure time so as to ensure that, while we validate the right to work, we in no way validate or legitimate the exploitation of the worker.

Who Guarantees the Right to Work?

For every right there is a corresponding obligation so that a person's claim is guaranteed. The right to work must be of the nature to fit this model, and yet there is no one person or group of people responsible for finding dignified, unexploitative work for each and every human being. On the contrary, the right to work functions more like the right not to go hungry, that is, the right not to go hungry occasionally steps in to override another right, such as someone else's right to private property. For example, if my private property is such that it interferes with your ability to obtain food, then your right not to go hungry overrides my right to private property.[3] One could imagine a situation in which one individual's private property spanned the length of a river. The property owner, in an attempt to "do with his/her property as he/she wills," reroutes a substantial portion of the water of the river onto his/her property for irrigation purposes. The rerouting of the river, while not causing the original path of the river to be interrupted, severely decreases the flow of water over that original path, thereby causing a decrease in the amount of fish present in the river. In this scenario, one could certainly argue that the right of people inhabiting the village downstream not to go hungry overrides the right of the property owner to "do with his/her property as he/she wills."

Similar to the right not to go hungry, the right to work may function to limit other rights and inform other obligations. An example like the one above is the conflict between the right to private property and the right to work. A person's right to private property usually entails the right to use and dispose of the property as he or she wishes. If, then, as the owner of a factory, I decide to layoff *arbitrarily* three quarters of my employees with no advance warning and no unemployment insurance, I may be in violation of their right to work.[4] Similarly, as a property owner, one may be under the mistaken assumption that one could pay his or her employees unequal wages based on arbitrary standards or hire and fire based on those same arbitrary standards (*arbitrary standards* here might include such things as race, sex, and religion, but not such things as job performance, skill level, knowledge required, and degree of difficulty).

Do All Types of Work Fulfill the "Right to Work"?

Not all work supports or upholds the dignity of the individual. Some work may be demeaning and actually detract from a person's sense of personal autonomy or responsibility. When work goes against human dignity or is degrading, it does not fulfill the requirements of an individual's right to work. Adina Schwartz argues that, in order for work to respect people as autonomous subjects, it must be restructured so that the decision-makers and those who execute the decisions are not separate, hierarchically ordered workers.

Schwartz's argument is based on a notion of autonomy as a "process of integrating one's personality." In other words, autonomy means "coming to see all one's pursuits as subject to one's activity of planning and to view all one's experiences as providing a basis for evaluating and adjusting one's beliefs, methods, and aims."[5] This understanding of autonomy challenges the notion that one may be autonomous in one area of one's life while not being autonomous in other areas. Schwartz emphasizes that, insofar as work is degrading and does not allow for the exercise of autonomy, other aspects of one's life are also affected. For instance, if one experiences a lack of empowerment in the workplace, it may harm the worker's self-esteem or self-concept to such an extent that the worker's confidence in acting autonomously in other aspects of her or his life is hindered. Similarly, if decisions at work immediately affect one's life plans, projects, and prospects (as in the case when an employer stops providing health insurance for her or his employees or when employees are required to work longer shifts without freely choosing to do so),[6] then it follows that all aspects of life are affected by one's ability to be autonomous at work as elsewhere.

Following Schwartz, we might conclude that work must be structured such that individuals have some opportunity to participate in the decision-making and policy formation of those decisions that affect their working environment, long-term goals, and overall contentment at work. Such a plan would require that there be no strict distinction between the decision-makers and the persons carrying out the decision. Thus, employees become empowered in their work.

Michael Walzer has also discussed the question of whether all types of work fulfill one's right to work. Walzer dissects hard work—work that is "harsh, unpleasant, cruel, difficult to endure"—into three categories: grueling work, dirty work, and dangerous work.[7] Hard work, in this context, is work that is potentially degrading and also socially necessary. While others have proposed an equitable sharing of the work that needs to be done or even distributing hard work to those who are already degraded or alien (for example, prisoners and immigrants), Walzer's approach is different. He suggests that a fair distribution of potentially demeaning work is in fact impossible. On the contrary, a restructuring of the attitudes toward this type of work is called for. As an example, Walzer cites the Sunset Scavenger Company in San Francisco. This company has been immensely successful at challenging the notion that collecting garbage is demeaning work. The Sunset Company operates according to principles similar to what Schwartz proposed, that is, no one is exempt from collecting garbage on the streets or from decision-making and policy formation, and the workers own the company. As a result, work that many people traditionally viewed as "dirty work" or undesirable work has become both desirable and dignified.[8]

It may be interesting to discuss here whether or not professional athletics/pro sports qualify as "work." Certainly an argument may be made that athletes provide a great deal of entertainment value to the community. However, one might also argue that such value may be achieved through amateur athletic contests. In addition, one could argue against the unreasonably high salaries of some professional athletes by pointing out the injustice in wage distribution. These considerations do not even mention the disadvantage to the community caused by gambling on professional sporting events, the increase in domestic violence linked to professional sporting events, and consumption of alcohol at such events.

Other types of work might not qualify as work that upholds human dignity. An example of this is monotonous work that does not allow for freedom of thought or creativity, such as assembly line work. These tasks, however, can be modified so as to facilitate the development of autonomy for the individual performing the task, thereby creating an atmosphere wherein human dignity might be able to flourish. I have discussed a few such modifications above. They include incorporating all workers into the decision-making process, allowing for a variety of tasks and worker input into modifications of workload or production alterations, providing adequate leisure time, and avoiding dehumanizing hierarchicalization of types of work.

Obligation to Work

Having determined that individuals have a right to work—that is, to perform some freely chosen skill or service to society—it now must be asked whether or not individuals have an obligation to work. In examining this question, I wish to focus on able-bodied adults. I do this both to exclude those adult individuals who are physically and/or mentally unable to work and to set aside the question of children working.[9] Note that bracketing children and mentally and physically challenged adults in the discussion of an obligation to work does not take away from their right to work. Indeed, society may have to find creative ways to accommodate some people's right to work and ensure that that right is not infringed upon.

First of all, what is the nature of an obligation? An obligation is a moral responsibility. When one has an obligation to do X, one must do X; X is one's duty. The nature of the obligation, however, may vary. For example, an obligation may be immediate, as when a person is asked to tell the truth about a particular event or when one must take care of a sick child or parent. Or an obligation may be less ruled by the contingency of time, such as when one has an obligation to speak out against injustice. It is in no way less of an obligation to speak out against injustice, but the individual must respond to situations of injustice in the manner in which he or she is most comfortable or prepared to do. This means that the individual must assess varying situations of injustice to determine which position to take, examine potential responses to injustice to see which is most effective and in accordance with Christian ethical principles as articulated in the gospel, and then respond to the particular situation of injustice.

Similarly, one may have an obligation to oneself or one may have an obligation to the community. An example of one's obligation to oneself might be to educate oneself or to treat one's body according to standards of human dignity. An example of an obligation to others might be, for instance, to provide for those in need.[10]

In the case of work, there is both an obligation to oneself and to one's community. First of all, work fulfills an obligation to oneself in that it encourages or even requires that the individual determine certain aims or goals for oneself. These aims generally make use of one's unique talents or gifts. For example, I might decide to be a philosophy teacher at a university. This work requires such skills as knowledge of philosophy, the ability to speak in public, the ability to clarify complex concepts and problems, the desire to work with colleagues and students on a daily basis, and so on. In choosing such a job, I am declaring that I have been given and have developed these or similar skills (this is not to say that this is the only sort of job I could take with this set of skills). If, on the other hand, I set my sights on being a mathematics teacher, a form of work for which I have no particular skill or knowledge, I deceive myself and fail to recognize or make use of my true gifts and talents (I may also be depriving the community). The point of this discussion is that our uniqueness helps determine our obligation to work. We are obligated to develop our talents in order to actualize our own potential. It is, in part, in fulfilling this obligation that we take seriously the value of each individual life as a unique gift from God. Additionally, in fulfilling our obligation to work, we provide an example or role model for others: "Make it a point of honor to remain at peace and attend to your own affairs. Work with your hands as we directed you to do, so that you will give good example to outsiders and want for nothing" (1 Thes 4:11–12).

In addition, our obligation to work extends to the community. The community provides certain social goods, ranging from simple support to more detailed structures of exchange. Membership in a community entails reciprocal relations whereby one gives of oneself in the form of time, talent, and goods while also receiving from others similar forms of support. These reciprocal relations allow individuals to pursue more specialized tasks precisely because they are ensured that those tasks related to daily living will be reciprocally exchanged for the specialized task some individuals perform. So, too, the New Testament tells us that we have a responsibility to care for all peoples, especially those who are poor, suffering, or oppressed: "You yourselves know that I have worked with these hands of mine to provide everything that my companions and I have needed. I have shown you in all things that by working hard in this way we must help the weak, remembering the words that the Lord Jesus himself said, 'there is more happiness in giving than in receiving'" (Acts 20:34–35).

Obligation to the Poor

One of the unique characteristics of Christian ethics is the normative value of social responsibility. We are, in other words, responsible for our fellow human beings, requiring both an understanding of the way our actions affect others and recognizing our call to service.

First of all, understanding the manner in which our actions have an effect on others requires a reflective attitude toward day-to-day actions. For instance, the manner in which one makes use of resources greatly affects the potential availability of resources to others both near to us and in distant lands. One example might be found in the beef industry. Beef cattle consume a significant portion of the world's grain and provide a certain amount of protein. However, the grain would in fact provide much more protein if it were directly consumed by humans rather than "processed" into beef for our consumption. Thus, the beef industry challenges the First World to assess its impact on the Third World's need for grain. This fact alone, or coupled with the knowledge that beef cattle breeding is also a primary cause for the destruction of the rain forest, might lead us to reduce significantly our consumption of beef.[11]

Catholic social teaching under the guidance of Pope John Paul II has used the notion of "solidarity" to capture this attitude. Solidarity, very simply stated, is the recognition that near and distant peoples are interconnected with me and thus what happens to them affects my life plans and vice versa. Pope John Paul II argues that solidarity is a virtue grounded on global interdependence, and thus we need to adopt the attitude that what is done to the least of our brothers and sisters is done also to us. The global family can only truly flourish when all are free from unjust suffering and oppression.[12]

Additionally, as Christians we are called to serve. This aspect of our social responsibility has been described as both a "testimony for Christ" as well as a doing unto Christ,[13] that is, what we do for the needy, we also do for Christ. We ought to keep this in mind as we carry out our social responsibility to those in need. So, too, in our service to others, we provide witness for the message of Christ. As Matthew reports the words of Christ in the Gospel: "I assure you, as often as you did it for one of my least brothers and sisters, you did it for me" (Mt 25:40) and "I assure you, as often as you neglected to do it to one of these least ones, you neglected to do it to me" (Mt 25:45).

The Christian ethical position regarding an obligation to the poor might be contrasted with both the Kantian position and the utilitarian position. The Kantian position prescribes an imperfect duty to care for those in need. As an imperfect duty, an individual must fulfill this obligation, but may have some input into the determination of when and how the obligation is fulfilled.

John Stuart Mill, basing his moral theory on the normative value of utility, argues that we must care for those in need because that will bring about a greater amount of utility or happiness than if we were to let some in our society go hungry. The idea here is not that we have a duty or obligation to the poor, but rather that when one weighs the consequences of giving to the poor or not giving to the poor, one finds that there is a maximum amount of happiness, with a minimal amount of pain, for all concerned if those who have the means come to the aid of those in need.

The Christian ethic bridges the Millian perspective and the Kantian perspective. According to the Christian ethic, we have a social responsibility to provide for our brothers and sisters. This is our duty. However, it is done so as to advance the common good. In other words, the community flourishes only if each individual member is able to flourish, and each individual flourishes (reaches his or her full potential) only when he or she has as an end the common good. Not merely the presence of pleasure and the absence of pain, the common good is based on the harmony of the community rather than the sum of individuals' pleasures.

Other traditions have made similar proposals for how we might live out a Christian obligation to the poor. In Latin America, for instance, liberation theology challenges us to make a "preferential option for the poor." This radical rereading of the Gospels in light of the plight of the poor calls us to live in solidarity with near and distant peoples who suffer economic and political marginalization. Thus, all daily life decisions and actions must be made after reflecting on how those actions and decisions affect the least among us. This reflective action, or *praxis,* reshapes our lives as individuals and as a political community as we attempt to live the Gospel message.

Working with one's hands, mind, and heart for the well-being of self and community is one way we give glory to God. God's gifts for each unique human individual need to be exercised in order to flourish. As we work in this world, we are better able to respond to the challenge to build the Kingdom of God.

Is There a Just Economic Distribution?

The appropriate question for this section might instead be: "Is there an *unjust* economic distribution?" Rather than formulating a just system of distribution, a Christian ethical perspective calls on us to recognize and challenge unjust systems. We do this by examining the ways in which all peoples are treated according to any given economic system or policy. In other words, each economic system, policy, or change ought to be judged in part by whether or not it upholds the human dignity of each person affected by it.

Suppose, for example, that a major industrial country was considering abolishing its current welfare system. Some of the issues to be considered might include how well funds are allocated, the success rate of the welfare program in providing adequate basic need resources, and the future potential for welfare recipients to provide fully for themselves. The principles of Christian ethics presented above also ask us to consider the extent to which the dignity of the person is upheld and fostered. Thus, according to Christian ethics, other issues to consider in any discussion of the change to the welfare system must also include the extent to which the individuals involved can freely participate in the decisions that affect their lives—thereby participating in community; the ability to provide for oneself and one's family—thereby valuing all life; and the impact of the policy change on those who are poor and suffering—thereby upholding human dignity. Finally, the reform must also be checked for the impact it might have on distant peoples, that is, in considering how welfare reform affects the poorest among us, we must consider not only the poor in our own community, but also the poor of the global family. If a welfare reform policy adversely affected the amount and type of aid given to developing countries, then it may be judged as unjust. Or, for example, if the welfare reform was designed in order to allocate more money to the defense industry, then it may be judged as contrary to the principles of Christian ethics, which stress a value for all human life and an imperative to live in solidarity with all members of the global community. Indeed, if the reallocation supports any industry that functions contrary to human dignity or adversely affects the poor, it is judged unjust according to Christian ethical principles. Thus, the Christian ethic challenges us to evaluate welfare reform not only on the basis of distribution of economic resources, but also on the basis of the distribution of human rights and dignity.

Notice that this proposal goes beyond the United Nations Declaration of Human Rights, which stipulated that if a wage for any given form of work was insubstantial for the support of a worker's family according to the minimal levels of human dignity, then it was the responsibility of the society, community, state, or nation to supplement the wage. Thus, in addition to discussing when a wage is insubstantial, a Christian ethical perspective calls for an evaluation of all potentially unjust economic policies, including situations in which a wage is excessive or a policy unjustly favors a particular social group.

The United States Catholic bishops put forth a strong statement on just economic conditions and the injustices of capitalism in *Economic Justice for All: Pastoral Letter on Catholic Social Teaching and the U.S. Economy*. Included in this document is the notion that economic institutions must serve human beings rather than human beings being treated as a mere means to uphold the functioning of those institutions. With this criterion in hand, we are called to evaluate the economic systems we tend to take for granted. Thus, we must look not only at the outcome of economic policy on individuals' human dignity, but also reflect on the structure of economic institutions.

Conclusion

Work provides each human person with purpose and an avenue to freely exercise the gifts given by God. It is a source of self-esteem as well as an obligation to others. The dignity of work is evident when the work allows the unique individual to creatively contribute to the community through a freely chosen skill or service. Pride in work is not measured by the material wealth one accumulates or the social status one achieves. Rather, the Christian ethical perspective challenges us to measure our pride in our work according to the flourishing of human dignity—our own and that of others in the community.

Endnotes

1. Joseph Fahey and Richard Armstrong, eds., United Nations General Assembly (Dec 10, 1948) "Universal Declaration of Human Rights" in *A Peace Reader* (New York: Paulist, 1992) 337.

2. See also the U.S. Catholic bishops statement to this effect in *Economic Justice for All: Pastoral Letter on Catholic Social Teaching and the U.S. Economy* (Washington, DC: United States Catholic Conference, 1986) #28.

3. Amartya Sen, "Property and Hunger," *Economics and Philosophy* 4/1 (April 1988).

4. This example excludes instances of forced layoffs due to external economic conditions.

5. Adina Schwartz, "Meaningful Work" in *Social Justice in a Diverse Society*, Rita Manning and Rene Trujillo, eds. (Mountain View, CA: Mayfield, 1996) 263.

6. The air traffic controllers in the United States in 1995 were required to work a six-day week. This long workweek was on top of having one of the most stressful jobs in the nation, as well as relying on outdated equipment. *Time* (February 19, 1996) 52–53.

7. Michael Walzer, *Spheres of Justice: A Defense of Pluralism and Equality* (New York: Basic, 1983) 165–183.

8. Ibid. 177–180.

9. Walzer examines the possibility of having children do the "dirty work," as suggested by Fourier. For example, children might be commissioned to collect the garbage because children generally enjoy playing in the dirt anyway. Walzer, wisely I think, rejects this possibility in part because it is hardly the case that what garbage collectors do is "play." Walzer, *Spheres of Justice* 168, 174.

10. These categories of obligation roughly correspond to Kant's perfect and imperfect duties to self and others as articulated in the *Foundations of the Metaphysics of Morals*. They differ in that Kant's duty is a categorical imperative, while the

duties I have articulated are based on human understanding of the commands of God. Immanuel Kant, *Foundations of the Metaphysics of Morals* translated by Lewis White Beck (New York: Bobbs-Merrill Company, 1959) 39–41.

11. Peter Singer, *Practical Ethics* (Second Edition) (New York: Cambridge University Press, 1993), 220.

12. This point is reiterated by the U.S. Catholic bishops in *Economic Justice for All: Pastoral Letter on Catholic Social Teaching and the U.S. Economy* (Washington, DC: United States Catholic Conference, 1986) #322–325.

13. Norman Geisler, *Ethics: Alternatives and Issues* (Grand Rapids, MI: Zondervan, 1971) 191–192.

10

IS TOLERANCE ENOUGH? THE CATHOLIC UNIVERSITY AND THE COMMON GOOD *

DAVID HOLLENBACH

Boston College

Catholic and Jesuit higher education today faces a major challenge: how to retain and strengthen its distinctive religious identity while educating students for life in a world increasingly aware of its pluralism. This challenge reflects the more general contemporary problem of how Western culture can retain its commitment to reasoned efforts to understand what is truly human while grappling in an equally serious manner with the different ways of thinking of and living in our world. Jesuit colleges and universities, in other words, are sharply confronted with the tension between their commitment to sustain and advance the Catholic tradition's understanding of the human good and their efforts to serve the common good of our diverse world.

Catholic thought has long held that the common good is the overarching end to be pursued in social and cultural life. Since education is the activity through which culture is sustained and developed, the success or failure of a society to realize its common good will be largely dependent on its educational endeavors. But that is the rub. A pluralist society, by definition, is one in which there is disagreement about the meaning of the human good. This definition leads some to conclude that the idea of the common good and the reality of pluralist diversity are utterly incompatible. In such a context, the pursuit of the common good and the existence of educational institutions committed to particularistic traditions may seem self-contradictory. The corollary for Jesuit education is an apparently stark choice: either remain rooted in the Catholic tradition and abandon efforts to serve the larger good of our diverse world, or intensify efforts to address the demands of diversity and abandon the Catholic tradition.

For two reasons, however, I will argue that this is a false dilemma. The time is opportune for an important contribution to the advancement of the common good of a deeply pluralistic world by education rooted in the Catholic tradition. First, some of the most urgent contemporary cultural and social problems we face today are immune to solutions built on individualistic presuppositions that downplay the importance of the notion of the common good because of perceived diversity. The need for stronger bonds of social solidarity across cultures and for efforts to attain a greater degree of shared moral vision is increasingly evident in our world today. Second, the Roman Catholic tradition possesses some distinctive resources that can be brought to bear on these challenges.

The Problem: Pluralism or Social Conflict?

Today we face an array of issues that make the need to address the interdependence of persons on one another increasingly evident. A very partial list of such issues would include the following: continuing crisis in American life evident in even a cursory look at the statistics on the growth of economic inequality; the chaos in family life and sexual relationships in an age of single parenthood and of AIDS; the obstacles posed to the reform in the provision of health care by business-as-usual, interest-group politics, the serious dangers posed by environmental degradation regionally and globally; the clashes of "identity politics" within the United States and the rising national and cultural conflicts that have led to the tragedy in Bosnia and the genocide in Rwanda; the lack of even an approximation of economic justice in a world where the very notion of a domestic economy seems anachronistic.

In the background of these pragmatic social issues stands the deeper cultural question of whether we can achieve even a minimal consensus on the values that might enable us to address such pressing problems in a positive way. Many students today seem to have abandoned all expectation that such consensus is possible. This abandonment is evident in the often-observed hesitancy of contemporary undergraduates to make value judgments that go beyond the expression of personal preference or choice. Much literary, political, and philosophical theory rightly supports such reticence by pointing out how strong claims to know what is good for all people often mask the privileged power and desire for domination of those who make such claims.

The elusiveness of such a consensus on values goes very deep. Today many Americans recognize that they cannot go it alone in the face of the complexities of contemporary life. We know we need a connection to others if we are to find meaning and a sense of direction in life. But this quest for community can have pathological results if misdirected. For example, Robert Bellah has argued that among upper-middle class suburbanities it often leads to the development of what he calls "lifestyle enclaves." People in such enclaves find and express their identities through "shared patterns of appearance, consumption, or leisure activities." These relationships are based on sharing some feature of private rather than public life. People in such enclaves act as friends together in a kind of club, not as fellow citizens sharing a common fate with people who are different.[1] So they are not likely to translate their need for community into ways of thinking and acting that address issues such as the divisions between core cities and suburbs or between clashing religio-cultural identities in international politics. In fact the need for community, when expressed in lifestyle enclaves, can lead to the construction of walls and moats, in the form of bigger and better malls and tougher zoning ordinances that strengthen the locks that protect the privileged from those who are different. The adoption of a similar enclave strategy by those who seek to enhance the religious identity of Catholic higher education is equally dangerous.

Such an enclave is very different from the stronger community described by Aristotle as the *polis,* or by Cicero as the *res publica,* which can be translated the "public thing," the "commonwealth," the "commonweal," or simply a "republic." These stronger communities are places where people are truly interdependent on each other through their participation in, discussion concerning, and decision-making about their common purpose. Such strong communities are, therefore, political communities, where people make decisions together about the kind of society they want to live in together.

In the United States today, citizenship has itself became a problematic concept and we are experiencing an "eclipse of citizenship."[2] The low percentage of Americans who exercise their right to vote and the slogan "no new taxes" are visible evidences for this. This situation, I think, is caused largely by a lack of confidence that individual people can have any meaningful influence in a political society as vast as the United States in the complex context of today's global scene. Many people, including many in the middle class, feel politically powerless. E. J. Dionne, in a book tellingly titled *Why Americans Hate Politics,* argues that this alienation from citizenship results from the fact that current political discourse does not address the real needs of communities.[3] This failure is itself partly the result of the fact that interest-group politics is frequently incapable of even naming the social bonds that destine us to share either a common good or a "common bad." Politics is perceived as a contest among groups with little or no concern for the wider society and its problems, for example, suburbanites versus the urban "underclass," or American workers versus the poor who labor in Mexican or El Salvadoran *maquilladoras.* Lifestyle enclaves seem the only form of communal connection realistically available.

This tendency was discussed at some length in the United States Catholic Bishops' 1986 pastoral letter, *Economic Justice for All.* The bishops noted the deep structural causes for the contemporary devaluation of citizenship. Modern societies are characterized by a division of labor into highly specialized jobs and professions. Individual lives are further fragmented by the way family life, the world of work, networks of friendship, and religious community are so often lived out in separate compartments.[4] It is increasingly difficult to see how our chopped-up segments of experience fit together in anything like a meaningful whole.[5] This fragmentation makes it very difficult to see how the kinds of lives we lead really make any difference for the common good of the whole community. The resulting lack of public discussion of the common good in turn generates a heightened sense that individuals are powerless over larger social forces. It also helps explain the prevalence of single-issue styles of political action.

Tolerance as Alienation?

The standard response to the diversity of groups and value systems in Western political culture has long been an appeal to the virtue of tolerance.

Tolerance is a live-and-let-live attitude that avoids introducing conceptions of the full human good into political discourse. This stance is the prescription of the eminent political theorist and moral philosopher, John Rawls. Rawls recommends that we deal with the fact of value-pluralism by what he calls "the method of avoidance." By this he means that in political life "we try, so far as we can, neither to assert nor deny any religious, philosophical or moral views, or their associated philosophical accounts of truth and the status of values."[6] This appeal hopes to neutralize potential conflicts and to promote democratic social harmony. But if my analysis is correct, it actually further threatens democracy by deepening alienation and anomie. A principled commitment to avoiding sustained discourse about the common good can produce a downward spiral in which shared meaning, understanding, and community become even harder to achieve in practice. Or, more ominously, when the pluralism of diverse groups veers toward a state of group conflict with racial or class or religious dimensions, pure tolerance can become a strategy like that of the ostrich with its head in the sand.

In my view, this strategy is just what we do not need. The basis of a functioning democracy is not the autonomy of individuals who agree to leave each other alone by "avoiding" the question of the good they share in common or the "bad" that jointly threatens them all. The exercise of real freedom in society depends on the strength of the communal relationships that give persons a measure of real power to shape their environment, including their political environment.[7] Solitary individuals, especially solitary individuals motivated solely by self-interest and the protection of their rights to privacy, will be incapable of democratic self-government. Democracy requires more than this. It requires the virtues of mutual cooperation, mutual responsibility, and what Aristotle called civic friendship and concord.[8]

Of course, Aristotle knew that there were limits to how wide a circle of friends one might have, as he knew there were limits to the size of a city-state. Today we are acutely aware that a nation as vast and diverse as the United States cannot hope to achieve the kind of social unity that might have been possible in the Athenian *polis*. While the virtues of mutual cooperation, responsibility, and friendship can exert positive influence in small communities governed by town meetings, we hardly expect this to occur on a national—much less an international—scale.

But here our social situation reveals its paradoxical nature. As the scale and diversity of society tempts us to conclude that community is achievable only in private enclaves of the like-minded, *de facto*, technological, political, and economic interdependence grows stronger each year, indeed each day. For example, the notion of a "domestic economy" is virtually obsolete and a technological tool in use on virtually all American campuses is called the World Wide Web. These realities cry out for conscious acknowledgement and for a renewed commitment to our *moral* interdependence. Stress on the importance of the local, the small-scale, and the particular must be complemented by a kind of solidarity that is more universal in scope. This wider solidarity is essential if the quest for community is to avoid becoming a source of increased conflict in a world already riven by narrowness of vision. Commitment to communities with particular ways of life must be complemented by a sense of the national and the global common good and the need for a vision shaped by hospitable encounter with traditions and peoples that are different from ourselves.

The Catholic Tradition of the Common Good

The tradition of Catholic social thought, especially as it has developed over the past century, is positioned to make a significant contribution to the recognition of the importance of both small-scale and wider forms of community. It is particularly noteworthy that several commentators from outside the Catholic tradition have commented on this. For example, William Lee Miller suggests that the Catholic tradition's commitment to the idea of human interdependence in community can contribute resources that both Protestantism and secular liberalism lack to the complex and uncertain future of the American republic. He calls this solidaristic vision of interdependence "personalist communitarianism." In his view, "something like such a personalist communitarianism is the necessary base for a true republic in the interdependent world of the third century of this nation's existence. And the Roman Catholic community is the most likely single source of it—the largest and intellectually and spiritually most potent institution that is the bearer of such ideas."9

This personalistic communitarianism is based on the recognition that the dignity of human persons is achieved only in community with others. To paraphrase John Donne's words, no person is an island. This understanding of the human has biblical roots in the notion of covenant—the fact that God called Israel precisely as a *people,* not as individuals one at a time.

It also has Greek roots in Aristotle's understanding that the human being is a social or political animal *(zoon politikon),* whose good is essentially bound up with the good of the polis. This understanding of the person has direct implications for the way freedom is understood. Freedom's most important meaning is *positive,* the ability to shape one's life and environment in an active and creative way, rather than the negative state of privacy or being left alone by others. For the ancient Greeks, privacy was a state of deprivation, a fact echoed in the etymological link of privacy and privation. Similarly, the biblical understanding of freedom, portrayed in the account of the Exodus, is not simply freedom *from constraint* but freedom *for participation* in the shared life of a people. Liberation is *from* bondage *into* community.[10] To be sure, freedom from oppression demands that persons' dignity and rights be protected from infringement by other people, by society, or by the state. Freedom in its most basic form is freedom from oppression. But freedom will be understood in a truncated way if its meaning is understood only as the negative immunity that protects one from interference by others. Individualistic isolation is finally a prison, not a liberation.

Pope John Paul II has stressed this social dimension of freedom in his frequent discussion of the moral basis of democracy. Catholicism, of course, has often been regarded with justifiable suspicion in discussions of democracy because of its history of opposition to democratic movements in the modern era. Since the Second Vatican Council, however, the Catholic Church has become one of the strongest advocates and agents of democratization visible on the global stage today.[11] In his role as advocate of democratic government, John Paul II has been critical of ideas of democracy based on individualism and on strictly negative understandings of freedom. His analysis echoes some of the founders of the American experiment in its insistence that the success of democracy over the long haul is dependent on the virtues present in the citizenry and the link between the life of virtue and commitment to the common good.

This is most evident in John Paul's discussion of what he calls "the virtue of solidarity." This virtue will not be found on the classical lists that include prudence, justice, temperance, and fortitude. Nevertheless, the fact that it belongs there is evident from the Pope's definition. He calls solidarity "a firm and persevering determination to commit oneself to the common good; that is to say to the good of all and of each individual."[12] For Christians, such a commitment is rooted in the commandment of love of neighbor. Thus "Solidarity is undoubtedly a Christian virtue. . . . [There are] many points of contact between solidarity and charity, which is the distinguishing mark of Christ's disciples (cf. Jn 13:35)." It is recognition of one's neighbors as fundamentally equal because they are "living images of God, redeemed by the blood of Jesus Christ and placed under the permanent action of the Holy Spirit."[13] The promotion of the common good therefore flows from the heart of Christian faith.

At the same time, solidarity as the pope understands it is not far removed from the virtue that Aristotle called "civic friendship" or "civic concord."[14] Precisely as commitment to the common good, the virtue of solidarity ought to link Catholic Christians with the larger community of non-Catholics, non-Christians, and non-believers. Indeed, John Paul II expresses the hope that all people, "whether or not they are inspired by religious faith, will become fully aware of the urgent need to *change* the *spiritual attitudes* which define each individual's relationship with self, with neighbor, with even the remotest human communities, and with nature itself." Such a change in attitudes arises from a recognition of "higher values such as the *common good.*"[15] Thus, the effort to nurture this virtue of solidarity not only has distinctively Christian warrant in theology but is also proposed as a worthy and in fact essential task in a secular, pluralistic context.

Justice: Prerequisite for a Good That Is Common

The linkage of solidarity with the demands of Christian charity should not be mistaken as limiting this virtue to the domain of affectivity. Commitment to the common good requires a hard-nosed recognition of the reality of human interdependence, "sensed as a *system determining* relationships in the contemporary world."[16] This commitment puts solidarity in continuity with Thomas Aquinas's claim that all virtues are oriented to the promotion of justice.

For Aquinas, the premier moral virtue is justice, which directs a person's actions toward the good of fellow human beings. Because all people are both individuals and also participants in the common life of the civil community, virtuous citizens must seek not only their private good but the good of the community as well. Thomas Aquinas calls such concern for the common good of the community "general justice." He contrasts it with "particular justice," the virtue that specifies obligations to individuals, for example, the obligations of parents to their children or the duties of employers to pay their employees a just wage. These latter concerns are of course indispensable in any life that is virtuous. But they are not the whole of virtue, just as the duties of justice toward one's children or employees are not the whole of justice. When one possesses the virtue of general justice, one's actions will be habitually directed toward the good of the more encompassing community of one's fellow human beings. Justice, therefore, is the virtue of good citizens. In Thomas's words, "the virtue of a good citizen is general justice, whereby a person is directed to the common good."[17] The achievement of the common good requires a citizenry nurtured in ways that enable them both to understand the meaning of justice in society and to work for its achievement in the systemic patterns of social organization that shape common life in our cities, in the United States as a whole, and globally.

Thus it should come as no surprise that John Paul II states that solidarity is a moral bond or responsibility of more influential persons for those who are weaker. It is a bond that links the poor with each other in asserting their needs and rights in the face of the inefficiency or corruption of public officials. It is opposed to every form of imperialism, hegemony, greed, or unrestrained quest for power. It is the path to both peace and genuine economic development.[18] This strong language is intensified when the pope lists manifestations of human sinfulness that are directly opposed to solidarity. These include trampling upon the basic rights of the human person: attacks and pressures against the freedom of individuals and groups; racial, cultural, and religious discrimination; violence and terrorism; torture and repression; arms races and military spending that divert funds that could be used to alleviate misery; and the increasing inequality of the rich and poor. All of these phenomena divide persons and communities from each other and undermine human solidarity on a social, structural level. In the pope's words, they shatter the world to "its very foundations."[19]

An adequate discussion of the full meaning of justice is impossible here. The task can be simplified, however, by noting the United States Catholic bishops 1986 description of the bottom-line demands of justice. They said, *"Basic justice demands the establishment of minimum levels of participation in the life of the human community for all persons."* Put negatively, "The ultimate injustice is for a person or group to be treated actively or aban-

doned passively as if they were nonmembers of the human race."[20] The
United States bishops call this exclusion "marginalization"—exclusion
from social life and from participation in the common good of the human
community.

Unjust exclusion can take many forms, as justice can take many forms.
There is political marginalization: the denial of the vote, restriction of free
speech, the tyrannical concentration of power in the hands of a ruling elite,
or straightforward totalitarianism. It can also be economic in nature.
Where persons are unable to find work even after searching for many
months or where they are thrown out of work by decisions they are powerless to influence, they are effectively marginalized. They are implicitly told
by the community: we don't need your talent, we don't need your initiative,
we don't need *you*.[21]

When citizens acquiesce in such situations when remedial steps could
be taken, they promote injustice. One can hardly think of a more effective
way to deny people any active participation in the economic life of society
than to cause or allow them to remain unemployed. Similarly, persons who
face hunger, homelessness, and the extremes of poverty when society possesses the resources to meet their needs are treated as non-members. Citizens who permit or abet such conditions when effective action could be
taken to change them for the better fail to exercise their responsibility
toward the common good. As Michael Walzer puts it with respect to
meeting the basic material needs of the poor: "Men and women who
appropriate vast sums of money for themselves, while needs are unmet, act
like tyrants, dominating and distorting the distribution of security and
welfare."[22] In the same way, the United States bishops state that the hungry
and homeless people in this nation today are no part of anything worthy of
being called a commonwealth. The extent of their suffering shows how far
we are from being a community of persons. The willingness of citizens to
tolerate such conditions and even to take action to perpetuate them shows
how far we are from an effective commitment to the common good in this
nation.

Against the background of this normative understanding of justice and
the common good, the fear that introducing substantive notions of the
human good into our public life will be divisive and lead to intolerance
seems rather quaint. We live in a dangerously divided nation and world. If
we are to begin the task of securing even minimal justice, we need to

confront these divisions, not "avoid" or "tolerate" them. The root of many of the conflicts dividing the nation today is not the different conceptions Americans have of what makes for full happiness or what private "life-plans" are worth pursing. The problem is that many would prefer not to reflect on what it means to say that poor and marginalized people are members of the human community and that we have a duty to treat them as such.

Consequences for Education

The difficulty of specifying how citizens might respond to this duty is obvious. Individuals, at least when acting one at a time, are simply incapable of shaping the quality of community life on such a vast scale, ranging from the nearest of our neighbors to persons half way around the globe. Rather, whatever the more specific duties of civic virtue or solidarity may be, they are necessarily mediated and specified through our roles as citizens, our roles as economic agents, our positions of responsibility on the job, the location that we have within particular geography, and so on. One of the most important roles through which this responsibility is exercised is the role of individuals and the community at large in the sphere of education.

The links among education, virtue, and the common good were made explicit in the writing of one of the most influential representatives of the Catholic tradition a generation ago. In the 1950's, John Courtney Murray argued that concern for the common good translates directly into concern for the moral substance of public affairs. The relevance of this concern to education is clear from the fact that, in its many forms and dimensions, education shapes the values that become operative in a republic by helping to shape the virtues and character of its citizenry. As Murray put it, "the great 'affair' of the commonwealth is, of course, education."[23] Put negatively, worries about the quality of public life in a democracy lead directly to worries about the whole process by which each generation prepares its progeny to assume their responsibilities as citizens. This preparation is the entire undertaking of education broadly conceived. Education in virtue is education that guides the development of students in ways that enable them to become good citizens, men and women dedicated to the service of the common good.

Education in virtue might sound like a rather antiquated phrase to describe the task of the contemporary university. I agree that the days when the university functioned in *loco parentis* in a moralistic way are over. However, the long tradition of Catholicism possesses some distinctive *intellectual* resources that are much needed on the American university scene today. Let me call the chief of these resources a commitment to intellectual solidarity. By *intellectual solidarity* I mean a willingness to take other persons seriously enough to engage them in conversation and debate about what makes life worth living, including what will make for the good of our deeply interdependent public life. Such a spirit includes, but goes well beyond, an appeal to tolerance. Tolerance is a strategy of non-interference with the beliefs and way of life of those who are different. The spirit of intellectual solidarity is similar to tolerance in that it recognizes and respects these differences. It does not seek to eliminate pluralism through coercion. But it differs radically from pure tolerance by seeking positive engagement with the other through both listening and speaking. It is rooted in a hope that understanding might replace incomprehension and that perhaps even agreement could result. Where such engaged conversation about the good life begins and develops, a *community* of freedom begins to exist.

The history of Catholic tradition provides some noteworthy evidence that discourse across the boundaries of diverse communities is both possible and potentially fruitful. This tradition, in its better moments, has experienced considerable success in efforts to bridge the divisions that have separated it from other communities with other understandings of the good life. In the first and second centuries, the early Christian community moved from being a small Palestinian sect to active encounter with the Hellenistic and Roman worlds. In the fourth century, Augustine brought biblical faith into dialogue with Stoic and Neoplatonic thought. His efforts profoundly transformed both Christian and Greco-Roman thought and practice. In the thirteenth century Thomas Aquinas once again transformed Western Christianity by appropriating ideas of Aristotle he had learned from Arab Muslims and from Jews. And though the church resisted the liberal discovery of modern freedoms through much of the modern period, affirmation of these freedoms has been transforming Catholicism once again through the last half of our own century. The memory of these events in social and intellectual history as well as the experience of the Catholic Church since the Second Vatican Council leads me to the hope that communities holding different visions of the good life can get somewhere if they are willing to risk serious conversation and sustained argument about these visions. Injecting such hope back into the public life of the United States would be a signal achievement.

What might such public discourse look like? Broadly speaking, it will be conversation and argument about the shape of the culture the participants either share through their common traditions or could share in the future through the understanding of each other they seek to achieve. The forum for such discussion is not, in the first instance, the legislative chamber or the court of law. It is the university and all the other venues where thoughtful men and women undertake the tasks of retrieving, criticizing, and reconstructing understandings of the human good from the historical past and transmitting them to the future through education. It occurs as well wherever people bring their received historical traditions on the meaning of the good life into intelligent and critical encounter with understandings of this good held by other peoples with other traditions. It occurs, in short, wherever education about and serious inquiry into the meaning of the good life takes place.

Further, the achievement of such a truly free dialogue about the meaning of the good life has direct implications for the role of religion in the university. Our culture needs much more conversation about the visions of the human good held by diverse religious communities and real intellectual engagement with these religious visions. The Catholic tradition and many Protestant traditions as well reject the notion that religious faith must be irrational and, therefore, out of bounds within the intellectual forum of the university. In both the Catholic and Calvinist views of the matter, faith and understanding are not adversarial but reciprocally illuminating. This viewpoint invites those outside the church to place their self-understanding at risk by serious conversation with religious traditions. At the same time, the believer's self-understanding will be challenged to development or even fundamental change by dialogue with the other—whether this other be a secular agnostic, a Christian from another tradition, a Jew, a Muslim, or a Buddhist.[24]

Serious dialogue is risky business. At least some religious believers have been willing to take the risk. The future of the common good in our society could be considerably enhanced by the willingness of a considerably larger number of people to take this risk of cultural dialogue and intellectual solidarity, whether they begin as fundamentalists convinced of their certitudes or agnostics convinced of their doubts. Our society needs more imagination about how to deal creatively with its problems than it appears to possess today. Religious traditions and communities are among the principal bearers of such imaginative sources for our understanding of the human. They can evoke not only private self-understanding but public vision as well. Both believers and unbelievers alike have reason to risk considering what contribution religious traditions might make to our understanding of the public good. For a society to try to exclude religious narratives and symbols from its public culture solely because they are identified with religion would be to impoverish itself intellectually and culturally. This impoverishment deprives society of one of its most important resources for a more publicly shared cultural self-understanding. Religious communities make perhaps their most important contribution to public life through this contribution to the formation of culture. If they seek to make this contribution through a dialogue of mutual listening and speaking with others, it will be fully congruent with the life of a free society. The principal place where this can happen is the university, as the Catholic tradition has long known. Today, the Catholic university ought to embody such dialogue in a preeminent way. Were it to fail to do so it would betray its identity both as university and as Catholic.

Finally this intellectual solidarity must be accompanied by a *social solidarity* that opens the minds of the students and faculty of the university to the reality of human suffering in a world marred by the grinding poverty of so many in the world, by lack of health insurance for large numbers of Americans, by the attempts at genocide in Bosnia and Rwanda, by the fate of refugees throughout the world—to name only a few of the most obvious manifestations of the long history of human beings' sinful propensity to treat each other in inhuman ways. As Michael Buckley has noted, the origins of the Catholic university in the Middle Ages and its development by the Jesuits and other religious communities at the dawn of the modern period were manifestations of the conviction that a Christian humanism is both possible and required by the dynamic of Christian faith itself. The challenge of Christian humanism remains central to the identity of Catholic universities. But today that humanism must be a social humanism, a humanism with a deep appreciation not only for the heights to which human culture can rise but also for the depths of suffering to which societies can descend.[25] There are strong currents in American life today that insulate both professors and students from experience of and academic reflection on these sufferings. A university that aspires both to be Catholic and to serve the common good must do more than include nods to the importance of social solidarity in its mission statement. It must translate this commitment into teaching and research priorities, and actualize these priorities in day-to-day activities in classroom and library—a posture that takes both the courage and the humility that the privileged learn only when they encounter the reality of poverty and other forms of suffering.

The virtue of solidarity as commitment to the common good, therefore, has both intellectual and social dimensions. Indeed, these intellectual and social dimensions are profoundly interconnected—neither is possible without the other. Both raise significant challenges in the life of the university today. Both hold out opportunities for the university that are worthy of our deepest aspirations. Both intellectual and social solidarity can give new life to the identity of colleges and universities that are both Catholic and Jesuit by tradition and that seek to be so in the future.

Endnotes

*This essay previously appeared in *Current Issues in Catholic Higher Education* 16 (Summer 1995) 3–15, and in *Conversations,* Spring 1998, and is used with permission.

1. Robert Bellah, Richard Madsen, William M. Sullivan, Ann Swidler, and Steven M. Tipton, *Habits of the Heart: Individualism and Commitment in American Life* (Berkeley: University of California, 1985) 335.

2. The phrase is from Robert J. Pranger, *The Eclipse of Citizenship: Power and Participation in Contemporary Politics* (New York: Holt, Rinehart and Winston, 1968). See also Michael Walzer, "The Problem of Citizenship," in *Obligations: Essays on Disobedience, War, and Citizenship* (Cambridge, MA: Harvard University, 1970) 203–228.

3. E.J. Dionne, Jr., *Why Americans Hate Politics* (New York: Simon & Schuster, 1991).

4. National Conference of Catholic Bishops, *Economic Justice for All: Pastoral Letter on Catholic Social Teaching and the U. S. Economy* (Washington, DC: USCC, 1986) no. 22.

5. See Bellah et al., *Habits of the Heart* 277.

6. John Rawls, "The Idea of an Overlapping Consensus," in *Oxford Journal of Legal Studies* 7 (1987) 12–13.

7. John A. Coleman, "Religious Liberty in America and Mediating Structures," in his *An American Strategic Theology* (New York: Paulist, 1982) 226.

8. See *Nicomachean Ethics* 1167 a, b.

9. William Lee Miller, *The First Liberty: Religion and the American Republic* (New York: Alfred A. Knopf, 1986) 288–89. For other perspectives along these lines by non-Catholic thinkers see also R. Bruce Douglass, "First Things First: The Letter and the Common Good Tradition," in Douglass, ed., *The Deeper Meaning of Economic Life* (Washington, DC: Georgetown University, 1986); Charles R. Strain, ed., *Prophetic Visions and Economic Realities: Protestants, Jews, and Catholics Confront the Bishops' Letter on the Economy* (Grand Rapids, MI: Eerdmans, 1989); Charles Lutz, ed., *God, Goods, and the Common Good* (Minneapolis, MN: Augsburg, 1986); Thomas Gannon, ed., *The Catholic Challenge to the American Economy* (New York: Macmillan, 1987) especially essays by Ronald Green and Norman Birnbaum; Michael Katz, *The Undeserving Poor* (New York: Pantheon, 1989) 180–84.

10. See National Conference of Catholic Bishops, *Economic Justice for All* no. 36.

11. For a discussion of the transformation of the role of the Catholic Church in efforts to secure democratic forms of government since Vatican II, see Samuel P. Huntington, "Religion and the Third Wave," in *National Interest* 24 (Summer 1991) 29–42.

12. John Paul II, "Sollicitudo rei socialis," in David J. O'Brien and Thomas A. Shannon, eds., *Catholic Social Thought: The Documentary Heritage* (Maryknoll, NY: Orbis, 1992) no. 38.

13. Ibid. No. 40.

14. Aristotle, *Nicomachean Ethics* 1167 a, b.

15. John Paul II, *Sollicitudo rei socialis* no. 38, emphasis in the original.

16. Ibid. No. 38, emphasis in the original.

17. Thomas Aquinas, *Summa Theologiae* II-II, q. 58, art. 6.

18. John Paul II, *Sollicitudo rei socialis* nos. 38–39.

19. John Paul II, "Apostolic Exhortation on Reconciliation and Penance" in *Origins* 14 (Dec. 11, 1984) 432–58 no. 2.

20. National Conference of Catholic Bishops, *Economic Justice for All,* no. 77.

21. See the documentation provided in National Conference of Catholic Bishops, *Economic Justice for All,* chap. 3. The bishops' numbers are for 1986, but the situation is very similar today.

22. Michael Walzer, *Spheres of Justice: A Defense of Pluralism and Equality* (New York: Basic, 1983) 76.

23. John Courtney Murray, *We Hold These Truths: Catholic Reflections on the American Proposition* (New York: Sheed and Ward, 1960) 9.

24. See Michael J. Perry, *Love and Power: The Role of Religion and Morality in American Politics* (New York: Oxford University, 1991). See also Robin Lovin, "Perry, Naturalism, and Religion in Public," in *Tulane Law Review* 63 (1989) 1517–39. Both Perry's earlier work and Lovin's theological reflection on it are discussed in my "Religion and Political Life," in *Theological Studies* 52 (1991) 87–106.

25. See Buckley, "The University and the Concern for Justice: The Search for

a New Humanism," in *Thought* 57 (1982) 219–33, and "Christian Humanism and Human Misery: A Challenge to the Jesuit University," in Michael J. Buckley et al., eds., *Faith, Discovery, Service: Perspectives on Jesuit Education* (Milwaukee, WI: Marquette University, 1992) 77–105.

INDEX